Forms of the Cinematic

Forms of the Cinematic

Architecture, Science, and the Arts

Edited by
Mark E. Breeze

BLOOMSBURY ACADEMIC
NEW YORK • LONDON • OXFORD • NEW DELHI • SYDNEY

BLOOMSBURY ACADEMIC
Bloomsbury Publishing Inc
1385 Broadway, New York, NY 10018, USA
50 Bedford Square, London, WC1B 3DP, UK
29 Earlsfort Terrace, Dublin 2, Ireland

BLOOMSBURY, BLOOMSBURY ACADEMIC and the Diana logo are trademarks of
Bloomsbury Publishing Plc

First published in the United States of America 2021
This paperback edition published 2022

Volume Editor's Part of the Work © Mark E. Breeze

Each chapter © of Contributors

Cover design: Carolyne Hill

All rights reserved. No part of this publication may be reproduced or transmitted
in any form or by any means, electronic or mechanical, including photocopying,
recording, or any information storage or retrieval system, without prior
permission in writing from the publishers.

Bloomsbury Publishing Inc does not have any control over, or responsibility for, any third-
party websites referred to or in this book. All internet addresses given in this book were
correct at the time of going to press. The author and publisher regret any inconvenience
caused if addresses have changed or sites have ceased to exist, but can accept no
responsibility for any such changes.

Library of Congress Cataloging-in-Publication Data
Names: Breeze, Mark E., volume editor.
Title: Forms of the cinematic: architecture, science and the arts / edited by Mark E. Breeze.
Description: New York City: Bloomsbury Academic, 2021. |
Includes bibliographical references and index.
Identifiers: LCCN 2020033873 | ISBN 9781501361425 (hardback) |
ISBN 9781501361449 (epub) | ISBN 9781501361432 (pdf)
Subjects: LCSH: Motion pictures–Philosophy.
Classification: LCC PN1995 .F623 2021 | DDC 791.4301–dc23
LC record available at https://lccn.loc.gov/2020033873

ISBN: HB: 978-1-5013-6142-5
PB: 978-1-5013-7490-6
ePDF: 978-1-5013-6143-2
eBook: 978-1-5013-6144-9

Typeset by Deanta Global Publishing Services, Chennai, India

To find out more about our authors and books visit www.bloomsbury.com and
sign up for our newsletters.

Contents

List of figures — vii
List of contributors — viii

Forms of the cinematic: An introduction
Mark E. Breeze — 1

Part One
Rethinking: from Idea to Structure

1. Idea and image
   D. N. Rodowick — 17

2. The screen as barrier and support: Monitoring, projection and perfectionism in Brad Bird's *Tomorrowland: A World Beyond* (2015)
   Stephen Mulhall — 31

3. Surface thoughts: On the look of cinema
   John Ó Maoilearca — 42

4. The film event: From Bazin to Deleuze
   Tom Conley — 55

Part Two
Revisualizing: from the Tangible to the Intangible

5. What film studies is: Mapping the discipline
   Annette Kuhn and Guy Westwell — 75

6. A cinematic aided design approach and the need for (in)-disciplinarity
   François Penz and Janina Schupp — 92

7. Microcinematography and biomedical science
   Brian Stramer — 107

8	Cinematic forms and cultural heritage *Maureen Thomas*	122

Part Three
Reconstructing: from Writing to Architecture

9	The modulation of emphasis: Screenwriting as a literary art *Clare L. E. Foster*	145
10	Mapping Andrei Tarkovsky's *Stalker*: An architectural exploration of the 'Zone' *Stavros Alifragkis*	161
11	*Architecture Beyond Sight*: Filming blindness *Anna Ulrikke Andersen*	178
12	Towards an architecture of the cinematic *Mark E. Breeze*	190

Index   209

Figures

4.1	Still from *Stagecoach* (1939): The Stage to Lordsburg	56
4.2	Still from *Ride Lonesome* (1959): A lunar landscape	56
4.3	Bernard Salomon, 'The Creation of the World'	61
4.4	Still from Fritz Lang's *Fury* (1936): Joe meets the dog	65
4.5	Still from Fritz Lang's *Fury* (1936): The dog shares Joe's thoughts	66
4.6	Still from Fritz Lang's *Fury* (1936): Joe enters the apartment (in a dissolve)	67
4.7	Still from Fritz Lang's *Fury* (1936): A shimmer in the dark	67
4.8	Still from Fritz Lang's *Fury* (1936): Joe turns on the light	68
4.9	Still from Fritz Lang's *Fury* (1936): Joe reaches for the note	68
4.10	Still from Fritz Lang's *Fury* (1936): Joe reads the note	69
5.1	Dictionary planning mind map	77
5.2	Thinking through category overlap	79
5.3	Mind map showing main sub-areas of film studies	80
5.4	Film theory and some of its subsidiary fields	81
5.5	Template used for cognate discipline entries	83
5.6	Retrofitting identity	89
6.1	Data mining in *Kitchen Stories* (Bent Hamar, Sweden 2003)	95
6.2	A multitude of windows in *L'Eclisse* (Michelangelo Antonioni, Italy 1962)	96
6.3	The contemplative window in Ozu's *Tokyo Twilight* (Japan 1957) versus Hitchcock's voyeuristic approach in *Rear Window* (USA 1953)	97
7.1	Still from David Rogers' *The Chase* (c. 1950)	108
7.2	Still from Ronald Canti's *The Cultivation of Living Tissue* (1928)	113
8.1	*Queens Game* pre-production 3D dramatic atmosphere test, 2019	132
8.2	*Queens Game* Margrete and Ingegerd concept art, 2020	133
11.1	Still from *Architecture Beyond Sight* (2019): Two women drawing on a wall	179
11.2	Still from *Architecture Beyond Sight* (2019): A man sanding wood using power tools	183
11.3	Still from *Architecture Beyond Sight* (2019): A shot of a London street, captured from above	187

Contributors

Stavros Alifragkis is Adjunct Lecturer at the Hellenic Open University, Greece, and an architect by training (Diploma, 2002, Thessaloniki; Interdisciplinary Postgraduate Degree, 2003, Athens; MPhil, 2004, Cambridge; PhD, 2010, Cambridge). His doctoral thesis researches the reconstruction of the socialist city in the cinema of Dziga Vertov. Stavros studies models of representation of the modern city and its architecture in different mediums (drawings, photography, cinema, literature) and the narrative mechanisms of space in late nineteenth- and twentieth-century European cultures. His recent publications include the chapters 'The Mythical Landscape of Andrei Tarkovsky' (2020) and 'Constructing the Urban Cinematic Landscape: Theo Angelopoulos' Thessaloniki' (2017).

Anna Ulrikke Andersen is a Norwegian filmmaker, architectural historian and currently a postdoctoral researcher at the University of Oxford. She is interested in how filmmaking could be used to explore the built environment and our experiences thereof, where her work to date has focused on themes such as windows, translation, disability, and the life and work of Christian Norberg-Schulz. She holds a PhD in Architecture from the Bartlett School of Architecture, UCL. She was a 2018–19 fellow at Harvard Film Study Center and a Visiting Fellow at Vanderbilt University. She has published in *Architectural Research Quarterly*, *Screenworks* and *InForma Journal*.

Mark E. Breeze is a Harvard-trained architect, an Emmy-nominated documentary filmmaker and the Director of Studies in Architecture at St John's College, University of Cambridge. He completed his postdoctorate at the University of Oxford, and he has held fellowships at the US Library of Congress and The Huntington, Los Angeles. His academic and creative practice explores the intersections between architecture and film. His work has been built, exhibited, published and broadcast internationally.

Tom Conley is the author of *The Self-Made Map* (1996), *Cartographic Cinema* (2007), *An Errant Eye* (2011), *À fleur de page* (2015) and other titles; he is the co-editor of the *Wylie-Blackwell Companion to Jean-Luc Godard* (2014) and the *Anthem Handbook of Screen Theory* (2018). In 2020, he was a fellow at the American Academy in Berlin, completing a study of cartographies of media and engineering.

Clare L. E. Foster is a British Academy postdoctoral fellow at Centre for Research in the Arts, Social Sciences and Humanities (CRASSH) and Affiliate Lecturer in the Faculty of History at the University of Cambridge. From 1994 to 2009 she was a full-time screenwriter based in Los Angeles. While a PhD student and research fellow at Cambridge, she founded and ran two research networks, about the concept of performance (CIPN) and cultural repetition (the 'Re-' Network). She teaches theatre and film history and leads practical workshops in playwriting and screenwriting.

Annette Kuhn FBA is Professor and Research Fellow in Film Studies at Queen Mary University of London and a former editor of the journal *Screen*. Her books include *The Women's Companion to International Film* (1990); *Family Secrets: Acts of Memory and Imagination* (2002); *An Everyday Magic: Cinema and Cultural Memory* (2002); *Ratcatcher* (2008, 2020); and *Little Madnesses: Winnicott, Transitional Phenomena and Cultural Experience* (2013). She is co-author, with Guy Westwell, of the *Oxford Dictionary of Film Studies* (2012, 2020), and is currently working on an AHRC-funded project, 'Cinema Memory and the Digital Archive'.

John Ó Maoilearca is Professor of Film at Kingston University, London. He has also taught philosophy and film theory at the University of Sunderland, England, and the University of Dundee, Scotland. He has published eleven books, including (as author) *Bergson and Philosophy* (2000), *Post-Continental Philosophy: An Outline* (2006), *Philosophy and the Moving Image: Refractions of Reality (142010)*, *All Thoughts Are Equal: Laruelle and Nonhuman Philosophy* (2015), and (as editor) *Bergson and the Art of Immanence* (2013) and *The Bloomsbury Companion to Continental Philosophy* (2013). He is currently working on ordinary modes of time-travel (so far with only modest success).

Professor Stephen Mulhall is the Russell H. Carpenter Fellow in Philosophy at New College, Oxford. Prior to this appointment, he held a Prize Fellowship at All Souls College, and then a Readership at the University of Essex. His research interests include Wittgenstein; Nietzsche; Heidegger and Sartre; the philosophy of religion; and the relationship between philosophy and the arts. His recent publications include the third edition of *On Film* (2016) and *The Great Riddle: Wittgenstein and Nonsense, Theology and Philosophy* (2015).

François Penz directs the Digital Studio for Research in Design, Visualization and Communication at the University of Cambridge. He recently published a monograph *Cinematic Aided Design: An Everyday Life Approach to Architecture* (2018). His current Arts and Humanities Research Council (AHRC) project, *CineMuseSpace: A Cinematic Musée Imaginaire of Spatial Cultural Differences* (2017–20), expands the ideas developed in his monograph to other cultures, China and Japan in particular. He is also the Principal Investigator for the *CineGenus* Global Challenges Research Fund project (2019), which expands the *CineMuseSpace* methodology to Indian fiction films staged in low-income habitats. He is a professor, former Head of the Department of Architecture and a Fellow of Darwin College, Cambridge.

D. N. Rodowick is Glen A. Lloyd Distinguished Service Professor at the University of Chicago, where he teaches in the departments of Cinema and Media Studies, and Visual Arts. He is the author of numerous essays as well as eight books, including, most recently, *What Philosophy Wants from Images* (2018). His newest book, *An Education in Judgment: Hannah Arendt and the Humanities*, will be published in 2021. Rodowick is also a curator and an award-winning experimental filmmaker and video artist.

Janina Schupp is an Affiliated Lecturer and Research Associate in Architecture and the Moving Image at the University of Cambridge and a documentary film producer. Her research focuses on representations of the home and urban spaces in screen media. Her publications include an upcoming co-edited book *Slices of Everyday Lives*, and contributions to *Filmurbia: Screening the Suburbs* (2017) and *Urban Noir: New York and Los Angeles in Shadow and Light* (2017). She held fellowships at the Library of Congress in 2015–16 and the Camargo Foundation in 2017, and was a Visiting Scholar at Nanjing University, China in 2019.

Brian Stramer is a Professor of Cell and Developmental Biology. His laboratory pioneered the use of fruit flies as a model system to understand the role and regulation of cell migration during embryogenesis. His group developed techniques to image fly macrophages at high resolution during their normal development in living embryos. Through this system, they have revealed the role of migration machinery and cancer-associated genes in cell motility (Yolland *et al.* 2019; Zanet *et al.* 2009); the functions of cellular interactions during developmental migrations (Davis *et al.* 2012); and the relationship of the extracellular matrix with cell motility (Matsubayashi *et al.* 2017).

Maureen Thomas, Professor of Narrativity and Interactivity and Senior Artistic Researcher at the Norwegian Film and Television School, Oslo, is a dramatist, story architect and director with a special interest in Old Norse/Icelandic myth, poetry and literature. Her most recent (award-winning) feature film script is *Homo Novus* (2018). Previously, she was a Senior Creative Research Fellow at the Interactive Institute, Malmö University and a Senior Research Fellow at Churchill College, Cambridge. She publishes widely on interactive narrativity.

Guy Westwell is Reader in Film Studies at Queen Mary University of London and author of *War Cinema: Hollywood on the Front-line* (2006) and *Parallel Lines: Post-9/11 American Cinema* (2012) and co-author, with Annette Kuhn, of *The Oxford Dictionary of Film Studies* (2012, 2020). His current research focuses on the war and anti-war film, with a particular focus on peace, pacifism and conscientious objection.

Forms of the cinematic

An introduction

Mark E. Breeze

At the end of 2020, few spheres of life are not affected by moving images, either directly or indirectly, shaping how we think, visualize and construct the world around us, from the sciences to the arts. The increasingly easy reproducibility and visually captivating nature of moving images has been supercharged by the almost all-pervading digitality of our daily existence. Their reach is global, transcending disciplinary, social, economic, political, cultural and demographic boundaries to varying degrees. Informing even the most unstructured and banal moving images – narrative or otherwise – are the histories, theories and ever-evolving methods, tools and techniques of cinema. Indeed, cinematic forms have a special claim on our realities through their ability to document (and thus also archive), create and recreate pasts, presents and possible futures, sometimes simultaneously (see Ferro 1988, and Davies 2002, for example); and they familiarize, enable and perpetuate actions and events, including even violence and war (see Virilio 1989, and Zimmer and Leggett 1974, for example). Building on these axioms, this interdisciplinary volume examines a diverse variety of forms of the cinematic to explore its transformative nature to rethink, revisualize and reconstruct the worlds that we inhabit. In so doing, this book explores how cinema questions its own frames of reference, how its forms become the matter of its thoughts and how those forms reframe the matter of our lives.

Cinema has been a form and means of research since its very inception in the late nineteenth century, as the practice-based research of the scientist Étienne-Jules Marey or the photographer Eadweard Muybridge elucidate. Indeed, the filmmaker Jean Painlevé stated that it would 'never have occurred to the pioneers of film to dissociate research *on* film from research *by means* of film': film is shared experiments through technical manipulations of space, time, light and framing (Painlevé [1955] 2000: 161–9). The nature of film enables both the tangible and intangible to be examined and visualized, separately and together:

from animal movement (e.g. Étienne-Jules Marey, Eadweard Muybridge); cell behaviour (e.g. Michael Abercrombie, Ronald Canti); and city-planning (e.g. *Die Stadt von Morgen* (dir. Erich Kotzer and Maximilian von Goldbeck, 1930), *Architectures d'Aujourd'hui* (dir. Le Corbusier and Pierre Chenal, 1930); to our thoughts and memories (e.g. Henri Bergson, Germaine Dulac); and even our subconscious (e.g. Jean Cocteau, Ricciotto Canudo, Emile Vuillermoz). Avant-garde and experimental cinema explicitly explores many of these intersections (e.g. the work of Hans Richter or Walter Ruttmann), and as an art form in itself film implicitly touches on what Burch (1973) would describe as its 'poetic function'. Moreover, cinema has been envisaged as analogous to the human mind itself (e.g. Hugo Münsterberg) and as a medium that provides access to a 'reality of another dimension', to the 'concept of life as such . . . life as a powerful entity' (Kracauer 1960: 53, 169); as theorists from Jean Epstein to Gilles Deleuze have elucidated, it can be a type of thought-machine, producing purely mental images. Thus, we can understand film as more than just a device to 'defamiliarize' (as Shklovsky (2015) and the Russian formalists might have described it); it is a medium that can manifest new forms of thought and, thus, think with its spectators (see Deleuze [1986] 2003, and Deleuze [1989] 2003). This volume aims to explore and expand such understandings through a broad but focused exploration of how cinematic forms can be methods to think differently, tools to visualize the world afresh and techniques that transform the understandings and constructions of the discipline outside itself, and so starts to enable access beyond itself.

All moving images are forms of the cinematic to some degree: a series of images in a rapid sequence, creating the effect of movement over time, shaped by the tools, techniques and histories of its use. Movement is the essential trait of the cinematic – from the physical, to the illusory, to the suggested – as indeed Münsterberg argued (see Münsterberg 1970). Movement occurs on many levels: within the frame, of the frame, through the pull of the focus, to the cut of the edit. Indeed, Bergson argues that the image itself is always moving, given its position *between* a thing and its representation (Bergson 1991: vii–8). Through movement, the cinematic can create, fragment and immobilize time, and so shape space, as Bergson (1983) elucidates. And as Badiou argues, the cinematic 'makes time visible' (Badiou 2013: 209). Indeed, for Deleuze, 'the essence of cinema is the adventure of movement and time' (Deleuze 1989: xiii). And it is this essence that creates the impression of reality through a sensation created by movement: motion creates 'transformation and continuity' (Gunning 2007: 52).

Rhythm and pacing are extremely important too: the presence, control or lack of continuous linear movement transforms meanings; indeed, Vertov would always highlight the pauses and the intervals as intrinsic features of montage and, consequently, as a way of constructing and communicating meaning. The cinematic is a fluid system of motion, which enables it to constantly shift between notions of reality and fiction, freely creating its own sense of speed, rhythm, space and hence time and change: it is a highly adaptable system.

The cinematic has a complex web of roots in the static image. Gunning (2007) acknowledges the predominance of the photographic in thinking the cinematic – from Kracauer and Benjamin, to Bazin. Indeed, Benjamin argued how the image (especially slowed images) 'can bring out those aspects of the original that are unattainable to the naked eye . . . [and] can capture images that escape natural vision' (Benjamin 2008: 331). The motional form of the cinematic enables it to draw selectively on these roots, be it a Bazinian collapse of the distinction between the model and the object or the Piercian mediation between the object and viewer through symbolism, iconology and indexicality: it offers the possibility of its own images, languages and styles, as its extensive history shows. It enables us to form new relations with objects and other images more generally. In this sense, it is beyond the traditional realist readings of Bazin (1967), but not of the illusory nature that Langer (1953) argue. Similarly, this cinematic core is neither a language nor a language system, but more of an expression, following Metz (1974); and as Wollen notes, in the semiologically complex media of film there is no way of knowing what an image connotes – 'there is no pure cinema' (Wollen 2013: 132). The cinematic can provide detached and transparent representations, subjective and more objective visions, as well as embodied and disembodied viewpoints: it is a highly flexible and mutable mode of visioning.

The cinematic reconstructs vision and experience through its optical techniques, as the formative Muybridge movement studies elucidate. In the terms of Virilio (1989), the effect is to create a *different* form of visibility that uses illusion or its implicitly incomplete three-dimensional experience to create new spatial and experiential possibilities: it not only shapes these by its framing, editing and post-production, but also selectively documents and controls the duration and qualities of momentary phenomenon to construct, deconstruct and reconstruct our understandings of such. Everything shown becomes an object of observation, a construction of associations and dissociations in time and space, mutating our relations to – and impressions of – reality. What is *not* shown is vital too: how off-screen space becomes alive, and how the boundary of the frame can be creatively manipulated through source (off-screen) sound and movement, something Noël Burch describes as having a 'fluctuating existence during any film' (Burch 1973: 21). Extra or non-diegetic material (such as cutaways or sound, etc.) further multiplies the dimensions of the cinematic: to crudely modify Rudolph Arnheim's dictum, the cinematic is simultaneously two-dimensional, three-dimensional and something in-between (see Arnheim 1969: 20). The cinematic in this sense becomes more than Vertov's 'kino eye' that constructs, as it emphasizes continual change and transformation: it is a form that is constructing, deconstructing and reconstructing the viewer's subjective experience. The cinematic experience is by nature subjective, a thing to explore the world and present ourselves with symbols of reality. As Metz states – implicitly invoking Vertov – 'it is I who make the film': we are the screen, the projector and the camera – we receive, process, project and impose forms on what we see (Metz 1982: 48). The cinematic spectator is synthetically both passive and active in constructing and reconstructing it: the cinematic itself is in this sense never complete, as it depends on us – it is a process and in this sense a subjective tool.

The camera uniquely fixes and explores spatial and temporal relationships as Benjamin notes, and so can open up 'a new realm of consciousness' into being (Benjamin 2008: 264, 329). Indeed, Münsterberg and Arnheim explored film's unique capacity to manipulate reality, and convey thoughts and feelings (see Arnheim 1969; and Münsterberg 1970); Bazin (1967) and Kracauer (1960) explored its ability to re-present reality; and Balázs (1952) explored film as a process that can shows us a different reality, not capturable by the human eye. The cinematic in this sense is something other, something that can reconfigure our experience of the world in which we participate. The cinematic subjectively reproduces reality and manipulates it to explore specific conceptual effects and possibilities.

Through its ability to offer new and possibly unexpected configurations of the world (be it through sequencing, or in a particular focus on specific objects or effects), the cinematic can both reconfigure our understandings and embody philosophical thought (Cavell 2005). As Deleuze argues, it can generate new philosophical concepts and problems (Deleuze 1989). As such, the cinematic can be understood as a 'vector of thought' exactly because it 'alters the possibilities of synthesis' and in the process 'invents new syntheses' (Badiou 2013: 207–16). The work of Stephen Mulhall (2002) is relevant here, in conceiving film as a mode of philosophy using metaphor, symbolism and imagery to reflect and evaluate;

and in turn the Deleuzian argument that film thinks with images is implicit here too (Deleuze 1989). Indeed, D. N. Rodowick's elucidation of cinema as a mode of knowing is especially pertinent here in his emphasis on its 'elusiveness with respect to systematic thought' (Rodowick 2001: 167): the cinematic helps us think abstractly, but not systematically. In this sense the cinematic becomes a mode of thought that explores possibilities rather than dictating any particular understanding: it is a moving image with an elusive, shape-shifting form.

The cinematic is more than a mere mechanical recording, as Münsterberg articulated (see Münsterberg 1970). The formative work of Muybridge and Marey clearly elucidates the core nature of the cinematic as a spatially and temporally curated movement sequence, with specific intentions and effects. Interestingly, Benjamin noted that the German term 'operateur' refers to both a surgeon and a projectionist (Benjamin 2008: 233): both are skilled, temporally spatial undertakings. Indeed, as Deleuze notes, movement is an 'immediate given' of the cinematic image (Deleuze 1989: 64): the subtractive nature of 'framing' is counteracted by the editing and camera movement, which 'restores temporal and spatial connections' (Deleuze 1989: 58); the Soviet school of montage would probably go as far as to say that cinema is all about montage, as the work of Kuleshov, Eisenstein and Vertov shows. The cinematic is different to the 'simulacrum' of Baudrillard (1983) – where through the process of reproduction, reality and unreality blur to produce a representation of something that has never existed; rather, it is the selective use of movement to create a sequence that emphasizes or highlights specific temporal or spatial effects of the selected situation. The cinematic movement sequence is still a participatory movement, directing what effect to experience, at what distance, from what angle and for how long. The essence of the cinematic in this understanding is not a form of 'unseeing' as Cavell (1979) argues, where people and things are de-presented, but rather it is a movement of highly selective participatory sequences of effects: its form and effects are constantly moving.

The cinematic in its raw form has at best the most basic of narrative structures – a beginning, a middle and an end; but it can be but a fleeting snapshot without any such structure. (By this understanding, narrative is an additive element, rather than a fundamental core part of the cinematic.) Indeed, by the terms of narrative defined by Barthes, there is no progressive integration of functions, actions and narration (Barthes 1975: 243); similarly the sequence is not necessarily a whole within which nothing is repeated (Barthes 1975: 271). Such an understanding highlights the layered meaning to Stephen

Heath's argument that 'film takes place as narrative' (Heath 1976: 107): any filmic act is narrative, and the 'place' constructed by film is the narrative. The post-modern tradition opens up the complexities of what constitutes narrative – let alone the text, author and subject – as the film work of Peter Greenaway illustrates. This potential for meaningful storytelling via less structured or completely unstructured (random) narrations is particularly pertinent now in the new media and new technology landscape of the twenty-first century (see Manovich 2001). In many senses, this fluid complexity of narrative forms makes the cinematic closer to the 'neutral' described by Barthes: a structural thing, which can refer to intense and unprecedented states; a category, not a discipline; a 'stubborn affect', which has shed meaning (Barthes, Clerte and Marty 2005: 6–13). In this sense, the cinematic has no specific physical form in achieving specific affects.

In such an understanding, the objects represented are reduced to a mere image of particular effect (or affect); for example, the mammals of the motion studies of Muybridge and Marey are no longer individual animals of any specificity, but rather images of the physiology of movement. Although the initial basic intent of effect might be clear, any broader meaning is to be negotiated, as the cinematic reconfigures our personal experience of the world. To modify Barthes (in his 1970 essay 'The Third Meaning'), the informational and the symbolic are reconfigured to create the obtuse (see Barthes and Heath 1977: 44–68). And as Cavell (2015) argues, we can never be sure exactly what has been communicated. The cinematic is closer to Sobchack's (1992) understanding of film as a subjective, mediative act, which is both presentational and representational: it is a form of subjective inter-objectivity – it is never complete in itself. We are each shaped by our subjective experience of its relational sequence of focused effects, and we reshape it in how we experience and use it. In this sense, the cinematic is constantly exploring, engaging and articulating – and in the process re-forming – domains outside of itself: it is an incomplete, constantly re-articulating form.

In this process of articulating a participatory sequence of effects, the cinematic performs experience momentarily, and so it creates and constitutes our experience with a particular intensity. In framing and focusing our attention on particular effects, events and actions, for a particular duration of time, it overlaps our own experience of them in their context within our own individual temporal, cultural and social context. While Münsterberg claims film does 'not imitate reality but changes the world, selects from it special features for new purposes, remodels the world' (Münsterberg 1970: 114), the core cinematic performs a selected reality for the viewer to experience: its lack of definitive form enables it to constantly re-articulate the world. In this understanding, the cinematic is less a model for measuring the real, as Baudrillard claims (Baudrillard and Gane 1993: 47); rather, the cinematic is a sociocultural tool for dynamically performing a moment of its specific context in time, which reflexively enables us to rethink our engagement with the world.

Like the origins of cinema itself, this book is richly interdisciplinary and methodologically diverse. From still photography to moving images and digital augmented reality, cinematic forms continue to evolve with and through advancements in equipment, processes, disciplines and understandings of reality itself – how we theorize it, represent it and tell stories about it. As such, this volume draws on a wide variety of methodologies in a rich range of disciplines that continue to engage with – and be transformed by – film. Through a breadth of approaches by both academics and practitioners from a diversity of disciplines, this collection reveals the depth and nature of cinematic forms – from architecture, biological science and philosophy, to filmmaking, scriptwriting and many fields in-between. Through this strategic, inclusive and intra-disciplinary engagement, this collection will begin to elucidate the dynamic range, nature and implications of these forms of the cinematic to think, visualize and construct our own realities.

The contributions are grouped in three key parts: Rethinking, Revisualizing and Reconstructing. As inadequate as these categorizations may be, they nevertheless demarcate three fundamental qualities of the forms of the cinematic, none of which is mutually exclusive. Part One, 'Rethinking: from Idea to Structure', explores the cinematic as a different mode of abstract thought that can not only illustrate philosophical concepts but also think conceptually in its own right through its structure and forms. Part Two, 'Revisualizing: from the Tangible to the Intangible', examines the cinematic as a tool, exploring how it can make dynamic physical and conceptual processes that are not fully visible to the human eye, visible, and thereby provide a unique means of analysis for us to revise our understanding of the world around us. The final part, 'Reconstructing: from Writing to Architecture', examines the cinematic as a technique, exploring how it can work performatively, and in so doing enables us to critique and remake the experiential world in which we all share.

Part One, 'Rethinking: from Idea to Structure', examines the cinematic forms of its own practice as *methods* of thinking. Reflecting on his own experimental film and installation art practice, D. N. Rodowick asks what it would mean to propose seriously that creative work is a philosophical practice. He examines, in Chapter 1, how thinking in concepts and thinking in images intersect in points of contact and exchange as forms of creative intuition. In reading his own moving image practice as posing new philosophical questions or problems, he asks how one can creatively extract or produce different dimensions of sensation. His investigations pose new questions about the ontologies of analogical and digital media, while creatively producing new varieties of digital time images, new strategies for aspect seeing in time and novel ways for apprehending the rhythms of history and memory.

In Chapter 2, Stephen Mulhall focuses on how films can not only think about the sorts of problems philosophers characteristically think about but also make a contribution to a reflective conversation about them. Affirming that some films are capable of questioning our prior faith in our general theories as they are of confirming that faith, he suggests that some films can be understood as critically engaging with the work of specific philosophers. Through juxtaposing Stanley Cavell's claims about the distinctive nature of the screen in cinema with a reading of Brad Bird's commercial film *Tomorrowland: A World Beyond* (2015), he elucidates their shared interest in a version of moral perfectionist thinking. In showing how each of them critically evaluates the screen's way of disclosing and barring us from the world of its films, he argues for the role of the screen itself as a barrier and support.

In Chapter 3, John Ó Maoilearca reframes the exploration of how film can be philosophical in its own way by demonstrating a philosophical approach that emerges directly from the formal structure of film itself. To explicate his argument, he uses the cinematic model of Lars von Trier's and Jørgen Leth's *The Five Obstructions* (2003) – a film that documents Leth remaking one of his own early films five times under different creative constraints set by von Trier – to introduce the non-standard philosophy of François Laruelle. Noting that Laruelle claims his philosophy is itself modelled on artistic practices, Ó Maoilearca thus remakes this film of philosophy, thereby demonstrating a philosophical approach that emerges directly from the look of film.

What of the *task* of philosophy in relation to film? In Chapter 4, Tom Conley reminds us that Deleuze assumed it to be the production of *events*, and, following Bergson, Peirce and Bazin, he correlated that task with what cinema does via its image types. But, as Deleuze himself asked in *Le Pli: Leibniz et le baroque* (1988), 'What is an Event?' Conley carefully elucidates how cinema inflects Deleuze's response to this question through a concept Deleuze draws from Bazin and Proust – the 'image-fact'. Through studying Fritz Lang's *Fury* (1936), Conley shows how an otherwise passing sequence can be taken as an unsettling 'event' in its strongest philosophical and cinematic inflection: the cinematic simultaneously thinks itself and outside itself.

Part Two, 'Revisualizing: from the Tangible to the Intangible', examines the cinematic as a *tool* of observation and analysis that enables us to visualize afresh the physically tangible and intangible. In Chapter 5, Annette Kuhn and Guy Westwell ask how we should visualize and thus map the simultaneously tangible and intangible elements of the discipline of film studies itself. In guiding us through the process of creating and revising their seminal *Oxford Dictionary of Film Studies* (2020), they reveal how the dictionary is both a picture and an enactment of interconnections between, and fluctuations in the status of, various areas of inquiry within film studies.

In Chapter 6, François Penz and Janina Schupp consider films as a tangible visual archive of the practice of everyday life in domestic spaces, and thus how films can make intangible cultural differences spatially tangible. Through overviewing the aims, objectives and methodology of their recent Cinematic *Musée Imaginaire* of Spatial Cultural Differences project, they elucidate how they have begun to construct a cinematic ontology of spatial cultural differences between the Western 'naturalism' tradition and the Eastern 'analogism' tradition: the cinematic form is here a global, historical, visual source of constructed and recorded spatial differences.

Brian Stramer continues this exploration of the cinematic form as a mode of visual observation and analysis through examining the history of cinemicroscopy in the context of his own biological research and teaching, in Chapter 7. He elucidates how the controllable temporal nature of film makes it a critical experimental tool to observe and analyse cellular processes in new ways, leading to significant biological discoveries. By making the intangible tangible, these biomedical films enable more engaged and effective forms of education, and new forms of entertainment. Noting the entwined relationship at the end of the nineteenth century between the origins of the moving image, biological research and novel forms of entertainment, he sees a renewed opportunity now for scientists and filmmakers to collaborate to engage wider audiences.

In Chapter 8, Maureen Thomas further develops these understandings of cinematic forms as simultaneously historical sources, types of entertainment, educational resources and critical tools, through examining how cultural heritage has been constructed, reconstructed and expressed in a diverse range of audiovisual narrative forms that visualize mythopoeia – from films and television series, to immersive and interactive works. She elucidates how changing cultural constructions in audiovisual media follow a long tradition of cherishing, questioning and developing the tangible and intangible cultural heritage that reflects and shapes our values.

Part Three, 'Reconstructing: from Writing to Architecture', examines the cinematic as a *technique* of making which transforms disciplines and their disciplinary acts, and in so doing creates new forms of engagement with the world. Clare L. E. Foster opens the section by examining the cinematic techniques of narrative construction in screenwriting, drawing on her own experience as a movie scriptwriter. She understands screenwriting as a means to an end rather than an end in itself, and in that sense quintessentially instrumental. As in music, the art of film is characterized by duration and sequence; the meaning of an image is a function of how much, and when, we get to look at it. She explores how screenwriting is the practice of suggestion, and anticipated effect – in short, of emphasis – where space on the page becomes time. She reflects on this new status of screenplays both as a literature in their own right – separate entities from the end product for which they are functionally a tool – and as the opposite – not 'stories' in the conventional sense at all, but 'content' that is endlessly transferable to as many media and platforms as possible. Screenwriting becomes a kind of anti-writing: writing that succeeds by writing itself out of the game. As such, she elucidates how the cinematic transforms writing into a spatial and temporal performance of the unfolding narrative experience – a form of writing which envisages the film as the audiences it implies.

In Chapter 10, Stavros Alifragkis explores how cinematic techniques can construct and remake spatial and temporal experiences of architecture and landscape. Through an original reading of the Zone in Andrei Tarkovsky's *Stalker* (1979), he correlates different spatial categories with Tarkovsky's itinerant camera to discuss his film poetics from a chiefly architectural point of view. He debates how Tarkovsky's disjointed film sets become meaningful narrative spaces and a monumental architecture of procession, thereby enabling a better understanding of both the filmmaker's distinct screen language and the construction of his personal and idiosyncratic filmic landscape. In so doing, he shows how cinematic techniques can subtly yet dramatically remake spatio-temporal experiences and so open up different possibilities for the built and natural environment.

Anna Andersen directly uses cinematic techniques herself in Chapter 11 to bring new understanding to how disability can be considered in architectural design. She argues that instead of universal design solutions, architects should aim to engage with the messiness, complexities and contradictions of all human bodies, disabled or not. Through a self-inflected process of making an essay film and then writing about that process, she asks how filmmaking as a practice can be used as a critical tool in architectural thinking. With a specific focus on radio microphones and the Bolex H16 film camera, she discusses filmmaking as a critical spatial practice, well suited to tackle the complicated relationships between body and building. In this way she elucidates how the cinematic means of audiovisual recording is a powerful technique to access inhabited space and lived experience, enabling a different understanding of the implications and potentials of architectural design to engage and transform bodily experiences.

In the final chapter, I evaluate the architectural implications of the early relationship between the disciplines and practices of architecture and cinema. Through analysing selected key works of the architectural historian Auguste Choisy, the trained engineer, architect and filmmaker Sergei Eisenstein, and the architect, theorist and sometime filmmaker Le Corbusier, I argue that the evolving and increasingly intertwined architecture–cinema relationship opens up richer ways of thinking and conveying the emotional and physical experiential qualities and possibilities of architecture. I show how these cinematic approaches re-centre the subjective human experience and emphasize architecture as a performative act that constantly shapes, frames, orients and moves us – both physically and emotionally – just as we shape it through our bodily presence, experiences and use of it. The cinematic in this sense can become an enabling condition for a different mode of architectural understanding and practice – architecture as a form of the cinematic.

The approach and scope of this volume certainly has many limits, both practical and theoretical. Given its very nature as a small, static, black-and-white object, the ability to engage the reader fully in many of the examples cited – especially moving images – is necessarily limited. Within these constraints I gave the authors relatively free reign over whether to use images or not, as they felt appropriate to tactically elucidate their arguments; hopefully, the result helps to illustrate the meaningful diversity of styles and approaches represented in this volume. Furthermore, for the sake of clarity and consistency across so many different approaches and disciplines, many complexities have been simplified, and nuances grotesquely blurred. I know some will find the almost-cavalier shifting between the terms 'film', 'moving image' and 'cinema' especially egregious – as well as the similarly fluid use of 'cinematic' as the adjectival form encompassing all those terms; the nuances of these distinctions are well dissected and debated elsewhere, and so for the purposes of this volume and to avoid confusion, these terms are used quite broadly except where explicitly called out.

Given the brevity of this volume, not all fields, theories, methodologies, broader discussions and contributors that one would want to include ideally in an intra-disciplinary collection such as this could be accommodated. However, the histories and theories of the cinematic form itself are deliberately not discussed or analysed here, as this volume seeks to complement that extensive literature by looking beyond the discipline itself, to how its forms infiltrate, inflect, modify and make anew fields beyond its own.

This book hints at the richness of cinematic forms that permeate so many aspects of our contemporary existence, and the different narratives, realities and affective worlds to which they give us access. There is deliberately no conclusion to the volume, as it seeks to open up broader discussions about the nature, range and roles of cinematic forms, as methods, tools and techniques to rethink, revisualize and reconstruct the world that we inhabit. Through exploring these latent and manifest forms of the cinematic, this volume begins to think cinema outside of itself.

References

Arnheim, R. (1969), *Film as Art*, London: Faber and Faber.
Badiou, A. (2013), *Cinema*, ed. A. de Baecque, trans. S. Spitzer, Cambridge, MA: Polity Press.
Balázs, B. (1952), *Theory of the Film: Character and the Growth of a New Art*, London: Dennis Dobson.
Barthes, R. (1975), 'An Introduction to the Structural Analysis of Narrative', trans. L. Duisit, *New Literary History*, 6 (2): 237–72.
Barthes, R. and S. Heath, eds (1977), *Image Music Text*, trans. S. Heath, New York: Hill and Wang.
Barthes, R., T. Clerte and E. Marty, eds (2005), *The Neutral: Lecture Course at the Collège de France, 1977–78*, trans. R. Krauss and D. Hollier, New York: Columbia University Press.
Baudrillard, J. (1983), *Simulations*, trans. P. Foss, P. Patton and P. Beeitchman, New York: Semiotext(e).

Baudrillard, J. and M. Gane, eds (1993), *Baudrillard Live: Selected Interviews*, London: Routledge.
Bazin, A. (1967), *What Is Cinema?* Vol. 1, trans. H. Gray, Berkeley: University of California Press.
Benjamin, W. (2008), *The Work of Art in the Age of Its Technological Reproducibility and Other Writing on Media*, ed. M. Jennings, B. Doherty and T. Levin, Cambridge, MA: Harvard University Press.
Bergson, H. (1983), *Creative Evolution*, trans. A. Mitchell, Boston: University Press of America.
Bergson, H. (1991), *Matter and Memory*, trans. N. Paul and W. Palmer, New York: Zone Books.
Burch, N. (1973), *Theory of Film Practice*, London: Secker and Warburg.
Cavell, S. (1979), *The World Viewed: Reflections on the Ontology of Film*, New York: Viking Press.
Cavell, S. (1984), *Themes Out of School: Effects and Causes*, San Francisco: North Point Press.
Cavell, S. (2005), *Philosophy the Day After Tomorrow*, Cambridge, MA: Harvard University Press.
Cavell, S. (2015), *Must I Mean What I Say?: A Book of Essays*, Cambridge: Cambridge University Press.
Davies, N. Z. (2002), *Slaves on Screen: Film and Historical Vision*, Cambridge, MA: Harvard University Press.
Deleuze, G. ([1986] 2003), *Cinema 1: The Movement-Image*, trans. H. Tomlinson and B. Habberjam, Minneapolis: University of Minneapolis Press.
Deleuze, G. ([1989] 2003), *Cinema 2: The Time-Image*, trans. H. Tomlinson and R. Galeta, Minneapolis: University of Minneapolis Press.
Ferro, M. (1988), *Cinema and History*, trans. N. Greene, Detroit: Wayne State University Press.
Geraghty, C. (2007), 'Re-examining Stardom: Questions of Texts, Bodies and Performance', in S. Redmond and S. Holmes (eds), *Stardom and Celebrity: A Reader*, 93–105, London: Sage.
Gunning, Tom. (2007), 'Moving Away from the Index: Cinema and the Impression of Reality', *Differences*, 18 (1): 29–52.
Heath, S. (1976), 'Narrative Space', *Screen*, 17 (3): 68–112.
Kracauer, S. (1960), *Theory of Film: The Redemption of Physical Reality*, New York: Oxford University Press.
Landecker, H. (2006), 'Microcinematography and the History of Science and Film', *Isis*, 97 (1) March: 121–32.
Langer, S. (1953), *Feeling and Form: A Theory of Art Developed from Philosophy in a New Key*, London: Charles Scribner & Sons.
Manovich, L. (2001), *The Language of New Media*, Cambridge, MA: MIT Press.

Metz, C. (1974), *Film Language; A Semiotics of the Cinema*, trans. M. Taylor, New York: Oxford University Press.

Metz, C. (1982), *Psychoanalysis and Cinema: The Imaginary Signifier*, trans. C. Britton, London: Macmillan.

Mulhall, S. (2002), *On Film*, London: Routledge.

Münsterberg, H. (1970), *The Photoplay: A Psychological Study; The Silent Photoplay in 1916*. New York: Arno Press.

Painlevé, J. ([1955] 2000), 'La Technique Cinématographique', in A. M. Bellows and M. McDougall (eds), *Science Is Fiction: The Films of Jean Painlevé*, trans. J. Herman, 160–9, Cambridge, MA: MIT Press.

Rodowick, D. (2001), *Reading the Figural, or, Philosophy after the New Media*, Durham: Duke University Press.

Shklovsky, V. (2015), 'Art, as Device', *Poetics Today*, 36 (3): 151–74.

Sobchack, V. (1992), *The Address of the Eye: A Phenomenology of Film Experience*, Princeton: Princeton University Press.

Virilio, P. (1989), *War and Cinema: The Logistics of Perception*, London: Verso.

Wollen, P. (2013), *Signs and Meaning in the Cinema*, 5th edn, London: Palgrave Macmillan.

Zimmer, C. and L. Leggett (1974), 'All Films Are Political', *SubStance*, 3 (9) Spring: 123–36.

Part One

Rethinking: from Idea to Structure

1

Idea and image

D. N. Rodowick

Compare a concept with a style in painting.
    Ludwig Wittgenstein, *Philosophical Investigations*

Whether classic or modern, the great philosophers are often inventive stylists. It takes only a slight direction of attention to recognize suddenly that Plato or Wittgenstein are poets of philosophy, no less than Emerson, Nietzsche, Cavell, Deleuze and indeed many others. How is it possible to separate their art of thinking from the writerly composition of concepts in a space and time whose weaving of voice, rhythm, polyphony and counterpoint seem so close to musical creation? In fact, one cannot. Thinking and the expressive line are inextricably intertwined in the great philosophical stylists.

Deleuze himself beautifully voiced this perspective in a lecture entitled 'What is the Creative Act?', presented at La Fémis in 1991, which opens with the question, 'What does it mean to have an idea in cinema?' Deleuze notes an experience all too familiar to every creative mind – having an idea is an event worth celebrating because its occurrence is rare and unpredictable. To think, one must prepare a terrain and a context where an idea can germinate and unfold because, as Deleuze says,

> No one has an idea in general. An idea – like the one who has the idea – is already dedicated to a particular field. . . . Ideas have to be treated like potentials already *engaged* in one mode of expression or another and inseparable from the mode of expression, such that I cannot say that I have an idea in general. Depending on the techniques I am familiar with, I can have an idea in a certain domain, an idea in cinema or an idea in philosophy. (Deleuze 2006: 312)

One of the principal lessons expressed here is that there is no difference between theory and practice. I have often been asked to explain how I understand the relationship between my philosophical work and my creative practice. For many years, my habitual response was simple though perhaps not very clear or revealing: I am thinking, and these are two media or practices wherein or through which I feel compelled to think. Or, as Deleuze might say, I am thinking but in the two different domains of concept and image.[1]

The inescapable impulse to create experimental images and to write what is sometimes called 'theory' has for me always arisen simultaneously, as if springing from the same barely conscious point of origin. Many years later, I discovered that Henri Bergson named this experience as 'intuition' and made it the source of his creative philosophy. There is nothing mysterious or occult about intuition: it is a concrete philosophical practice where thinking deeply engages with the matter and time of human and inhuman life; its modes of attention are open to everyone, whether artist or philosopher. What Bergson calls intuition is a way of engaging thoughtfully with the world – and all the complexities of spatial and temporal experience of being in a world – with the fullness of your combined mental, perceptual and bodily attention. In its deepest sense, philosophical intuition involves thinking directly in and through sensory experience both perceptually and mentally, where body and mind resonate in their multiple relations with the world's forces, energies and matters of sensation. Thoughtful investigation through intuition may lead to philosophy (conceptual expression) or unfold itself in perceptual experience (say, images or percepts), but somewhere their borders always touch and interpenetrate, flowing into and out of one another in a domain whose point of departure may be mental experience (thinking as philosophy) or a perceptual experience (thinking through the image).

The scandal remains but must be directly confronted: What would it mean to propose seriously that creative work is a philosophical practice? Take as one point of departure the relation between problems and ideas as related to intuition. Here, the philosophical question one might ask of any given creative work is: How does an intuition give rise to an idea that is formulated in response to a problem?

If there is any unifying thread to my creative practice – and I believe there is – it arises in intuiting ways of making movement and time 'problematic' in relation to perception and thought as discovering new forms of the cinematic. Investigating critically the mediation of temporal experience by technicity – the logical design of cameras, lenses and recording media, whether analogue or digital – is another special concern. All of my moving image works may be read as posing new questions or problems about temporal and sensory experience by experimentally testing the normative design of recording devices and programmes with respect to the capture of light, space, colour, movement, duration and time. In this respect, I have a continuing interest in amateur or consumer recording technologies and programmes because these are machines designed to reproduce automatically a restricted set of perceptual norms of space and time. The question then arises: How can one creatively extract or produce different dimensions of sensation by experimentally testing these technologies in ways that push them beyond their design parameters and thus submit them to an internal critique?

Take for example two of my own short film works made thirty years apart: *Southcote Road: Frame Displacement* (1982, 16 mm silent film, colour, three minutes) and *Waterloo* (2012, HD video, colour, sound, three minutes fifty-eight seconds).[2] One obvious commonality between the two works is their internal time structure and the fact that they are made through improvised performative actions that are territorially delimited in space and duration. The basis of both works is circular walks in defined locations: *Southcote Road* documents the street where I lived in London on the last day of a seven-week stay in the summer of 1981; *Waterloo* documents an urban any-space-whatever in contemporary London. The brevity and temporal discipline of the second walk is inspired by the first. Editing plays no role in either work apart from starting and stopping a process.

Like many of my earlier films, *Southcote Road* is structured by a gestural performance, a dialogue or dance between a hand-held camera and a shaving mirror, improvised within an automated protocol: in this instance, programming the camera with an intervalometer to capture one frame per second until, after three minutes, the film runs out. Unlike digital capture, which is limited in duration only by the memory capacity of digital devices, here time is a finite resource that expires in a fixed interval. In *Waterloo* and my other digital 'walking' works, I apply this durational constraint as an abstract discipline in order to restore the value and density of time to a digital domain where time is in principle unlimited and thus increasingly devalued.

Absent from the projected space of *Southcote Road* is evidence of the physical exhaustion and actual duration of the performance, which took nearly one hour to record. In *Waterloo*, however, the time of the work is the time of the walk. Just under four minutes long, *Waterloo* captures in 'real-time' a thoroughly mundane location and situation: two circular trajectories through an underground passageway connecting the London Imax theatre to Waterloo station. Using an iPhone on a hand-manipulated monopod, I follow a figurative line drawn by the electrical conduit running along the top of the tunnel walls. Of course, this is not what one sees in the image. Similar to *Southcote Road*, *Waterloo* is recorded in a single take using a capture rate of one interval per second. As I move through the space, focus, exposure and effective shutter speed are allowed to float. The initial images begin as almost-abstract colour fields that are blurred, textured and fluid before resolving into a new series of volumes that emerge as if roughly extracted from the electrical conduit: jagged tubular shapes expand, contract and torque while dissolving and reshaping themselves unpredictably against the varying and textured colour fields. These tonalities emerge in response to the shifts in colour temperature and luminance produced by the tunnel's sources of artificial illumination. The sound is captured in real time along with these images – distant traffic, rumblings, footsteps, drunken laughter and snippets of animated conversation. The off-screen presence of real-time synchronized audio is an important temporal marker, for the rhythmic succession of (only) apparently still images are shaped by a duration every bit as real as the sound.

Despite other similarities, I think of these two works as experiments aimed at extracting novel dimensions or varieties of time from a given duration by exploring how spatial intervals produce tensions between stillness and movement. There is also something like an 'epistemological' difference between the two works as defined by their improvised, gestural performances in the analogue and digital domains. *Southcote Road*'s compositional gestures are photographic and 'reflexive' while *Waterloo*'s are immersive and sensory.

The automated operations of the intervalometer in *Southcote Road* compress time and duration so as to unveil the materiality of the filmstrip in a stuttering series of sequential images that shape a perceptual mise en abyme where the camera hand works to frame the mirror hand – there is a constant doubling of frame and screen as rotations of the mirror produce a cascade of reflected images from off-screen space. This is a reflexive gesture where the image sees itself seeing itself. Alternatively, in *Waterloo* the gestural hand paints a digital space where the interval is stilled, and space is stretched and blurred because the algorithms for maintaining focus, exposure and colour rendering lag behind the movements of the hand in this low light environment. On top of – or alongside – the uninterrupted duration of the soundtrack, there unfolds in the replacement of one image by another a digital domain whose framing of movement has a different phenomenological status than an analogue photogram – it is more a phase space of fluid and abstract transitions where time is suspended than a series of animated stills. Call this a digital time that appears in the image because the automated and algorithmic functions built into the camera continually fail to maintain the representational norms for which they were designed. Nevertheless, everything presented onscreen in *Waterloo* is data drawn from the actual environment – volumes, movements, surfaces, light intensities, colour temperatures and so forth. This is the prosaic world in which we situate ourselves, but it is not the world of the so-called natural perception, which is still apparent in *Southcote Road*'s staccato series of images.

These first two examples demonstrate the central formal and philosophical thread of my creative practice: with one or two exceptions, none of my works present movement in what is conventionally called 'real time'. Almost all devices for recording moving images, especially consumer devices, are designed to capture and present time as if it were a homogenous medium that unfolds through linear and chronological movements presented as uniform and continuous changes in space: either uninterrupted duration or the quantitative addition of continuous spatial sections (long take or continuity editing). How can one imagine creatively other forms of temporal experience?

Taichung (2012, HD video, colour, sound, four minutes fifty seconds) is one work that seems to be an exception to my investigation of alternatives to the so-called 'real time' recording. Rather than interrupting movements by recording at unconventional frame rates, *Taichung* is a phenomenological exploration of the infinite density of the physical reality of a world location and its space–time architecture. The work was recorded at sunrise from the thirty-seventh floor of a hotel in Taiwan's second city, Taichung. At first the image appears to be perfectly still, as if a photographic slide of a cityscape accompanied by the off-screen sound of a blaring television. The sound is incomprehensible for non-Mandarin speakers, but its genre is unmistakable. It is in fact a measure of mundane media time – a news and weather report leading up to a change of hour – and similar to the soundtrack of *Waterloo*, it is an obvious measure of chronologically unfolding duration. Real time takes on a different meaning, however, as presented by the perceptual discrepancy between a prosaic sonic time and the only apparently still image, which actually frames an infinite variety of barely perceptible interconnected micromovements: the early morning passage of minuscule cars and trucks; tiny bursts of light throughout the frame, which are actually car headlights on the horizon; the passage of clouds so slow as to be barely detectable; and towards the end, the rising sun, only a few pixels in size, that appears above the mountains before disappearing into the clouds. The idea of *Taichung* is to recover from a singular duration a dense matrix of physical and natural actions in all of their incalculable contingency and complexity. For viewers willing to redirect their perception and phenomenological attunement, the image is anything but static, minimal and empty of content – there are entire worlds to discover there if one can release oneself from an alienated and mediatized clock time to intuit more deeply the infinite density of movement and time bustling in this interwoven matrix of human and natural actions.

Center (Inside Out) (2013–14, HD video, colour, silent, one minute thirty seconds) presents another stark alternative both related to – yet different from – the temporal tactics I have discussed so far. I have mentioned my interest in testing the technological limits of consumer recording devices. What is the difference here between the analogue and digital domains? Working with 'tricked-out' iPhones and iPads, I began to discover that digital cameras were fundamentally distinct, perhaps even ontologically distinct, from analogue video recorders; indeed, they are more like programmable computers with lenses than recording devices. This realization inspired a number of new experiments with non-standard frame rates and shutter speeds. However, I found myself missing a special capability of Super-8 cameras: the possibility of 'triggering' images one photogram at a time and using in-camera editing to build up animated image clusters of various metrical lengths and combinations. Both Rose Lowder and Kurt Kren have created compelling work with these strategies. Turning a video recorder on and off is not the same as triggering a single film frame because, as can be seen in the contrast of *Waterloo* with *Southcote Road*, the digital image is not a photogram; it is rather a pixel matrix. Unlike Super-8 or 16 mm film, it is difficult to animate images in camera because digital recorders capture dynamic data streams rather than whole frames. Change occurs not in the displacement of one 'image' by another, but rather through data operations in a logical space that samples light values and encodes them as symbolic notations of colour, intensity and position. Individual pixels in the matrix correspond to memory locations that are dynamically updated during capture and playback; pixel values are continually changing but the matrix itself does not move. At a fundamental level, the digital apparatus conditions time, movement and space in ways that are profoundly different from the photochemical filmic apparatus, and acknowledging these conditions shape intuitive responses to a new philosophical problem: What is a digital time image? I will return to this question. But for the moment, it is important to acknowledge that digital cameras do capture still images, that is, 'photographs'.

Center (Inside Out) is a love letter to Le Corbusier's Carpenter Center for the Visual Arts at Harvard University (where I spent nine stimulating years) and a video postcard to the colleagues I left behind when I moved to Chicago in 2013. The idea informing *Center* was to invent a strategy of in-camera digital animation analogous to what is very simply done in the analogue domain. The solution was to adapt a time-lapse programme for the iPhone, although using it to record only one image at a time at disjoined temporal intervals of one-thirtieth of a second – the elapsed interval between any given image in *Center* can range from several minutes to several months, although this is invisible to the viewer in the flood of images passing onscreen at thirty frames per second. *Center* is related to both *Southcote Road* and *Waterloo* through the idea of investigating different ways of relating stillness and movement in non-standard times and frame rates. It is also another unedited work, though this time 'hand animated' by taking a series of over one thousand sequential still images over a period of a year. The successive images follow a planned trajectory circling around the outside of the building, and then descending in circular movements from the top floor to the basement. Individual details are composed to assure maximum discontinuity through a precise compositional discipline: each successive image is framed to maximize contrast in terms of scale, shape, colour, texture and other formal values. Despite the apparent rapid-fire continuity, because there is an indefinite interval between each image, the composed fragments assembled on the timeline involve a radical compression of time into an image crystal or constellation where a life lived over twelve months is condensed into one minute and thirty seconds. Perhaps *Center* and *Taichung* can be read as two variations on a digital time image where the intensive intervals of *Center* turn the durational image of *Taichung* 'inside out', thus revealing between and across each image micro-intervals of time whose interval duration and division fall below perception, yet makes themselves perceptible, perhaps, as rhythm.

The deeper problem I am trying to define here is the ontological distinctiveness of the presentation of time in digital images, which in my creative work is often intuitively expressed by exploring different varieties of stillness in relation to movement. There is an absolute stillness at the bottom of cinematographic movement, which is the individual photographic frame on the filmstrip, where time congeals into a space that cannot be further subdivided. This segmented time then becomes a building block for assembling fixed spatial intervals at various scales – from Eisenstein or Vertov's metrical editing, to the sequence shots of Orson Welles or Béla Tarr – that define the pulse of time in every filmic image.

Alternatively, everything in the digital image is a numerical *process*, and this intuition leads to two fundamental facts whose potential creative significance is very great. First, digital images can express change, but they do not *move* because their fundamental form is symbolic notation, tokens of numbers within a pixel matrix that neither occupies space nor changes through time. Rather, time values are assigned to groups of pixels as output instructions in the form 'retain value *x* for time interval *y*'. The stilled digital interval is less a 'freeze frame' than a suspension of time within the matrix or designated regions of the matrix. We may perceive 'movement', but ontologically the electronic image is never wholly present in either space or time, nor does it 'pass' in any way analogous to the unreeling filmstrip. Instead, the digital image is constructed through dynamic changes in information inputs and outputs within a pixel matrix that is fundamentally discontinuous – it is never identical to itself in a given moment of time, but rather is presented in a mosaic of oscillating pixels.

This discontinuity at the heart of the digital image leads to the second fundamental intuition: one can construct micro-intervals of time and assemble them into constellations that interact at scales above and below the frame, or even as fractional divisions within the frame.[3] Unlike the chemical photogram embedded on the film strip, the digital interval is almost infinitely variable, scalable and divisible. Finite extension in space is always the measure and limit of photochemical time. Alternatively, within the digital image, composed space and time may be compressed or expanded at will on the editing timeline – any given interval may in principle be digitally re-timed in durations ranging from fractions of seconds to minutes or even hours.

Again, I turn to paired examples. *Pyramid* (2016, HD video, colour, silent, three minutes fifty seconds), is the result of experiments inspired after visiting an exhibition at London's Tate Museum that same year: *Conceptual Art in Britain, 1964-1979*. The title of the work and its 'protagonist' refers to Roelof Louw's *Soul City (Pyramid of Oranges)* (1967), a sculpture composed from a pyramid of fresh oranges whose geometry is gradually disrupted as visitors 'consume' the work by taking away its organic elements one by one.

However, the mathematical protocol and the aesthetic idea informing my *Pyramid* was more directly inspired by John Hilliard's matrix of seventy photographs entitled, *Camera Recording its Own Condition (7 Apertures, 10 Speeds, 2 Mirrors)* (1971).[4] In contrast to *Center*, *Pyramid* was animated in Final Cut Pro on the digital timeline, in full knowledge that the digital image has no fixed interval but rather its duration can be digitally re-timed along both horizontal and vertical compositional axes. The work is composed from 482 sequential photographs of Louw's eponymous orange, captured with systematic variations in light and dark bracket exposures, which were then assembled into a baseline video of twenty-second duration, which is itself repeated ten times. The internal time structure of the work resulted from assembling a time 'pyramid' in which six layers of the baseline video are superimposed one on top of the other; each layer is then re-timed systematically for shorter and shorter durations, thereby creating more and more compressed speeds. Viewed as a static graphical picture within the editing programme, the stacked layers appear geometrically in the form of a pyramid, thus giving this digital time image its name. But when displayed on the screen, the fixed matter of the orange shatters into bursts of flickering quanta of light or energy that pulse in heterogenous waves or flows until receding into darkness. The rigid spherical form gradually and systematically dissolves as micro-intervals of time accumulate within it as if an intensive temporal mise en abyme.

Untitled (2017, HD video, colour, silent, nine minutes), sometimes referred to as *Augustine on the Beach*, exemplifies another tactic of using time pyramids to work with intensive and heterogenous durations. The video opens with a citation from Augustine's *Confessions*, 'Time never lapses, nor does it glide at leisure through our sense perceptions. It does strange things in the mind', and concludes with the philosopher's question:

> What, then, is time? If no one asks me, I know what it is. If I wish to explain it to him who asks me, I do not know. Yet I say with confidence that I know that if nothing passed away, there would be no past time; and if nothing were still coming, there would be no future time; and if there were nothing at all, there would be no present time.

Untitled is a creative response – in the form of another kind of digital time image – to the philosophical problem posed by Augustine's pointillist conception of passing time in which three temporalities coexist within any given interval: a time present of things past, a time present of things present and a time present of things future. Here the baseline is a simple long take of a sunset on the ocean at Étretat on the coast of Normandy, a site favoured by many Impressionist painters. But similar to *Pyramid*, this simple duration is interrupted and internally complicated by superimposing eight stacks or layers of the baseline image whose durations are increasingly compressed. In simple chronological time, the sun sets within seven minutes. However, the time pyramid in *Untitled* is constructed so that after thirty seconds a second layer is superimposed on top of the first, but re-timed so that the sun sets within a duration of about six minutes and so on incrementally until, at the peak of the pyramid, the movements of sun, clouds and waves are compressed into a duration of one minute. What one sees inside the work are internal cycles or repetitions of more and more compressed time that blur the image and cause it to vibrate internally with more and more intensive rhythms until its forms begin to dissolve into atmospheres, producing painterly effects not unlike Monet's 1872 *Impression, soleil levant*. In the final stages of the work, chronological time reasserts itself gradually as the superimposed durations conclude one by one.

The model of the time pyramid has become more and more frequent in my work, starting with the fourth part of *Plato's Phaedrus* (2016, HD video, colour, Dolby 5.1, sixty-eight minutes) and its companion piece, *Agora, or things indifferent* (2015–16, HD video, colour, Dolby 5.1, eleven minutes), and extending to more recent videos like *Lichtung Test No. 1* (2017, HD video, colour, nine minutes nine seconds). While the basic idea may seem simple, I discovered that an almost infinite variety of spatial effects can be produced within the temporal geometry of time pyramids by experimenting with mathematical formulas for manipulating the ratio of intervals aligned on the horizonal line in relation to the ratio of micro-intervals ascending into the vertical stacks. One might imagine these formulas as a kind of a digital alchemy or numerology.

I want to conclude, however, with another idea that is becoming more and more important to both my single-channel videos and my work with moving image installations. I call this 'aspect seeing in time'. Aspect perception is a phenomenon familiar to psychology, but its most well-known philosophical examination appears in the second part of Ludwig Wittgenstein's *Philosophical Investigations*. Wittgenstein invokes 'aspect seeing' to examine how a given form or picture can give rise to conflicting or contradictory perceptions and interpretations, as in the famous drawing that can be seen as either a duck or a rabbit, but not both simultaneously. However, the problems of interpretation raised by 'aspect seeing' are not limited to spatial illusions.

My moving image installation, *Interval* (2019), takes up this problem as an investigation of how remediations of the historical image – in other words, representing the mediated image under different temporal aspects – may affect our perception of time and processes of memory and forgetting. In 1983, I completed a film entitled *1963 (a meditation on history and violence)* (1983, 16 mm silent film, colour, ten minutes), which proved to be my last circulating analogue work. Made twenty years after the assassination of President John F. Kennedy, *1963* is a contemplative investigation of the relation between image and memory, and indeed image as a medium that obscures memory as much as preserving or transmitting it. The paradox here is that the more traumatic the historical event, the more images and documents proliferate around it, clouding or fogging the experience to such an extent that one only sees the obscuring haze.

The source material for *1963* was a copy of Abraham Zapruder's 8 mm footage of the Kennedy assassination, itself refilmed in colour Super-8 from the screen of a small black-and-white video monitor as it was broadcast on national television. Already twice mediated, these 26.6 seconds of images were then blown up to 16 mm and step-printed at one frame per second, slowing and obscuring the image while bringing forward the textures of its electronic and photochemical mediations. In *1963*, the step-printed sequence is repeated once – history repeats itself, at least in images.

In the intervals of time that have now elapsed between and beyond 1963 and 1983, I often thought about returning to these materials but in expanded form and using digital means. *Interval* is thus a new iteration of my ongoing interest in the fading of memory and historical experience as a function of image and medium. My intuition here is that the mediated images that comprise our collective memory of historical events are subject in complex ways to temporal erosion where duration becomes distended and elliptical, gapped and perforated, and space is clouded by a thickening or sedimentation of time perceived as indistinct layerings of the past and the present in uneven rhythms.

The Zapruder film comprises 486 frames exposed at 18 frames per second on Kodachrome II safety film, shot from Zapruder's vantage point on a concrete pedestal near Dealey Plaza in Dallas, Texas. *Interval*'s first temporal aspect shift is presented in eighteen cyanotype prints aligned in a continuous series on the gallery walls. (Printing digital files with this anachronistic photographic process presents another turn in *Interval*'s analogue-digital transformations.) Each individual print is an image sampled from *1963* by dividing the running time of the work by a factor of eighteen. Set equidistant from each other, the arrangement of these images in series recalls the unrolling of a strip of film, and their uneven textures and monochrome colour are reminiscent of Warhol's 'Disaster Series'.

Two video projections are set at either end of the print series. The time structure and duration of these works are very different; indeed, they present two different digital time images. The first video is a time pyramid (*Red Interval*) wherein a baseline sequence extracted from *1963* is copied, re-timed at different durations and stacked vertically on the editing timeline in different opacities. The effect of layering different intervals of the image one on top of the other suggests that a heterogeneous and a-rhythmic time is itself obscuring the image. Layers loop and retrogress, preventing actions from going forward while splitting, fraying and dissolving space as if to introduce new contingencies into the event, which nonetheless arrives at its foreordained conclusion.

The second projection (*Slow Interval*) is ideally set off from the rest of *Interval* in a quiet and darkened space. If the temporal aspect of the print series suggests an imagined external viewpoint and a linear though gapped trajectory in time, and if the first video presents a compression of historical time into densely packed heterogeneous series, the second video offers an impossibly elongated event, slowed to the point of indiscernibility. The space of the second projection is meant to give the impression of residing within our own heads or some solitary space disconnected from the outer world. This should be a floor-to-ceiling projection. Its material comprises a digitized file of the Super-8 source images for *1963*, re-timed to a duration of fifty-five minutes – the exact time elapsed between the landing of Air Force Two at Love Field in Dallas and the firing of the first shot in Dealey Plaza. For viewers unwilling to spend significant time in this meditative space, the images will appear almost completely still or moving forward at a rate just below the capabilities of human perception.

A central theme of *Interval* concerns the technological conveyance of historical experience through images in uneven rhythms and staggered durations where information is both elliptical and gapped, and either too present or too withdrawn. There is a lesson to be learned here that is no less important for the spectator than the artist. Any given image contains everywhere and on its surface all the information it will ever convey; nothing is suppressed or invisible. However, while every image presents a space of total visibility, every observer confronts the image from a perspective of limited intelligibility. Interested observers never perceive every data point that the image offers – information emerges or recedes according to the external perspectives and contexts from which images are perceived and interpreted, and these contexts are continually appearing and disappearing in entirely contingent ways. Wanted here is a better comprehension of how the intelligible is distinct from the sensible. The radical multiplication of images, documents and data in contemporary culture neither adds to nor subtracts from our ability or inability to derive sense from them. Images have no ethics, only interpretations of images, and these are inherently incomplete, contested and contradictory. Learning to see time differently may yet help us to experience time differently in new forms of the cinematic and new architectures of space and time.

Notes

1 For a deeper account these questions, see my book, *Philosophy's Artful Conversation* (2015), Cambridge: Harvard, especially pages 106–58.
2 Many of the works referred to in this chapter can be viewed at: https://www.vimeo.com/dnrodowick. Further information and documentation can be found at: https://www.bauleute.org.
3 Leighton Pierce introduced me to this concept and to various ways of implementing it in practice, which informs his own video work in beautiful and imaginative ways. I would like to thank him here for those generous conversations and his continuing influence on my own work.
4 Documentation for both works can be found online at: https://www.tate.org.uk/whats-on/tate-britain/exhibition/conceptual-art-britain-1964-1979

References

1963 (a meditation on history and violence) (1983), [Film] Dir. D. N.Rodowick, USA.
Augustine (1955), *Confessions*, Book Four, Chapter VIII and Book Eleven, Chapter XIV, trans. Albert C. Outler, London: SCM Press.
Center (Inside Out) (2013–14), [Film] Dir. D. N. Rodowick, USA.
Deleuze, G. (2006), 'What Is the Creative Act?' in D. Lapoujade (ed.), *Two Regimes of Madness*, trans. A. Hodges and M. Taormina, Paris: Minuit.
Interval (2019), [Moving Image Installation] Dir. D. N. Rodowick, USA.
Lichtung Test No. 1 (2017), [Film] Dir. D. N. Rodowick, USA.
peripatetikos 1. Agora, or things indifferent (2015–2016), [Film] Dir. D. N. Rodowick, USA.
peripatetikos 2. Phaedrus (2016), [Film] Dir. D. N. Rodowick, USA.
Pyramid (2016), [Film] Dir. D. N. Rodowick, USA.
Rodowick, D. N. (2015), *Philosophy's Artful Conversation*, Cambridge, MA: Harvard University Press.

Southcote Road: Frame Displacement (1982), [Film] Dir. D. N. Rodowick, USA.
Taichung (2012), [Film] Dir. D. N. Rodowick, USA.
Untitled (2017), [Film] Dir. D. N. Rodowick, USA.
Waterloo (2012), [Film] Dir. D. N. Rodowick, USA.
Wittgenstein, L. (2001), *Philosophical Investigations*, 3rd edn, Oxford: Blackwell.

2

The screen as barrier and support

Monitoring, projection and perfectionism in Brad Bird's *Tomorrowland: A World Beyond* (2015)

Stephen Mulhall

I've spent quite a few years now trying to hold open the possibility that films are capable of engaging reflectively with problems of the kind that philosophers are interested in, and in ways akin to the ways that philosophers articulate and develop those interests: this is something I'd be happy to call 'Cinematic Thinking'. In this chapter, I'd like to explore a little further exactly what I mean by this kind of thinking; and it may help if I begin by emphasizing what I don't mean by it.

I don't mean that films can be used to illustrate independently derived and analysed philosophical claims and positions, and I don't mean that films can raise questions for philosophers in just the way that any other natural or cultural phenomenon might raise philosophical questions. Although I believe that film can legitimately function either as an ornament to a philosophical investigation or as its raw material, as decoration or subjectmatter, I'm not here interested in either function. In my view, cinematic thinking takes place when a film can be shown to be thinking about the sorts of problems philosophers characteristically think about, as opposed to unreflectively instantiating them. Those problems may have nothing in particular to do with cinema (they might be ethical, political or ontological), or they may have a distinctively cinematic inflection (being the kinds of problems that the philosophy of film characteristically addresses – the nature of the screen image, the relation between film actor and film character, etc.). But the critical requirement is that the films concerned can be seen and shown to be actually thinking about those problems – making a contribution to a reflective conversation about them to which philosophers might also make a contribution.

This model of a fruitful conversation is intended to contrast with what still seems to me to be a very common alternative, according to which films are discussed as objects to which specific theoretical edifices (originating elsewhere, in such domains as psychoanalysis or political theory) could be applied. Even the most useful of these discussions usually begin with a long explanation of the relevant theory, and turn to the specific film only at the end, and only as a cultural product whose specific features served to illustrate the truth of that theory – as one more phenomenon the theory rendered comprehensible. Of course, I have no objection to anyone making use of whatever intellectual resources they find pertinent in coming to understand a film's power and interest; Stanley Cavell's work has long served as such a resource for me, here and elsewhere. But the alternative approaches I have in mind tend to see in films only further confirmation of the truth of the theoretical machinery to which the theorist is already committed. The film itself has no say in what we are to make of it, no voice in the history of its own reception or comprehension, of a kind that might contribute to an intellectual exploration of the issues to which these pre-established bodies of theory also contribute, or even serve critically to evaluate those theories, to put their accuracy or exhaustiveness in question. It's my belief that some films are in fact as capable of putting in question our prior faith in our general theories as they are of confirming that faith; and in the present remarks, I want to suggest more specifically that some films can be understood as critically engaging with Stanley Cavell's own work – both on topics of general philosophical interest and on topics that are usually regarded as the province of the philosophy of film. I hope that this will allow me to make it clearer why my own use of Cavell's thought does not amount to succumbing to a version of the theory-application model that I have followed him in criticizing.

Of course, the best way to establish that cinematic thinking of the kind in which I am interested is a real possibility is to identify actual instances of it. In this chapter, I propose to do so by looking in some detail at *Tomorrowland: A World Beyond* (Brad Bird: 2015). My claim will be that it addresses in concrete detail not only the distinctive physiognomy of moral perfectionism as that is articulated in Cavell's work, but also his equally idiosyncratic treatment of an exemplary issue in the philosophy of film – the nature and status of the cinematic screen. One feature that I hope will be of particular interest is that these two issues appear to implicate one another, so that matters often assigned to the philosophy of film turn out to be internally related to issues usually taken to fall outside that branch of my subject, and that this complexity is something that shows up in the work of mainstream Hollywood directors (not all of whom have become darlings of the critics).

Cavell's conception of the screen is handily encapsulated in the following passage:

> The world of a moving picture is screened. The screen is not a support, not like a canvas; there is nothing to support, that way. It holds a projection, as light as light. A screen is a barrier. What does the silver screen screen? It screens me from the world it holds – that is, makes me invisible. And it screens that world from me – that is, screens its existence from me. That the projected world does not exist (now) is its only difference from reality. (Cavell 1971: 24)

Rather than attempting to elucidate these remarks in the abstract, I propose instead to allow their significance to emerge more gradually in the context of another aspect of Cavell's thinking, which does require some initial contextualization – his advocacy of moral perfectionism. Cavell's version of that ethical vision – which he distinguishes from other forms of perfectionism by calling it 'Emersonian', thereby declaring its distinctively American physiognomy – cuts across more familiar moral preoccupations with doing one's duty or maximizing the general happiness or cultivating one's virtues, preoccupations whose theoretical expression are associated with the names of Kant, Mill and Aristotle, respectively. It embodies an idea of the individual's truth to herself or to the humanity in herself, but it sees that self-concern as inseparable from a concern with society and the possibilities it holds out for others. For it understands the soul as on an upward or onward journey that begins when it finds itself lost to the world, and it requires a refusal of the present state of society in the name of some further, more cultivated or cultured, state of society as well as of the soul. This species of perfectionism further assumes that there is no final, as it were absolutely or perfectly cultivated, state of self and society to be achieved; rather, each given or attained state of self and society always projects or opens up another, unattained but attainable, state, to the realization of which we might commit ourselves, or alternatively whose attractions might be eclipsed by the attained world we already inhabit.

In that sense, every attained state is (i.e. can present itself as, and be inhabited as) perfect – in need of no further refinement; hence, the primary internal threat to this species of moral perfectionism is that of regarding genuine human individuality as a realizable state of perfection (even if a different one for each individual), rather than as a continuous process of self-perfecting (selfhood as self-improvement or self-overcoming). The most extreme version of that threat is realized when an individual's investment in her attained self is so unquestioning that the very possibility of her present state being otherwise is occluded; in such circumstances, overcoming this false sense of perfect self-coincidence (of the self's being identical with its current state) may require a relationship with an other – one who exemplifies in their own lives the possibility of things being otherwise, and exhibits an impersonal interest in recalling particular others to their own ways of becoming other than they currently are.

Cavell summarizes this perfectionist vision in the terms of one of its founding articulations, in Plato's *Republic*:

> Obvious candidates features are its ideas of a mode of conversation, between (older and younger) friends, one of whom is intellectually authoritative because his life is somehow exemplary or representative of a life the others are attracted to, and in the attraction of which the self recognizes itself as enchanted, fixated, and feels itself removed from reality, whereupon the self finds that it can turn (convert, revolutionize itself) and a process of education is undertaken, in part through a discussion of education, in which each self is drawn on a journey of ascent to a further state of that self, where the higher is determined not by natural talent but by seeking to know what you are made of and cultivating the thing you are meant to do; it is a transformation of the self which finds expression in the imagination of a transformation of society into something like an aristocracy where what is best for society is a model for and modelled on what is best for the individual soul, a best arrived at in the view of a new reality, a realm beyond, the true world, that of the Good, sustainer of the good city, that of Utopia. (Cavell 1990: 6–7)

Cavell's perfectionism thus envisions the self as internally split or doubled, as essentially non-self-identical even when it relates to its attained state as if it could not be otherwise (for to adopt such a relation is itself something that could be otherwise); and part of what is both inspiring and frustrating about this vision of self-perfecting is that our unattained state presents itself as attainable, as within our grasp if we will but admit its attractiveness and turn towards it. Its very closeness to us – the fact that our distance from it is internal to us, hence not strictly speaking a measurable distance from us at all – is what makes its non-realization peculiarly maddening, as well as deeply motivating; but in order to experience that frustration, to reach the point of realizing that a better state might only be a step away, we stand in need of inspiring examples of successfully holding oneself open to self-overcoming – exemplary individuals (Emerson would call them 'friends') whose orientation towards their own better selves is realized and displayed to us in such a way as to reveal our present state as dissatisfying and to turn us away from it.

Existing as a self is thus a processual or active business of perpetual nextness to or neighbouring of oneself (or its failure) – what Emerson's disciple Thoreau calls being beside ourselves in a sane sense, and what Nietzsche (himself a lifelong venerator of Emerson) might express as a matter of Becoming (or its refusal) rather than Being. Cavell has recently taken this Nietzschean connection a step further, by pointing out that Nietzsche's call for a philosophy of tomorrow and the day after tomorrow deploys a German construction ('morgen und übermorgen') which parallels his more familiar invocation of the over-man ('übermensch'). If we assume that the man who attains self-overcoming is Nietzsche's way of articulating the Emersonian vision of an individual who privileges her unattained over her attained self, and recall the former's intimate neighbouring of or nextness to the latter, then we can infer that the day after tomorrow – the day in which we realize our own and our society's self-overcoming – is itself not a measurable distance away from our present moment, but rather haunts each such moment as its better or higher self, from which we are separated by nothing (nothing substantial, no external obstacle, only our own unwillingness to realize it).

In the light of this conceptual conjunction, it is not exactly surprising that an American film entitled *Tomorrowland: A World Beyond* should prove to stand in some relationship to the problematic of Emersonian perfectionism; but what may surprise some is that it should prove able to avoid helplessly reiterating either its corrupted variants or its ideal type in favour of reflectively interrogating the relationship between genuine perfectionist thinking and friendship and its counterfeits, between its past forms and its present possibilities, and between a perfectionist message and its cinematic medium.

The overarching myth of the film is that, ever since the end of the nineteenth century (the era of Tesla, Verne, Edison and Eiffel), a select group of outstandingly talented scientists and artists (called 'Plus Ultra') have taken up residence in a trans-dimensional universe that exists parallel to our own, and is (with great difficulty) directly accessible from it. In this world, free from politics, bureaucracy, distractions and greed, they have worked to bring the resources of human creative genius to bear on changing the world for the better. When that work was at the point of bearing fruit, they decided to reveal themselves by using advanced robots resembling human beings to distribute special pins (T-pins) which disclosed the existence and nature of Tomorrowland, thereby implanting the idea of a better and genuinely realizable future in the minds of its recipients. Each T-pin – being coded to the DNA of its new owner – thereby amounts to a highly personalized invitation to one individual in the actual world to help realize its unattained but attainable higher state. The film narrative begins when Casey Newton – a high school student with a flair for technology, an unemployed NASA engineer for a father, and an irritatingly undeviating refusal to admit that there is a problem that can't be fixed – comes across one of these pins, many years after its original fabrication.

The basic ontology of this myth is thus sensitive to Nietzsche's distinction between tomorrow and the day after tomorrow: Tomorrowland is not the realization of the actual world's unattained future, but rather an indispensable means for it. Its inhabitants have both a dream of how the world might be better, and a willingness to work hard to bring it about; but the culmination of their project is not Tomorrowland itself, but the transformation of the actual world as a whole along the lines incubated, developed and microcosmically realized in Tomorrowland. The goal is thus the realization of a world beyond Tomorrowland, the world that Tomorrowland's inhabitants turned away from only in order to return to it – the real world, only as it might be rather than as it is; the goal is to return that world to a real belief in the possibility of its improvement, to the perfectionist conviction that an improved state of itself is immediately available, and that the only thing standing in the way of its realization is the (un) willingness of its inhabitants to work to bring it into being.

Note, however, that reorienting those wills is an inherently individual matter: it can only be done by identifying and addressing each individual in terms essentially keyed to them (to which others will be oblivious), and it can only be done by individual representatives of Tomorrowland (in particular, by recruiters such as Athena, who gives her last T-pin to Casey and thereby engineers an encounter with an embittered exile from Tomorrowland named Frank Walker, who Athena also recruited at the 1964 World's Fair). In other words, an individual's access to Tomorrowland, and so to a vision of a higher state of self and world, is essentially mediated by others: it is initially discovered by the natural aristocrats of science and art, who dispatch emissaries designed to attract the actual world's dreamers towards it, but those dreamers are themselves accessible to such invitations because of their relations with actual others – role models or exemplars, whether positive or negative (in Casey's case her father, a NASA engineer, as opposed to her teachers; in Frank's case, Athena as opposed to Frank's father, whose perfect refusal to believe that his son's ideas might be successfully realized is what turns Frank away from his home and towards the World's Fair). The film's central plot explores what happens when the initial perfectionist aversion from the actual world comes unmoored from its intended ultimate turn back towards it, and how perfectionist friendships might both contribute to that unmooring and overcome its baleful consequences.

Tomorrowland's pin-mediated invitation to the actual world is never properly extended, because among its inventions was a piece of technology called the Monitor (based on tachyons – particles capable of travelling faster than light) through which information about the likely future state of the actual world could be visualized; and that future was one of apocalyptic annihilation. Tomorrowland's governor David Nix consequently decides to use the Monitor as a broadcasting device, in order to transmit its depiction of the future to the inhabitants of the actual world; but rather than being galvanized into aversive action by that vision of destruction, they gobble it up – by repackaging it as entertainment in television, movies and computer games, by sprinting towards it with gleeful abandon. As Nix tells Casey towards the end of the film, 'In every moment there lies the possibility of a better future, but you people can't believe it because to do so would be to ask something of you'; in short, the inhabitants of the actual world resign themselves to catastrophe because that licenses passivity. So Nix not only abandons any belief in those he originally aspired to invite and incite to self-overcoming; he also refuses to let any of them into Tomorrowland as pre-refugees, because they'll simply bring their apathetic savagery with them and so destroy Tomorrowland as well.

The film is careful to acknowledge the goodness of Nix's basic motives, and to sympathize with his entirely understandable rage and despair at the actual world's refusal to take responsibility for its own future. But his enactment of that despairing rage not only threatens the actual world; it wreaks terrible damage on Nix's world, and on himself. For by sealing off Tomorrowland from the actual world in order to seal it off from the future it was originally intended to shape, the film shows us that he has transformed it into a dilapidated shadow of itself; he has eviscerated the very thing he most wants to preserve by eliminating its point or purpose. And more importantly, he has made this decision on the basis of a perfectionist error; for he has forgotten that every moment contains within itself the possibility of a better future. The Monitor envisions the future as it will be if the present state of the world remains unchanged; and this extrapolation depends upon eliminating the possibility of change – more specifically, the possibility of a collective aspiration to favour the unattained but attainable state of the world over its attained state. Put otherwise: the Monitor privileges the world's attained state over its unattained state, a condition which in its most extreme version occludes the very idea of an unattained but attainable state of the world, and so the possibility that the world might ever be otherwise than it presently is.

By regarding the future as bound to be identical with the present, and so as absolutely determined, Nix overlooks a logical paradox that Casey immediately appreciates: that accepting annihilation might be an essential factor in bringing it about. Early in the film, when her father expresses a sense that the destruction of NASA and so of his employment prospects is inevitable, Casey recites to him a parable that he has recited so often to her. There are two wolves: one is darkness and despair and the other is light and hope; and they are constantly in conflict with one another. Which wolf wins? The (perfectionist) answer is: whichever one you feed. If you desire the attained over the attainable state of self and world, your desire will be satisfied; but if you desire the attainable over the attained, that desire too will be satisfied, in that simply to engender the desire is to become dissatisfied with that which is attained and so to begin to overcome it. This is why, when Casey is confronted with teachers who present the world as reducible to destructive politics, lethal climate change and dystopian art, she interrupts to ask: 'So how can we fix it?' And when she is later asked whether, if someone were certain of the date of her death, she would want him to tell her, she says that she would, but that she would refuse to believe it; for that refusal might alter the conditions on which the prediction is based, and so ensure its falsity. And the film shows us that even that 'hypothetical' act of dissent or aversion is enough to subvert the Monitor's 100 per cent certainty that the future will be apocalyptic, and thus to show that the attained and the attainable states of the world are not one and the same, unless we will them to be.

Where Nix's despair prevents him from acknowledging that slight flicker of hope, Frank finds in it a means of recovering his own perfectionist aspirations. Nix's decision to exile him from Tomorrowland after his algorithms had helped build the Monitor is never properly explained, although it is fairly clearly implied that he objects to Nix's way of putting that technology to use; but the matter is plainly entangled in his own mind with his belated, painful discovery that Athena – with whom he is besotted from their first meeting – is not human but a robot (more precisely, an audio-animatronic). This is the film's way of realizing the essentially impersonal nature of the perfectionist friend: although such a friend is always interested in her younger counterpart's state and fate, it is with a view to helping him to realize his own self-overcoming, not with a view to satisfying any of her own personal desires (in particular, not any romantic ones). Such an interest would in fact sabotage the perfectionist impulse, insofar as it would impose demands on the befriended one to conform to the friend's desires, and thereby substitute one form of conformity (with society's sense of what is possible) with another (the friend's sense of what is necessary, and in particular for her); and what the film presents in Frank is a case study of what may go wrong if the befriended one makes an analogous error. For the young Frank confuses one form of attraction with another – the attractiveness of Athena as an older girl and her attractiveness as a representative of his and the world's unattained but attainable higher state. His exile may be forced on him by Nix, but there is also a sense in which he accepts it because in his confusion he continues to conflate Tomorrowland's attractiveness to him with Athena's willingness to answer to his personal romantic desires, and so lives out his exile in a state of raging disappointment with the actual world that is strikingly analogous to that of Nix: it's as if Frank wants to deprive that world of its unattained future state because one inhabitant of it has lost all attraction for him.

What saves Frank is Athena's willingness to bear up under that disappointment and maintain their friendship, and, more specifically, her willingness to bring him into a relationship with Casey – one in which she takes over Athena's original role as exemplar of perfectionist self-overcoming, rekindles in him his lost perception of the difference between the world as it is and the world as it might become, and thereby motivates him to realize his own and his world's self-overcoming. In this respect, *Tomorrowland* emphasizes that Cavell's (which means Plato's and Emerson's) picture of the exemplary other as an older friend is itself open to question: with Casey and Frank it is the younger person who makes it possible for the older to recover perfectionist orientation, which makes it possible for us to re-conceive our appetite for self-overcoming as a kind of recovery of our youth, say of the adolescent aspect of ourselves – our capacity to think of the world as presenting itself to us as a whole for judgement, as something that we must determine to be either sufficiently attractive to motivate us to accept the obligations of adulthood or as deficient in this critical respect, and so as something to turn away from, in the name of a better world.

The film emphasizes the centrality of perfectionist friendship to perfectionist self-overcoming in its conclusion; for when Nix is overthrown and the Monitor destroyed, Casey and Frank work to revive Tomorrowland by resurrecting the T-pin strategy, and inviting the creative dreamers of the actual world to make the future real, to realize it. In every moment, there is the possibility of a better future, but you have to believe in it, to respond to its claim on you, if you and your society are to attain it.

But Brad Bird's film does not simply display a sophisticated understanding of the continued relevance of American perfectionism to contemporary life despite its own inherent vulnerability to deformation at the level of narrative content; it also declares an internal relation between perfectionist aspirations and the medium of cinema. This further claim begins to be articulated when Casey first touches the T-pin that Athena has secreted among her personal effects, and which is returned to her as she is released from the police station. She immediately finds herself in Tomorrowland, a world with which she can interact, although without ever leaving the car in which she is travelling with her father, to which she returns the moment she breaks contact with the pin. And as later instances of this transposition emphasize, every move she makes in Tomorrowland is one she simultaneously performs in the very different environment of the real world.

In other words, Casey discovers that she simultaneously inhabits two worlds – the actual world and Tomorrowland – which neighbour one another everywhere and at every moment; they are separated from one another by nothing whatever, although each is capable of screening the other from her. More precisely, whereas the actual world usually screens Tomorrowland from her, one element within it (the T-pin) can convert reality as a whole into a screen on which Tomorrowland is projected. That projection is visually indistinguishable from reality in its full three-(or four-)dimensionality, entirely overlaying and so apparently displacing it, but it remains light as light, essentially immaterial; for as Casey's repeated bruising and her climactic drenching attest, the actual world's material reality always invisibly underlies it and stubbornly obstructs her full immersion in it.

And here we return to Cavell's conception of the screen. All projected worlds need a support, which must be a part of the real world, and so can screen us from other things in that world, and cannot dematerialize altogether. It must at least include or proffer a two-dimensional surface onto which that world can be projected; but it doesn't follow that the projected world is two-dimensional, or that its denizens lack any of the features or attributes of the real world. The only difference between these worlds is that one does not exist (now); and existence is not a predicate. But this ontological condition has a perfectionist moral: for any world that does not exist now is not necessarily non-existent, and so might exist.

In other words, nothing differentiates a projected world from a real one except our relation to it, and in particular our desire that it might become real, which invites us to begin the work of realizing it.

Hence, this film's study of perfectionism, its vulnerabilities and its possibilities also shows that certain ontological conditions of cinema continue to hold open perfectionist possibilities. This is not just a film about the importance of privileging unattained but attainable states of the world over attained states in the light of unforeseen threats to the sheer possibility of a human future; it embodies just such a privileging, insofar as its projected vision of such a world is itself a means of communicating such ideas and inviting its audience to absorb and act upon them in the actual world – to overlay the attained state of the world with its unattained but attainable state, while appreciating that we can only get to there from here, in all its recalcitrant material reality. In this respect, viewing a film is unlike monitoring a transmission or broadcast: monitoring (which is made for registering events against the background of the uneventful) discourages enactment, whereas projecting a world that differs from the actual one only in that it does not (yet) exist invites it.

So, Casey's relation to the world disclosed by her T-pin figures our relation to the cinematic world in which this event is disclosed. This is why the film begins with an excerpt from the cinematic content Frank and Casey plan to attach to their new generation of T-pins – an opening which explicitly locates the film's viewers in the position of the recipients of those pins within the film, thereby inviting each of them to consider whether he or she is a dreamer, a perfectionist aspirant. It is also why, at the very end of the end credits, the screen on which *Tomorrowland* is projected displays a T-pin, and a hand coming into the field of the camera to touch it: this identifies the film we have just seen with its chosen embodiment of the perfectionist invitation. Taken together, they register this film's understanding of itself as posing a question to each member of its audience, namely: Which wolf will you feed?

References

Cavell, S. (1971), *The World Viewed*, Cambridge, MA: Harvard University Press.
Cavell, S. (1990), *Conditions Handsome and Unhandsome*, Chicago: University of Chicago Press.
Tomorrowland: A World Beyond (2015), [Film] Dir. Brad Bird, USA: Walt Disney Pictures.

3

Surface thoughts

On the look of cinema

John Ó Maoilearca

Introduction: Content following cinematic forms

In my previous work, especially *Refractions of Reality: Philosophy and the Moving Image* (2009), I have pursued a pluralist approach towards film-philosophy that looks at different philosophies of cinema without privileging any one position over the other. This was often done by adopting a 'non-philosophical' materialism (in François Laruelle's sense), that is, one that understands each and every theory of film as a material part of the Real – the part being immanent to the Real rather than a representation of it. Each theory, *qua* material part, was related to film mereologically rather than in immaterial terms of epistemic right (absolutism) or wrong (traditional relativism). Film merely reflects, or illustrates, the rightness of a philosophy. In other words, I argued that if one *materializes theory* itself, then it is futile to keep looking for one transcendent discourse that will somehow maintain a privileged access to film (such as cognitive neuroscience, Lacanian psychoanalysis and Deleuzian ontology). In addition, as film is itself one other part of the Real, this stance allows one to see film itself as philosophical through *its own material form of expression* (in audiovisual art – the look and sound of film).

Arguably, however, one flaw with this 'materiality of theory' approach was that it retained a textual and exegetical form that still, perhaps, *resembled* Laruelle's written philosophy too closely such that this stance too could be taken as just one more application of a superior 'theory' (Laruelle's) in a transcendent manner. Moreover, film itself would still be being used as purely illustrative of philosophy rather than being seen as philosophical in its own right. Form followed content, so to speak (if we can be allowed this binary for a moment), that is, film was made to illustrate Laruellean philosophy. Alternatively, what if we could reverse this hierarchy and make content follow form? This would be an endeavour to develop a non-philosophical approach *directly* out of the structure of film itself, *from forms of the cinematic* – the look of film. Though still communicated in textual form, this would be, nonetheless, a further step towards a genuinely autonomous film-philosophy that does more than merely illustrate philosophical (textual) ideas with filmic image. The form of the text would follow (a) film.

Films, non-philosophy and Laruelle

Consequently, in my subsequent book, *All Thoughts Are Equal* (2015), I explored the idea that film is philosophical while allowing *it* to introduce Laruelle's ideas about 'non-philosophy' or 'non-standard philosophy'. I go about this *equation* of film and philosophy by showing how the two might think *in their own way*. But I do this without any definitions (of film or philosophy), and I avoid such definitions for important reasons. For, conversely, should one say that film is philosophical *because* it is a *defined type* of philosophical act (it creates concepts, for example, or pursues fundamental questioning, or logical analysis, etc.), then one adds a third, defined element, a definition of philosophy in which film is *allowed* to participate. Yet even this definition can always be defined in such a way as still to make the *type* of concept creation or questioning or analysis that *philosophy first* instantiates different and superior to the concept creation or questioning or analysis of film. When saying that film equals philosophy, *and* then *how* they are equal (the third element), one thereby creates a new and potentially arbitrary definition that, again, can be made to make one half of the equation the privileged, exceptional instance. Alternatively, if there were no third element or property, then their equality is not defined but *invented*: in other words, it is *performative*.

And yet, have I not just said that film and philosophy are equally thoughtful, or at least that they both *think*? Isn't that a third property? Well, yes and no. The reason I say 'no' is because I have not defined what thought or thinking is. I have simply said that film and philosophy equally think, *but in their own way*. This is a pluralistic gesture to be sure, but, according to Laruelle at least, it is also a *non-philosophical* gesture, because the job of philosophy (by contrast) is to attempt to enforce one or other image alone of what counts as thought. Despite what appears to many as philosophy's benign, abstract and consequently (perhaps) even irrelevant status, Laruelle takes philosophy to be the supreme form of thought control, or, to be clear, a device for controlling what counts as 'proper' or 'fundamental' thought. By contrast, his non-philosophy is 'the manner of thinking that does not know *a priori* what it is to think' (Laruelle 2012a: 67).

So, when saying that 'cinema is a philosophy', one must not take this equation – this equality – as one conflating two defined entities. Rather, stating that 'film is philosophical' is an invention, an exploration of how this pair can be equalized, but without defining either of the two – nor their union – at the outset. For, inversely, if everything were equally philosophy *as defined as* X, we would still have to account for the *appearance* of those films or philosophies that also *unarguably look* like a film or a philosophy (standardly understood at any one moment), and those others that do not (and thereby need to have their participation defended with argument).

Alternatively, to say that film is philosophical *in a non-standard philosophical manner* is not another logical equation, but an invention, a hypothesis to be explored, a new comparative that must be only one among many. Saying that 'X equals Y' here is also to say that 'X could equal Z or Q or R' and so on. Of course, this multiplication of identities could explode into triviality, but only in a theory separated from practice. In practice, that is, performatively, the identifications have each to be invented in actual spaces and times (and not in one abstract position of everywhere and always). A film can be philosophical, in its own way.

Thinking democracy

Laruelle's non-philosophy aspires to bring democracy *into* thought. As a philosopher of 'radical immanence' everything is equal or equalized – no thing or thought transcends the rest. But, of course, all things do not look or appear equal. And Laruelle argues that philosophy is indeed the discipline that posits itself as the power to think at the highest level – the *unequal* thought: '*prima in dignitate, ultima in addiscendo*' in Aquinas's words (see Kielbasa 2013: 635–48). Despite appearances to the contrary, philosophy remains our dominant form of knowledge, according to Laruelle. Or rather, it is the very form of domination within knowledge. Adopting many positions, or 'decisions', as he puts it (empiricism, rationalism, idealism, materialism, scientism, even anti-philosophy), its fundamental pose is as a form of *exemplary* thinking. It is *the* model for all foundational thought, even when those foundations are differential or anti-foundational (multiplicity, alterity, *differance*, etc.). As Laruelle sees it, 'philosophy is not "first" for nothing; it is that which declares itself first and possessor' (Laruelle 2013a: 110). Even in our contemporary scientistic era, in epistemic relations

> philosophy holds the dominant place, science the dominated place. In positivism or scientism, the hierarchy is reversed or inverted; but it is still philosophy that dominates in anti-philosophy. The superior or dominant place is in effect always occupied by philosophy. (Laruelle 2013b: 43)

Hence, even scientism is a philosophy too (albeit a self-hating one).

Laruelle, on the other hand, believes that philosophy does *not* have a monopoly on (philosophical) thinking. In non-philosophy, all thoughts are equalized in value. However, this equivalence or conceptual democracy is not *political* in the philosophical and representational sense of the term (with all its attendant troubles). It is not a *theoretical* democracy – which would leave alone what counts as 'theory'– but the 'democracy of theory itself'. Such a non-representational democracy aims to resolve the traditional hierarchies of philosophy 'with experience, art, ethics, technology, mysticism, science, etc.' by mutating just what thought and theory might be – by 'universalizing thought beyond philosophy' (Laruelle 2013b: 49; Laruelle 2013a: 14).

There is a strange kind of materiality to Laruelle's approach here. I say 'strange' because, if he is a materialist, it is only in as much as he wants to treat *philosophy itself* as a material, yet *without* reducing it to any one or other *philosophical idea* of what (the relevant) matter is (borrowed from physics or neurology, say). This is a *material* philosophy rather than a philosophy of matter ('materialism' or 'physicalism'). The ideas of philosophy are no longer positions to be argued with, critiqued, accepted or promoted but a raw material or 'clone' to be utilized: it is not a question for him of how we should study philosophy 'philosophically' but rather that '*there is a body of philosophy, a philosophical materiality, a conceptual and lived material, and one can treat philosophy as a part of physical nature*' (Laruelle and Mackay 2012: 27). (Naturally, then, he leaves what physical nature is undefined.)

In pursuing this material treatment of thought and philosophy, we must first avoid the circular method of 'treating philosophy *philosophically*' and instead propose a 'means of causing thought to function otherwise than philosophically'

(Laruelle 2013a: 100). When speaking about his work, Laruelle describes his ongoing project to 'treat philosophy as a material, and thus also as a materiality – without preoccupying oneself with the aims of philosophy, of its dignity, of its quasi-theological ends, of philosophical virtues, wisdom etc.' He then adds: 'what interests me is philosophy as the material for an art, at the limit, an art' (Laruelle 2013a: 29).

A film of philosophy

One strand of my work, then, is to explain Laruelle's strange image of 'non-philosophy' – only without relying on terms of reference found in *philosophers'* explanations of philosophy. In order to introduce *non*-philosophy in a spirit of consistency, then, we have to think about it *non*-philosophically, that is, we have to acknowledge the importance of *extra-philosophical* materials as models for non-philosophy's modes of thought – what Laruelle describes as 'techniques of creation that would be pictorial, poetic, musical, architectural, informational, etc.' (Laruelle 2013c: 135). As mentioned at the outset, my own approach, modelled on Laruelle's own methods, involves film art by developing a non-philosophical model *directly from the structure of cinema*, in particular, the film structure of Lars von Trier's and Jørgen Leth's *The Five Obstructions* (2003). This is an attempt at making a 'Film of Philosophy' rather than a 'Philosophy of Film' (Resznitnyk 2014: 26).

A reorientation of philosophy through art material can also be seen in Laruelle's call for a 'non-standard aesthetics', which is described as 'an "installation" made up of multiple thought materials which are made at the edge of art and philosophy' (see Laruelle 2012b). *All Thoughts Are Equal* (2015), therefore, employs a visual art form (cinema) in order to perform a non-philosophical introduction to non-philosophy. And it does so because, if what Laruelle says is true – namely that 'it is precisely the model of art and its freedom of materials that have encouraged me in regards to non-philosophy' – then such an approach may be the only that one can consistently take.

The two most salient aspects of *The Five Obstructions* (2003) are, first, its peculiar composition and, secondly, that it is a collaborative work. *The Five Obstructions* (2003) is made up of five remakes of an original work by another filmmaker: Jørgen Leth. Leth, a mentor of von Trier, has to remake sequences from his own first film (a short, pseudo-anthropological study of human behaviour from 1968, *The Perfect Human*) five times, each with an obstruction or 'creative constraint'. The constraints are as follows:

1. That it be remade with no shot longer than twelve frames;
2. That it be remade in the most miserable place on earth;
3. That it be remade with *no* constraint at all (a form of meta-obstruction of total freedom);
4. That it be remade as a cartoon (*the* definition of a non-film for both von Trier and Leth); and finally,
5. That *von Trier* makes the fifth remake, though it must be both credited to – and narrated by – Leth.

The Five Obstructions (2003), consequently, is a work whose very form explores a number of issues, but especially those concerning aesthetic creativity and generative constraint.

However, because *The Five Obstructions* (2003) can be neither a mere application nor an illustration of Laruelle's non-standard philosophy (which would leave it unequal to his thought), it has to be its *own* non-philosophy. In *All Thoughts Are Equal* (2015), *The Five Obstructions* (2003) functions as a series of *surface tangents* rather than one essential determination (where 'this' cinematic element equals 'that' non-philosophical concept). These five cinematic tangents (in five chapters) touch on not only matters concerning Laruelle (e.g. philosophy, logic, behaviour, animality and performance) but also its own cinematic matter itself, *for itself* (e.g. the documentary gaze, editing, acting, animation and performativity). Consequently, Laruelle is introduced *tangentially* or *superficially* via this same constrained approach, multiplying images of non-philosophy according to *the film*'h fivefold cinematic structure. Non-philosophy is thus forced through five different remakes – beginning, ironically, with the most perspicuous one – philosophy – before continuing through paraconsistent logic, behaviourism, animality and performance (Bainbridge 2008: 158).[1]

Moreover, these five remakes can also be taken as experiments in 'cloning' – that is, in precisely what Laruelle does with non-philosophy in his materialist practice (treating philosophy as its raw material). *The Five Obstructions* (2003) might be said to enact the question of just what a remake, replica or clone is on a number of different levels: Who is in control? Who is the authority in this game of originals and remakes? And what exactly is being remade anyway (given the constant divergence between original and copy)? These are very much the questions animating the whole documentary as well as any 'philosophical' introduction to Laruelle.

A behavioural tangent: Being true to the idea (a film *du Look*)

It is the question of *what* is being remade, something deep or superficial, that I want to focus on here. *The Five Obstructions* (2003), as noted earlier, is a set of remakes of Jørgen Leth's original 1968 film, *Det Perfekte Menneske* (*The Perfect Human*). Krista Geneviève Lynes describes the film thus:

> Although the film has been described as having the cool aesthetic of Richard Avedon, it also insinuates other histories: the stark discipline of Eadweard Muybridge or Etienne-Jules Marey, and Alphonse Bertillon's physiological dissections. In it, Claus Nissen – dressed in a tuxedo – and Maiken Algren – in a white dress with radiant silver knee-high boots – perform daily activities in a white spaceless room: shaving, eating, jumping, sleeping, making love, falling, getting dressed and dancing. (Lynes 2010: 599–600)

In *The Perfect Human* (1968), various human behaviours are observed, often in close-up, dissected from the whole. They are sometimes ordinary and sometimes surreal actions, but all are viewed with the same supposedly transcendent camera eyes, accompanied by the narrator's detached voice:

> *Yes, there he is! Who is he? What can he do? What does he want? Why does he move like that? How does he move like that? Look at him. Look at him now. And now, and now. Look at him all the time.*

> *How does she lie down? Like that.*

> *We're going to see what the perfect human looks like and what it can do.*

Again, looks, and looking like. One way of reading *The Five Obstructions* (2003) is precisely as an enactment of Jean Renoir's adage – that each film-maker only makes one film, again and again – with von Trier forcing Leth to recompose *The Perfect Human* (1968) repeatedly following certain constraints. But the obstructions to each remake nonetheless ensure a creative reproduction, rather than a faithful replica. They look like each other, but only by degree. This has been accounted for partly through the use of *constant stylistic innovation*. As von Trier writes of his own work: 'you can become so good at producing things that they become nauseatingly boring to look at. That might have happened had I continued to make the same film again and again, as some people do' (Hjort

2008: 21). Von Trier is known for not repeating himself, *at least stylistically*. Yet, von Trier insists on a partial repetition in each task given to Leth, albeit that the added obstructions guarantee a certain creativity in style. Mette Hjort comments on this, saying 'the commitment [to renewing styles] throughout, it transpires, is to a form of self-provocation that involves *abandoning* the cinematic techniques as they are mastered in favour of new challenges' (Hjort 2008: 21).

Yet in writing (as I just have), 'at least stylistically', one should not see this as dismissing the issue of style: indeed, it becomes a highly significant approach – its seeming superficiality hides a depth that is all surface, so to speak. As Murray Smith also writes of the film,

> in *The Five Obstructions* the game of style is narrativised; the variations in style have an overt motivation in the narrative contest recounted by the film. Even so, the variations are not motivated in the traditional manner as apt stylistic expressions of theme. (Hjort 2008: 135)

In the opening obstruction (the twelve-frame one), a certain behavioural attitude is clearly assumed. Adopting the same pseudo-anthropological pose as its original, *The Perfect Human* (1968) asks questions such as 'What is the perfect human thinking? Is he thinking about happiness? Death? Love?' And yet the answers eventually provided to these and other questions are often superficial, pseudo-answers, at least for those who are looking for *deeper reasons*. Paisley Livingston describes the situation thus:

> The response to the question: 'Why does he move this way?' is a comical flaunting of Trier's injunction to answer the questions raised by the narrator of *The Perfect Human*; the proposed answer ('Because women like it') does not really answer the question, while seeming to do so in a blunt way; all the other questions remain willfully unanswered in the remake, which reinforces the thought that Leth has cleverly slipped past this obstruction. (Hjort 2008: 65)

However, I would say that questions such as 'what is he thinking?' and 'what are his motivations?' *are* answered, only through external, *surface* behaviour, or a style of movement, rather than *deep sufficient reasons*.

Significantly, we can see that when von Trier orders Leth to make *any* film, he wishes in the third obstruction, it is indeed an imposition of sorts: less the burden of responsibility than the burden of absolute creation. Naturally, Leth is free to escape from his freedom, in this third film at least, by reverting to his usual long-take, realist aesthetic. And yet, this is not what he does. Instead, he offers up a highly stylized, rather formal piece, using split screens, cryptic monologues and seemingly clichéd 'art-house' imagery (e.g. a mysterious man and woman, sexual encounters in anonymous hotel rooms, a sense of political or criminal intrigue, slow-moving limousines, clandestine meetings in rainy, desolate locations, etc.).

I already mentioned the pseudo-anthropological approach of Leth's original short. The narration of the remake (in English) compounds this impression:

Here's the man. Here he is. What's he want?

Here's the woman. Here she is. What does she want? What is she doing?

Here's a man. We don't know him. I don't know what to say about him. We love that he is special, unreasonable. The distant look, a loss of soul, the distant look.

I would like to know something more about him. I can see that he is here, and that he works. I have seen him smoke a cigarette. I didn't see him write. Is he good at describing death? Does he think about fucking? He is alone, preparing himself. He goes out and takes care of things. He's the perfect man.

In this and other sequences, the question as to what the man is thinking is reiterated but never answered. All we are given are external details, visuals of movement, of smoking, of shaving. Alongside this unanswered enquiry comes the peculiar mannerism of this version, with a certain 'type' of art-house cinema being replicated throughout (almost as in the *Cinema du Look* of the 1980s). Paramount in this, however, is the acting role of the male protagonist. Leth casts Patrick Bauchau (in Claus Nissen's role) almost entirely because of his presence and look. Murray Smith remarks on this as follows:

> the casting of Patrick Bauchau in *#3: Brussels*, for example, [was] inspired by Leth's admiration for his performance as the protagonist of Eric Rohmer's *La collectionneuse*. Intriguingly, Rohmer's film was, like *The Perfect Human*, released in 1968; it as if Leth has chosen a better-known counterpart to Claus Nissen – an equally handsome actor from the same generation, both born in 1938 – in order to stress the effects of time and experience on the model-like 'perfection' of the figures in his original film (Leth notes the importance of Bauchau's 'well-bruised' quality to his casting in *#3: Brussels*). (Hjort 2008: 130)

Nonetheless, it is not as if Bauchau is given much to do by Leth in this film, for he mostly poses in rooms, has little dialogue and even less interaction with other actors. He is there because of his 'look'. Leth is obviously delighted with his casting, stating that he is 'really pleased with him. He looks great. [. . .] He is . . . well-bruised as a person. He has experience of life. He has lived a life.

His story is fantastic' (Leth, 1968). Bauchau, then, stands for a certain type and remakes the Claus Nissen protagonist through a distinctive acting style, almost bordering on non-acting: he is a man who 'takes care of things' just by looking like such a man. Indeed, of all six films, the original and the third versions of *The Perfect Human* place the most emphasis on acting style (as opposed to editing in One, location in Two, animation in Four and performativity in Five). And it is Murray Smith, once more, who finds the right idea on this front when describing the original *The Perfect Human* (1968):

> *The Perfect Human* is an enigmatic, spare narrative film, depicting a man and a woman engaged in various generic activities – eating, dancing, undressing, shaving – mostly in isolation from one another. [. . .] The setting of the film is abstract in the extreme: the performers are afforded certain minimal props (a razor, a bed, a dining table) but the space behind them is so overexposed as to lead the eye into a white void. The man and the woman are beautiful, young, chic; much of the time they are doing little more than *striking poses* in the featureless zone that they occupy. (Hjort 2008: 118).

There is a further moment of what we might call this 'externalism' in Leth's remake that I would like to pause over here. In one 'behind the scenes' section of the making of third film, we see Leth talking with his assistants about a certain effect he is after, one that involves the arrangement and rearrangement of garden chairs on a building rooftop. He says that he sees this as a

> kind of ghostly ballet – with the chairs. We go up to them and move them around . . . haphazardly. Into a new, interesting arrangement. [. . .] 'Somebody has moved them around in the dark,' right? A mystery. *That's the idea we're keeping from the original scene.*

What is peculiar about this point in *The Five Obstructions* (2003) is that there is no scene in the original *The Perfect Human* (1968) that is in any way like that; there are barely any chairs at all visible, other than those glimpsed when a man is seated as he undresses or eats. So, what is the *idea* that is being reproduced? When, at one earlier point in *The Five Obstructions* (2003), von Trier accuses Leth's second remake of not being 'true to the idea' of his constraint, he was referring to the stipulation that Leth's subject (set in the most miserable place) should *not be seen*. It is ironic, then, that in this remake (which is actually set as a punishment for his prior wrongdoing on Obstruction #2), the idea from the original film that Leth tries to reproduce is itself invisible. Unless, of course, the idea simply *is* that of mystery, of haphazard movements (rearrangements) performed as if 'in the dark'? Both films have an air of mystery to be sure, though the first's is far less dramatically intriguing and more a matter of intellectual curiosity. There is really no deep idea (no 'concept' or 'propositional content') in either film, then, that might be transferred from the one to the other, but rather a manner, style or surface – the *behaviour* of the enigmatic, 'how it moves' so to speak. What is carried across is not an idea-in-translation (a copy), but a kind of gestural, postural materiality (that is also transformed as it is transferred).

Conclusion: How to behave like a film philosopher

In all then, be it through this externalization of ideas, the behaviourist and anthropological approach adopted, or the role of the actor as a type, this third version of *The Perfect Human* (1968) can be said to enact the question of just what a remake, replica or 'clone' is on a number of different levels. For the most peculiar thing is that, having been given the utmost freedom to make this version, the third film is probably the least like the original when compared to all the others.

What has this to do with Laruelle? How does this equate with Laruelle's thought – without merely illustrating it? According to one formulation, Laruelle's approach is radically *behavioural* too (rather than behaviourist) because it seeks, he says, 'a new conditioning or usage of philosophy itself' in the spirit of consistency. But this 'conditioning' is not philosophical (or Kantian), but material (in the non-philosophical sense). It operates 'through and on the *a priori* knowledges, by *universal* "condition" or "conditioning" rather than by general and regional laws' (Laruelle 2013b: 7, 73). It is behavioural or external, a surface conditioning.

For instance, in his book *Anti-Badiou* (2013a), Laruelle describes Alain Badiou's thought as an 'affirmation, a style, a posture, a statue that forms around it the type of circular void to which young badiolisers will gravitate'. Badiouism (as opposed to Badiou) is a void of circulations. Treating his thought in this manner transforms it into 'a body or a part of nature, a new philosophical object upon which we would carry out an experiment or provoke a reaction' (Laruelle 2013a: 61–2). Yet, as Laruelle continues, the 'characteristic, celebrated and foundational gestures' of other philosophies can also be transformed into verbal objects: 'founding, reducing, subtracting, withdrawing, suspecting, critiquing, anticipating/retarding, overthrowing, meditating, elucidating, analyzing, synthetizing, deconstructing and constructing, etc' (Laruelle 2013a: xxi, 212–13).[2] The philosophical pose or posture, then, is surface, the *look* of thought. Yet, it is not superficial at the expense of supposedly deep that belongs to something else (science, art, technology): all thoughts are equal or equalized, be they filmic or philosophical. If some look deeper, it is only because of a hierarchical optics formed through conventions that are both cultural and biological ('devices' in Bordwell's terms; Bordwell 1985: 48–57): and both such categories of 'nurture' and 'nature', be it in what they are themselves or what they categorize, are not only plastic and mutable but *philosophical* – products of decision.[3] Rejecting the decision for inequality allows the form(s) of cinema – its look – to function philosophically too – not in any defined way, but in an expanded form that democratizes thought.

Notes

1 Though turning to an art-house favourite like this is not totally contingent either given the attraction of von Trier's films to many 'philosophical' minds (his art is often deemed a great 'meta-cinematic work').
2 In Annette Baier's list of 'postures of the mind', she includes 'wondering, revising, correcting, rejecting, ignoring, welcoming, repenting, forgiving, redeeming' (Baier 1985: 39).
3 This chapter expands on ideas in Ó Maoilearca (2015).

References

Baier, A. (1985), *Postures of the Mind: Essays on Mind and Morals*, Minneapolis: University of Minnesota Press.
Bainbridge, C. (2008), *The Cinema of Lars Von Trier: Authenticity and Artifice*, New York: Columbia University Press.
Bordwell, D. (1985), *Narration in the Fiction Film*, New York: Methuen.
Det Perfekte Menneske (*The Perfect Human*) (1968), [Film] Dir. Jørgen Leth, Denmark: Laterna Film.
Hjort, M., ed. (2008), *Dekalog 01: The Five Obstructions Notes*, London: Wallflower Press.
Kielbasa, S. (2013), 'What Is First? Metaphysics as *Prima Philosophia* and *Ultima Scientia* in the Works of Thomas Aquinas', *Philosophia*, 41: 635–48.

Laruelle, F. (2012a), '"I, the Philosopher, Am Lying": Reply to Deleuze', in F. Laruelle, *The Non-Philosophy Project: Essays by François Laruelle*, ed. G. Alkon and B. Gunjevic, 40–73. New York: Telos.

Laruelle, F. (2012b), 'The Generic Orientation of Non-Standard Aesthetics'. Paper presented at the Weisman Art Museum, University of Minneapolis, 17 November 2012. Available online: https://performancephilosophy.ning.com/profiles/blogs/the-generic-orientation-of-non-standard-aesthetics-by-f-laruelle (accessed 25 February 2020).

Laruelle, F. (2013a), *Anti*-Badiou, trans. R Mackay, London: Bloomsbury Academic.

Laruelle, F. (2013b), *Principles of Non-Philosophy*, trans. N. Rubczak and A. P. Smith, London: Bloomsbury Academic.

Laruelle, F. (2013c), *Philosophy and Non-Philosophy*, trans. T. Adkins, Minneapolis: Univocal.

Lynes, K. G. (2010), 'Perversions of Modesty: Lars von Trier's *The Five Obstructions* and "The Most Miserable Place on Earth"', *Third Text*, 24 (5): 597–610.

Mackay, R. and F. Laruelle (2012), 'Introduction: Laruelle Undivided', in F. Laruelle, *From Decision to Heresy: Experiments in Non-Standard Thought*, 1–32, ed. R. Mackay, Falmouth: Urbanomic/Sequence Press.

Ó Maoilearca, J. (2010), *Refractions of Reality: Philosophy and the Moving Image*, London: Palgrave Macmillan.

Ó Maoilearca, J. (2015), *All Thoughts Are Equal: Laruelle and Nonhuman Philosophy*, Minneapolis: University of Minnesota Press.

Reszitnyk, A. (2014), 'Wonder without Domination', *Chiasma: A Site for Thought*, 1 (1): 24–53.

The Five Obstructions (2003), [Film] Dir. Lars von Trier, Denmark: Almaz Film Productions S.A.

4

The film event

From Bazin to Deleuze

Tom Conley

In the pedagogy of film theory, it almost stands as an axiom that, like Jack and Jill going up a hill to fetch a pail of water, students must read hand in hand *The Film Form* and *What Is Cinema?* Eisenstein, for whom form was the force of montage and the ideogram a grounding principle of cinematography, stands opposed to Bazin, the unyielding proponent of the long take in deep focus. In 'Montage interdit', the title of an article (first appearing in *Cahiers du cinéma*, 1953) that recalls René Clément's *Les jeux interdits* (Forbidden games) of the preceding year, Bazin would appear hell-bent against the principles of editorial craft that Eisenstein considered essential to the seventh art. Lo and behold, readers of *Qu'est-ce que le cinéma?* (*What Is Cinema?*) discover that polemics are not so much at issue, and even that Bazin's criticism holds montage in controlled or moderate esteem. Further, rightly or wrongly, they deduce that what Bazin advocates might be a theoretical poetics of classical French cinema: Lumière's single-takes of forty or fifty seconds, generally (but not always) of the order of a *plan-séquence*, remain at the core of an aesthetic by which cinema at once animates, becomes and even redeems reality itself.[1] Little wonder that Bazin would find a hero in Renoir, trained in silent cinema, deploying long takes, at least from sequences in *La Fille de l'eau* to much of *La Règle du jeu*, that would define the cinematic principle of a first great French *auteur* and even a national style. And then, beyond the hexagon, Welles, whose embrace of the 'abstract time of montage' marks *Citizen Kane* and *The Magnificent Ambersons*, would be enshrined in a nearby alcove in Bazin's imaginary pantheon. So also John Ford, when he follows a stagecoach rolling across the Monument Valley on its way Lordsburg (Figure 4.1) or Budd Boetticher, who sets his characters within vast

Figure 4.1 Still from *Stagecoach* (1939): The Stage to Lordsburg.

Figure 4.2 Still from *Ride Lonesome* (1959): A lunar landscape.

lunar landscapes where humans and horses, or for that matter, any living form, ought not belong (Figure 4.2). Were he alive, we can imagine Bazin ecstatic not only over the camera work of Tarkovsky, Kiarostami or, best of all, Belà Tarr – but maybe not quite so about the blindingly crisp visual field of digital cinema formatted in Blue-Ray.

A close reading of 'Montage interdit' shows that Bazin hardly beats his hobbyhorse to death. As much at stake as the white steed in *Crin blanc* or dying nag of *The Turin Horse* is the 'event' or the 'events' cinema brings to the screen when the long take is in dialogue with montage. Pocked with reference to events, the article that appeared in *Cahiers du Cinéma* can be countenanced veering into the direction of an essay on philosophy. For what follows, I should like to propose that in fact when it is shared among philosophers of continental inclination, possibly not on their own accord, but through dialogue, here and elsewhere Bazin's words gain different and even greater force than they may have had at the time of their writing. The stakes are simple: for Bazin, events are at the core of great cinema, and while they are generally motivated and conveyed through the long take and deep focus, within the regime of montage they gain autonomy beyond the confines of the seventh art. For Gilles Deleuze, one of Bazin's committed readers, albeit stated otherwise and with different consequences, the event is, no less, both philosophy and cinema itself. By means of reference to images to which both writers allude, juxtaposition allows us to see how the latter extends and refashions the former. Two different ways of thinking the event or events converge and diverge, the result becoming what both had hoped to be a politics and an aesthetics of consequence. A broader and more inclusive relation of film and event theory becomes for philosophers, filmmakers and spectators alike an 'operative function'.[2]

Bazin begins 'Montage Interdit' through reference to children's cinema, perhaps with indirect allusion to *Les Jeux interdits*, but clearly with direct reference to *Alice in Wonderland* and to the tales of Hans Christian Anderson (whose 'Little Match Girl' Renoir adapted for his eponymous silent feature of 1928). For Bazin, both are authors of fiction whose 'profondeur délicieuse et terrifiante (...) est au principe de leur beauté' (delightful and terrifying depth is the principle of their beauty). Later, reflecting on the revenge in Robert Flaherty's *The Louisiana Story* (1948) a boy takes on an alligator he believes has devoured his pet raccoon that had just saved an imperiled heron, Bazin writes: 'The spatial unity of the event must be respected at the moment its rupture would transform reality into its simple imaginary representation,' that is, when it is cut into the components of a montage to represent the event (Bazin 1985: 59). Flaherty realizes the stakes when he deploys the latter to dramatize the boy's capture of the beast and, earlier, the former to depict, 'in the same film, the sequence-shot [*plan-séquence*] of the alligator catching a heron, taken in a single panoramic' (Bazin 1985: 59–60). Bringing together the elements that the montage had just dispersed – in fact deleted from many copies of the films – this shot recovers the reality of the event itself, especially because it is shown and not explained through montage. The film event is marked by its concrete duration with emphasis placed on its 'spatial unity', which Bazin later describes as an 'opening of space', a 'feeling of space'

(Bazin 1985: 164) for which elsewhere finds mythic expression in neo-realism and in the American western.

In studying the 'aesthetic geology' of Rossellini's cinema, Bazin notes how *Paisan* (1947) is a layering (Deleuze will call it a stratigraphy) of six random sketches in a geography of the history of the liberation of Italy in the Second World War. The sixth, an episode portraying partisans and OSS soldiers in desperate battle with the Germans in the Po River delta, is crowned by a shot of a 'child [who] cries in the midst of his dead parents' who lay strewn on the ground in the crepuscule of dawn. 'That's it, it's a fact' (*Voilà, c'est un fait*). How did the Germans manage to know the actions of the peasants? Why is the child still alive? That's not the matter of the film. Yet a whole series of events are concatenated, leading up to its result' (Bazin 1985: 279). In these rich and dense pages, events are taken to be a dispersed series of 'facts' or effects of cinematographically uncertain causes. Each 'fact', a fragment of a brute reality, releases its 'sense' (Bazin puts *sens* between inverted commas, as if to meld inflections of sensation, direction and meaning) by dint of other facts to which it is juxtaposed. He concludes: 'Considerée en elle-même, chaque image n'étant qu'un fragment de réalité intérieure au sens, toute la surface de l'écran doit présenter une égale densité concrète' (Bazin 1985: 282) (Considered each in itself, every image being only a fragment of reality prior to meaning, the entire surface of the screen must present an equal concrete density). In short, the sentence tells us that in the final episode what had been a narrative suddenly becomes a film event. Attention is drawn to the *screen* that becomes an opaque surface on which swarming intensities of equal charge require the image to be seen as if it were a tableau or a painting, *all-over*.

Which is what, in another interrogative chapter of *Le Pli* (The fold), titled 'Qu'est-ce que ce qui est Baroque?' (Deleuze 1988: 38) (What is the Baroque?) Deleuze signals a fundamental trait: 'the Leibnizian monad would be . . . a room, an apartment entirely covered with lines of variable inflexion. It would be the obscure room [*chambre obscure* (or *camera obscura*)] of the *Nouveaux Essais*, furnished with a stretched canvas diversified by moving, living folds. Essential to the monad is that it has a *dark bottom* ["sombre fond"]' (Deleuze 1988: 38–9). At the fulcrum or axis on which *Cinéma 1* and *Cinéma 2* are balanced, at a line of demarcation between the two volumes, the author notes how the time image, generally belonging to modern cinema, comes forward when the event, what had been the essence of narrative film, scatters or becomes indiscernible because it shimmers *all over* the image. Recalling Bazin on *Paisan* at the beginning of

Cinéma 2, he shows how the *image-fact* is at the origin of cinemas emphasizing how the film itself is incapable of or incommensurable with the events it depicts. Events become unnamable, even unassimilable, visual 'facts' unto themselves.

Cinéma 2: L'image-temps was published in 1985. The following year, in *Foucault* (1986), an essay written in memory of the passing of his late friend, Deleuze noted closely and tersely how much *Ceci n'est pas une pipe* (This is not a pipe) and *Surveiller et punir* (Discipline and punish) were informed by – or were informing, possibly also informative of – contemporary cinema. At once marshalling Maurice Blanchot's famous 'Parler, ce n'est pas voir' (Speaking is not seeing) and invoking Robert Bresson to explain the nature of 'discursive' and 'visible' formations in which human subjects are born, Deleuze suggested that they could be discerned cinematically, as if they constituted the sound- and image-tracks of cultural forms shaping subjectivity (Blanchot 1969: 41–5). Two years later, Deleuze published his densely written *Le Pli: Leibniz et le baroque* (1988), from which allusion to cinema is evacuated but, it can be surmised, in which the principles of the seventh art are literally folded, notably in his exegeses of the early modern philosopher and the character of things baroque both then and now. The place where cinema and philosophy converge and become inextricably mixed might be the sixth and very slim chapter, situated near the middle, where, in light of Blanchot's preface to *L'Espace littéraire* (1969), who considers a book to be a picture whose force of attraction leads the eyes to a virtual vanishing or ever-moving median point, the title cannot fail to allude to Bazin: 'Qu'est-ce qu'un événement?' (What is an event?) seems grafted onto *Le Pli* from the style, temper and even the title of *Qu'est-ce que le cinéma* at the very time it anticipates the author's last major study published four years later: *Qu'est-ce que la philosophie?* What is cinema? What is philosophy? Each commands the same question mark.

Seen stratigraphically, as Deleuze advises readers of *L'Image-temps* to behold the landscapes in the films of Rossellini, Antonioni, Perrault and especially Alain Resnais, the three questions – concerning the nature of cinema, events and the baroque – suggest that in their very 'being', their *Dasein*, which implies design or *disegno*, events become the common ground of philosophy and cinema *tout court*. Which is and is not is what he announces in the first paragraph of the chapter when recalling how Alfred North Whitehead had three times asked the same question, 'What is an event?'[3] Writes Deleuze:

> Un événement, ce n'est pas seulement 'un homme est écrasé': la grande pyramide est un événement, et sa durée pendant 1 heure, 30 minutes, 5 minutes . . . , un

passage de la Nature, ou un passage de Dieu, une vue de Dieu. Quelles sont les conditions d'un événement, pour que tout soit événement? L'événement se produit dans un chaos, dans une multiplicité chaotique, à condition qu'une sorte de crible intervienne.

(An event isn't only 'a man is run over': the great pyramid is an event, and its duration for 1 hour, 30 minutes, 5 minutes . . . , a passage of Nature, or a passage of God, a view of God. What the conditions of an event so that everything becomes an event? Provided that a kind of screen intervenes, an event is produced in a chaos, in a chaotic multiplicity.) (Deleuze 1988: 103)

An accident, a fall, a cascade: the image of a man crushed or falling to his death, seen time and again in the visual records of the toppling of the World Trade Towers, or in our fantasies picturing Deleuze detaching himself from his dialysis machine, limping over to his window on the seventeenth floor of the building (8, Avenue Niel) in which he was living, climbing over the threshold, and letting himself plummet to the ground. Or famously, literature in 'De l'exercitation' (Of practice) in his (*Essais*, II, vi), Montaigne describes a similar occurrence. He sums up the essay with 'ce conte d'un si legier événement' (this tale of so slight an event), he has told about a grievous fall from his horse: Can these events, testing or approaching death as they do, be considered as affirmations of life (Montaigne 1950: 415)? An event can be both more and less than Deleuze's suicide or the accident that befell Montaigne. For the writer and the philosopher, an experience, understood as an essay on – or an experiment with – the proximity of death, may qualify as an event. But if the experience of duration is vital to the event, as Deleuze suggests, in cinema it might be manifest in the oft-unsettling effects of a long take. If a passage of Nature is in question, the long take would record the growth of grass in real time, or perhaps what James Benning approximates through the mediation and meditation of a continuous image of a lake whose waters stir at the shoreline ('Thirteen Lakes' (2004), studied in Conley 2018). Or if we were to behold a view of the world from the ichnographic standpoint of God, the event would be the contemplation of a photograph, the view of the earth emerging on the horizon of the moon much as we experience that of the sun at dawn in 'Earthrise, 1968', apparently the most famous picture ever recorded (NASA AS17-22727): the earth in the firmament, seen from the Apollo mission, 'ce grand monde' (this great world) much like the one Montaigne and Pascal had imagined, 'qui se presente, comme dans un tableau, cette grande image de nostre mere nature en son entiere magesté' (Montaigne 1950: 191) (bringing forward,

Figure 4.3 Bernard Salomon, 'The Creation of the World' in *La Metamorphose d'Ovide figuree* (Lyon: Jean de Tournes, 1557) (Harvard Houghton Library Typ 515.58.675).

as if in a picture, this great image of our mother nature in its entire majesty) (see 'The Modern Globe' in Cosgrove 2001). Following the drift of the words, we see how an event can be an invention of an origin of the world, perhaps like Bernard Salomon's illustrations of Marot's translation of Ovid's *Metamorphosis* of something emerging from an ever-given, 'already always' pictured – hence mediated – view of a formless condition (Figure 4.3) (Ovid 1557: f. aiii r°).

The intervention of a *crible* that makes an event possible would be a net or a screen that allows something 'One' to emerge from a 'pure Many, a pure disjunctive diversity' (Deleuze 1988: 103). Can we say that a filmic screen – be it a pendant sheet tacked to a wall, or a white screen coated with minuscule radiant particles mounted on a tripod, a computer's liquid screen, or the glass surface of an I-phone – is comparable to what Deleuze offers as *analogies*: the receptacle in the *Timaeus*, an electromagnetic field, or a porous elastic membrane? Where some kind of osmosis would take place, where a sifting or a 'triage', a passage through a mesh, is implied, what elsewhere he calls 'chaosmosis', the screen would make perceptible or visible the constitutive elements of nature. Nothing could be more cinematographic in Deleuze's description of what Leibniz brings out of chaos:

> Le chaos serait les ténèbres sans fond, mais le crible en extrait le sombre fond, le 'fuscum subnigrum' qui, si peu qu'il diffère du noir, contient pourtant toutes les couleurs: le crible est comme la machine infiniment machinée qui constitue la Nature. D'un point de vue psychique, le chaos serait un universel étourdissement, l'ensemble de toutes les perceptions possibles comme autant d'infinitésimales ou d'infiniment petits; mais le crible en extrairait des différentielles capables de s'intégrer dans des perceptions réglées'.
>
> (Chaos would be the depthless shadows, but the screen would extract from them its dark background, the *fuscum subnigrum* that however little it differs from blackness, nonetheless contains the spectrum of colors: the screen is like the infinitely machined machine that constitutes Nature. From a psychic point of view, chaos would be a universal giddiness, the sum of all possible perceptions, at once infinitesimal and infinitely small; but the screen would extract their differentials that can be integrated in regulated perceptions.) (Deleuze 1988: 104)

The reader senses the emergence of a moving image from the darkness of a movie theatre in which a viewer's eyes, rods and cones, unadjusted to the dimness, perceive and then watch illuminated or moving images as they come forward. It is the very mise-en-scène that Proust staged in remarking, at the outset of *À la recherche du temps perdu*, in these 'courts réveils d'un instant, le temps d'entendre les craquements organiques des boiseries, d'ouvrir les yeux pour fixer le kaléidoscope de l'obscurité' (brief awakenings for an instant, the time to hear the organic crackling of the woodwork, to open my eyes to stare at the kaleidoscope in the dark), an event forgotten when sleeping, later illuminated by a magic lantern he beheld an erotic fantasy projected the folds of a curtain (Proust 1954: 8):

> Au pas saccadé de son cheval, Golo, plein d'un affreux dessein, sortait de la petite forêt triangulaire qui veloutait d'un vert sombre la pente d'une colline, et s'avançait en tressautant vers le château de la pauvre Geneviève de Brabant. (. . .) Si on bougeait la lanterne, je distinguais le cheval de Golo qui continuait à s'avancer sur les rideaux de la fenêtre, se bombant de leurs plis, descendant dans leurs fentes.

(Full of frightening intentions, Golo going on his horse at a jerky gait, emerged from the little triangular forest, a velvet shimmer on its dark green slope, advancing and rearing toward the castle of poor Geneviève de Brabant. (. . .) If the lantern moved, I could distinguish Golo's horse that continued to advance on the curtains of the window, bulging from their folds, descending into their clefts.) (Proust 1954: 9)

For Proust, the screen is a curtain making palpable manifold fantasy, while for Deleuze, possibly imagining himself within the chamber of a monad, an event includes three components (*composantes*).[4] They include the following:

1. Infinite extension in space and time of things parts and whole discerned in series, felt in waves, through sonorous and luminous vibrations
2. Properties intrinsic to these series – pitch, timber, tint, chromatic saturation – that provide texture for whatever is in the *res extensa*, extension, yielding intensities, *intensions* or degrees of feeling
3. The 'individual', what Alfred North Whitehead calls a 'concrescence', a biological assimilation of elements, in other words a 'prehension'

Invoking Napoleon's troops passing by the pyramids to explain luminous prehension, Deleuze almost alludes to early cinema, to Lumière's famous fifty-second take of a caravan of ten dromedaries passing by a gigantic sphinx guarding a pyramid in the background, a film that Bertrand Tavernier calls a masterpiece (Tavernier 1998). In counterpoint to the men and camels moving across the foreground, the gigantic face of the human feline, immobile, at rest before a great triangle of stone, looks over a landscape near and away. In Deleuze's idiolect, forty centuries of obdurate time contemplate us through the implied screen of humans and animals cutting across the space. Hence, as if in free indirect discourse shared with Jean-Claude Dumoncel, in concert, he adds that 'echos, reflections, traces, prismatic deformations, perspectives, thresholds, folds' are as many screen-like surfaces, found in the world at large, that 'in some fashion anticipate psychic life'.[5] The eye of the pyramid or the sphinx beholding Bonaparte's soldiers or the caravan would be a vector of prehension going from a given or public world to the prehender (not a sub-ject but, because he or she relates to it, a super-ject), that the latter simultaneously objectifies from a 'public' standpoint ('a Lumière film' selling clichés of wonders its camera operators have photographed) and no sooner, makes 'private' or subjectifies (an almost uncanny, incommunicable sense of being seen by an inanimate object and sensing duration of time and space that even leaves commentator Bertrand

Tavernier, describing what he sees simply as 'incredible', at an uncommon loss for words).

In a baroque turn, as if recalling any of Mallarmé's swarms (as in 'L'Après-midi d'un faune'),[6] shifting from Whitehead's lexicon to his own, in which potentiation and possibility are keynote, he adds:

> Mais le datum, le préhendé, est lui-même une préhension préexistante ou coexistante, si bien que toute préhension est préhension de préhension, et l'événement, 'nexus de préhensions'. Chaque préhension nouvelle devient un datum, elle devient publique, mais pour d'autres préhensions qui l'objectivent; l'événement est inséparablement l'objectivation d'une préhension et la subjectivation d'une autre, il est à la fois public et privé, potentiel ou actuel, entrant dans le devenir d'un autre événement et sujet de son propre devenir. Il y a toujours quelque chose de psychique dans l'événement.

> (But the datum, the prehended, is itself a pre-existing or co-existing prehension, and the event, a 'nexus of prehensions'. Every new prehension becomes a datum, it becomes public, but for other prehensions that objectify it; the event is inseparably the objectivation of one prehension and the subjectivation of another. It is both public and private, potential or actual, entering into the becoming of another event and the subject of its own becoming. There is always something psychic in the event.) (Deleuze 1988: 104)

The sensation of becoming – and a becoming of one – event after another, in serial succession, assures any number of iterations of events. A pre-hension at once pre- (and co-) exists by virtue of the poetics of the word, *pré-* being the temporal and visual field that a screen brings to light or causes to take form in what seems to be a cognitive polyphony (see Ponge 1971; Derrida 1988, and 'The Titleer' in Derrida 2011, that takes up the relation of titles and events).

Three pertinent traits of an event become manifest within the confines of Leibniz's monad, a space and place our imagination cannot dissociate from a projection room or a movie theatre:

1. The subjective experience – active prehension – of a datum, such as the sphinx in Lumière's film, becomes an emotive or moving effect when sensed positively; contrariwise, when felt negatively, a 'bad vibe', it is sensed being 'excluded'.
2. The passage of one datum to another in a prehension – like moving images in either analogue or digital format – yields a perception of a 'becoming' that 'puts the past in a present filled with the future' (Deleuze 1988: 104).

3. Satisfaction or *self-enjoyment* (in English in the text) 'of its own becoming' occurs when the subject, say a cinephile, becomes replete with the data to its liking.

In a brief sequence in classical cinema, in Fritz Lang's *Fury* (1936) the process finds expression in a sublimely passing, insignificant, innocuous moment – call it an event – when a man named Joe Wilson (Spencer Tracy), a man who loves to gobble peanuts, has begun a commuter relation with his fiancée. After waving goodbye to her at a rail station, he walks in the rain to repair to his brother's apartment. Along the way, in a corridor, facing a poster under glass on an easel that leans against a dark wall he meets a stray dog (Figure 4.4). He looks at it with tenderness. A close-up of the dog, eagerly gazing at him (Figure 4.5) underscores an awakening force of attraction they have for each other. The sight of the solitary dog is matched on the sound track when Joe, speaking with empathy, conveys his thoughts. Voice-off, he utters, 'You look the way I feel, lonely and [wet and] small' (see the variations of the scene in Cormak 2004: 11). In the weakened deixis, his words could well be those the dog would be sharing with him. Joe objectifies (makes public) his feelings while the dog internalizes (makes private) what it feels and shares with Joe.

For an instant, man and dog find themselves in a nexus of prehensions. Turning about-face, Joe departs. A wipe from left to right – hence a screen-effect – draws him by an image or poster on an easel in angled into the frame to confront for a

Figure 4.4 Still from Fritz Lang's *Fury* (1936): Joe meets the dog.

Figure 4.5 Still from Fritz Lang's *Fury* (1936): The dog shares Joe's thoughts.

moment a wall that becomes a door (Figure 4.5). He finds a key and introduces it into the lock. Another wipe carries him beyond the door and into the space of a messy apartment where an unmade bed (contrary to what he had just seen with his fiancée through the window of a store) greets his entry (Figure 4.6). A tracking shot records him picking up a piece of dirty laundry, approaching a door and then stopping when, opening another it, he peers inside where, in the following take, we (and he, a common point of view is implied) happen upon a shimmering cascade of speckles of light behind six illuminated bars of what could be a carceral form or, we soon discover, a foot of a metal bedstead (Figure 4.7). An entirely oneiric scene, perhaps the inner wall of a monad, gives way to Joe's perception of a dark bedroom whose seeming 'fuscum subnigrum' would be the reflection on the wall of rain outside, pitter-pattering behind the window panes. The camera follows his entry before the scene becomes, for the slightest of instants, entirely abstract, then almost brutally concrete when he raises his right arm and turns on a pendant light fixture (Figure 4.8). In the bright light the nocturnal shimmer turns into a surface of wallpaper of an interlocking pattern of floral mesh. He lowers his arm. The shot cuts to the corner of a desktop on which is placed a portrait of his fiancée above a note (Figure 4.9) on which is penned, we learn when the man's hand grasps the sheet and brings it close to the camera lens, 'Gone to movie with Charlie. – Tom' (Figure 4.10).[7]

The note announces an unnamed movie or programme of movies. The words do not indicate to this point that *Fury* (1936) cues on the relation the burning of

Figure 4.6 Still from Fritz Lang's *Fury* (1936): Joe enters the apartment (in a dissolve).

Figure 4.7 Still from Fritz Lang's *Fury* (1936): A shimmer in the dark.

the Reichstag in 1933 holds with the blaze a crazed lynch mob sets in a prison in rural America in 1936. Identified by his craving for 'peanuts', Joe Wilson, falsely accused of having committed a murder, is jailed before the mob (whose dress and demeanour bear many German traits) sets fire to the building from which, miraculously, he escapes while his dog does not. A good deal of the critical work of *Fury* is made of director Fritz Lang's use of film within the courtroom sequence. The veracity of visible (albeit filmed) evidence or *enargeia* is debated, the prosecuting attorney (Walter Abel) defending the authenticity of the event

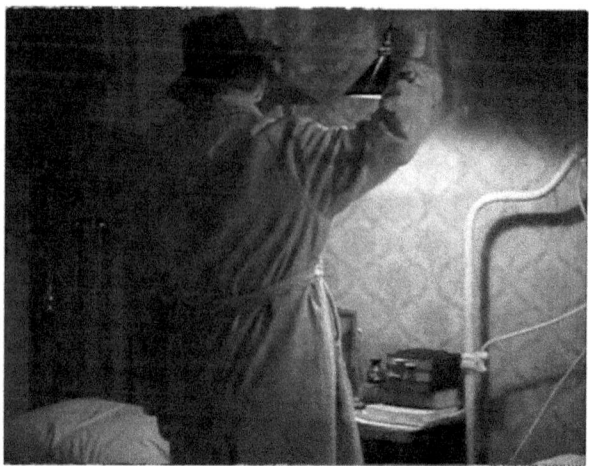

Figure 4.8 Still from Fritz Lang's *Fury* (1936): Joe turns on the light.

Figure 4.9 Still from Fritz Lang's *Fury* (1936): Joe reaches for the note.

when a team of newscasters (of the Movietone generation) is called to show the rushes of what they filmed. Yet the greater film event in the courtroom at the end of the feature has a miniature coequal where the hero, outside of a movie theatre where his brothers happen to be (as noted above), goes inside their apartment where he beholds an opaque screen whose shimmer of rain anticipates or 'prehends' the psychic nature at once of what will follow – an unsettling world, a *tout*, a movie, a world in itself. For Joe the promise of mutual self-enjoyment is shown, under a lampshade, in the illuminated portrait of his fiancée. Here

Figure 4.10 Still from Fritz Lang's *Fury* (1936): Joe reads the note.

the fourth and final aspect of an event pertains to Lang and Lumière alike. The extensions and prehensions

> ne cessent de se déplacer, gagnent et perdent des parties emportées par le mouvement; les choses ne cessent de s'altérer; (. . .) Les événements sont des flux. Qu'est-ce qui nous permet de dire, dès lors: c'est le même fleuve, c'est la même chose ou la même occasion . . .? C'est la grande pyramide. . . . Il faut qu'une permanence s'incarne dans les flux, qu'elle soit saisie dans la préhension. La grande pyramide signifie deux choses, un passage de la Nature ou un flux, qui perd et gagne des molécules à chaque moment, mais aussi un objet éternel qui demeure le même à travers les moments.

> (ceaselessly move about, gaining and losing pieces carried off by the movement; things are endlessly being altered; (. . .) Events are fluxes. What allows us to say, then: it's the same river, it's the same thing or the same occasion . . .? It's the great pyramid. . . . A permanence needs to be embodied in the fluxes, grasped in prehension. The great pyramid signifies two things, a passage of Nature or a flux which loses and gains molecules at all times, but also an eternal object that remains the same throughout time). (Deleuze 1988: 108)

Feelings (in English in the text) are eternal objects that ingress into an event as a quality (a colour, a sound, a filmic texture) while figures are matter (stone, a wall, a door, etc.). For Leibniz, the event is enclosed within the monad-theatre, whereas for Whitehead prehensions, vibrations, intensions belong to the reality of process, to the 'overture on a polytonality', what Pierre Boulez, notes Deleuze in admiration, called a 'polyphony of polyphonies' (Deleuze 1988: 112).

Fugacious and fleeting, but permanent too, the event takes place in what Deleuze calls a *chaosmos*, an osmosis of chaos and cosmos, in which a permeable membrane, what the context of *Le Pli* implies to be a bio-filmic screen, a *crible*, or a fold assures the possibility of the event. The screen becomes a liminal and psychically porous surface where subject and object move towards and through one another. For all its abstraction, the event could be a flickering surface of perceptions that in a viewing space or on a liquid screen become the matter and memories of events we carry with us.

Notes

1 Lumière in fact altered the long take. Raymond Bellour (2009) notes shifts and turns in the evolution of his work.
2 At the outset of *Le Pli: Leibniz et le baroque* (1988) Gilles Deleuze qualifies the 'baroque' less as a moment in the history of art and music than 'an operative function', perhaps in *Qu'est-ce que la philosophie?* (1991) what he calls a 'manner' or 'style' of thinking and doing.
3 At the outset of the chapter of *Le Pli* (p. 51), Deleuze invokes Whitehead for the first and only time in his writings. Three titles are mentioned: *The Concept of Nature* (1919), *Process and Reality* (1929), and *Adventures of Ideas* (1933).
4 Deleuze seems to rehearse Whitehead's reflections on the sentient qualities of the monad: Leibniz 'explained what it must be like to be an atom. Lucretius tells us what an atom looks like to others, and Leibniz tells us how an atom is feeling about itself,' in (Whitehead [1933] 1958: 136).
5 Jean-Claude Demoncel, *Whitehead ou le cosmos torrential*, in *Archives de la philosophie* (1984/85), cited in *Le Pli*: 103 fn1.
6 'Tu sais, ma passion, que, pourpre et déjà mûre, / Chaque grenade éclate et d'abeilles murmure;/Et notre sang, épris de qui le va saisir, / Coule pour tout l'essaim éternel du désir' (*Œuvres complètes*, ed. H. Mondor (Paris: Éditions Gallimard/ Pléiade, 1948), p. 52). (You know, my passion, that, purple and ripe already/ Every pomegranate explodes and murmurs with bees; / And our blood, taken with what will seize it, / Flows for the eternal beehive of desire.) An event, as Jacques Derrida noted, is a 'signature that is written' (in 'signature événement contexte', in *Marges de la philosophie* (Paris: Éditions de Minuit, 1976). The uncommon graphic design of the essay's title, in minuscule sans serif characters and without punctuation, suggests a gloss as *signature: événement qu'on texte* – signature: an event that is written). In Mallarmé's poem *essaim*, voiced as 'SM', would be an abbreviation of *S* téphane *M*

allarmé, also author of an English grammar, *Les Mots anglais* (that plays on 'angled words').

7   The shooting script does not make reference either to the rain or to the shimmer in the film: 'JOE enters followed by the dog. On his way to the bedroom of the flat he passes the in-a-door bed, stoops, picks up a pyjama jacket from the floor, tosses it onto the bed, and tiptoes on to the bedroom door. He cautiously opens it. *But the room is dark, except for a square of dim light through the window, beyond which is the top of a telegraph pole and wires*' (emphasis added), in Cormak 2004: 11.

References

Bazin, A. (1985 reprint), *Qu'est-ce que le cinéma?* Paris: Éditions du Cerf.
Bellour, R. (2009), *Le Corps du cinéma: hypnoses, émotions, animalités*, Paris: P.O.L./Trafic.
Blanchot, M. (1969), *L'Entretien infini*, Paris: Éditions Gallimard.
Conley, T. (2018), 'A Lake-Event', in N. Lübecker and D. Rugo (eds), *James Benning's Environments: Politics, Ecology, Duration*, 129–42, Edinburgh: Edinburgh University Press.
Cormak, B. (2004), *Fury: Shooting Script*, Alexandria: Alexander Street Press.
Cosgrove, D. (2001), *Apollo's Eye: A Cartographic Genealogy of the Earth in the Western Imagination*, Baltimore: The Johns Hopkins University Press.
Deleuze, G. (1988), *Le Pli: Leibniz et le baroque*, Paris: Éditions de Minuit.
Deleuze, G. (1991), *Qu'est-ce que la philosophie?* Paris: Éditions de Minuit.
Derrida, J. (1976), *Marges de la philosophie*, Paris: Éditions de Minuit.
Derrida, J. (1988), *Signéponge*, Paris: Éditions du Seuil, Coll. Fiction & Cie.
Derrida, J. (2011), *Parages*, ed. J. P. Leavey, trans. T. Conley et al., Stanford: Stanford University Press.
Fury (1936), [Film] Dir. Fritz Lang, USA: Metro Goldwyn Meyer.
Mallarmé, S. (1948), *Œuvres complètes*, ed. H. Mondor, Paris: Éditions Gallimard/Pléiade.
Montaigne, M. (1950), *Essais*, ed. A. Thibaudet and M. Rat, Paris: Éditions Gallimard/Pléiade.
Ovid (1557), *La Metamorphose d'Ovide figure*, trans. C. Marot, Lyon: Jean de Tournes, 1557, illustrated by B. Salomon.
Ponge, F. (1971), *La Fabrique du 'pré'*, Geneva: Skira, Coll. 'Sentiers de la creation' 11.
Proust, M. (1954), *À la recherche du temps perdu*, ed. P. de Clarac and A. Ferré, 3 vols, Paris: Éditions Gallimard/Pléiade.
Ride Lonesome (1959), [Film] Dir. Budd Boetticher, USA: Ranown Pictures Corp.
Stagecoach (1939), [Film] Dir. John Ford, USA: United Artists.

Tavernier, B., ed. (1998), *The Lumière Brothers' First Films*, New York: Kino on Video
Whitehead, A. N. ([1919] 1971), *The Concept of Nature*, Cambridge: Cambridge University Press.
Whitehead, A. N. ([1929] 1978), *Process and Reality*, New York: The Free Press.
Whitehead, A. N. ([1933] 1958), *Adventures of Ideas*, New York: Mentor Books.

Part Two

Revisualizing: from the Tangible to the Intangible

5

What film studies is

Mapping the discipline

Annette Kuhn and Guy Westwell

The title of this chapter, which borrows from that of Dudley Andrew's 2010 book, *What Cinema Is!*, suggests a way into thinking about what, through its interaction with other disciplines, film studies is now and what it is becoming (as well as about what other disciplines, through *their* interaction with film studies, are becoming) (Andrew 2010). On these issues, we have learnt much from our experience of collaborating on a work of reference that covers the entire field of film studies. In 2007, we were commissioned to produce the *Oxford Dictionary of Film Studies* (Kuhn and Westwell 2012).[1] Published in 2012, the dictionary was therefore the result of five years' work. Between us we authored all but a few of the nearly 500 entries (those on technical topics were commissioned from our colleague Eugene Doyen); and once the dictionary was in press, we continued updating our databases (and engaging in lively debate about changes in the discipline). As a consequence, we were well prepared when it came to putting together the revised and updated second edition (Kuhn and Westwell 2020).

Since the dictionary is a work of reference in **film studies** (and not in film), we felt that the only viable starting point would be to obtain a sense of the content and shape of the discipline.[2] And so we began by undertaking a systematic review of the field, both historically and as it is currently taught and researched. This process fed into the overall structure and organization of the dictionary and guided our practices of writing, editing and generally collaborating. In what follows, we explain the *process* of planning the dictionary and explain the carefully engineered *construction* of the finished product. The examples presented include an account of our coverage of **film theory**, the relation between film studies and what we call *cognate disciplines*, and our development for the revised 2020 edition of those entries related to **identity**. We conclude with some observations and questions of particular relevance for the present volume, including how film and film theory can rethink and redraw the terrain of traditional disciplines, enabling different modes of thought and practice within them.

Surveying the discipline

The initial step in the planning process was a three-part survey of the discipline. First, bearing in mind the dictionary's target readership (film studies students), we reviewed eight major English-language introductory film studies textbooks (Bordwell and Thompson 2004; P. Cook 2007; Dick 2010; Hill and Gibson 1998; Monaco 2009; Nelmes 2011; Nowell-Smith 1996) and looked at film studies curricula in UK secondary and tertiary education.[3] Secondly, we examined English-language reference works available at the time (Blandford, Grant and Hillier 2001; Hayward 2006; Katz, Klein and Nolen 2005; Konigsberg 1997; Thomson 2010).[4] These two exercises produced a listing of topics and areas of study widely regarded by practitioners and experts in the field as appropriate for inclusion in film studies courses, particularly introductory ones. Thirdly, because teaching and research are interdependent, and because we wanted to offer student readers the opportunity to delve more deeply into topics of special interest to them, as well as provide teachers and researchers with a source of basic information and recommended reading, we conducted a broad survey of the film studies *research* literature (Kuhn 2009). Coincidentally, while we were conducting this groundwork, a number of studies of the history and development of film studies as an independent discipline were published (Bolas 2009; Polan 2007; Grieveson and Wasson 2008).

These exercises, along with our own experience as teachers and researchers in the field – adding up to some six decades – initially produced a loose listing of topics and areas of research, scholarship and teaching in film studies (the core discipline, if you like). It also provided a sense of the changes that have taken place in the field over the years. We then tried to give this information some initial shape and structure using mind mapping software.

Figure 5.1 shows an early mapping of the field that was produced from the survey of introductory textbooks. It gives some idea of how we began to consider film studies as a relatively coherent discipline formed from different, but

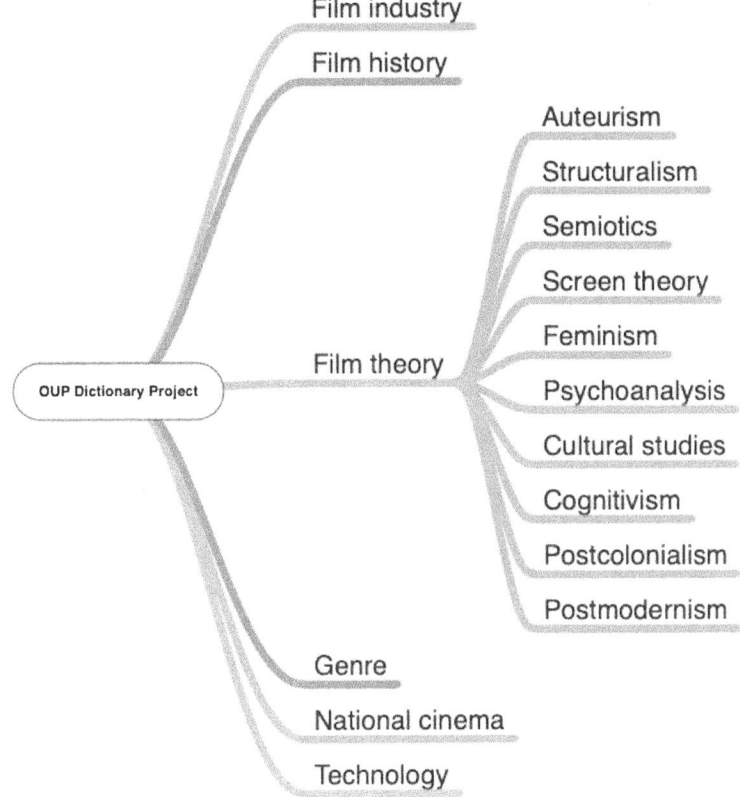

Figure 5.1 Dictionary planning mind map. Permission: authors' own.

interconnected, constituent parts. The film theory header has been expanded to show some of the key areas covered. From here, the mapping process continued over a considerable period of time, with our survey undergoing significant modifications and refinements. Ultimately, the aim was for exhaustive coverage of the discipline – an inclusive and yet concise map of the field that would eventually generate (and, importantly, contextualize) every topic addressed in the dictionary.

While at this point no dictionary entries had yet been drafted, as we moved on to research and write our individual entries, the mapping of the discipline continued; and as a preliminary to writing entries, a template or proforma was compiled for each broad sub-area of research, scholarship and teaching within film studies – the aim being to ensure consistency of entry structure and contents, while at the same time mapping out a system of cross-referencing.

The first sub-area we worked on was **national cinemas**, which ranged from entries on cinemas that have been subjects of long-standing and extensive study and can boast considerable historical, critical and theoretical literatures, to those on national cinemas that have not been widely researched or taught in Anglophone film studies. The template devised for drafting the 130 or so national cinema entries called for coverage of earliest films, key directors and stars, the national film industry and its associated organizations and institutions, film movements and significant genres, state involvement, censorship, current state of the industry, significant recent films and also – crucially, as we rapidly discovered – 'film studies interest', or how the national cinema in question has been covered or treated in film studies pedagogy and scholarship.

Some national cinemas can boast a substantial body of 'film studies interest', so much so that they have tended not to be thought, taught or written about under the *national* cinemas rubric. This is especially true of cinemas and cinema cultures that are associated with long-standing traditions of film-critical and film-theoretical interest: a prominent case in point being France, where the *politique des auteurs* was born, not to mention **psychoanalytic film theory** and much else besides, including, for instance, **beur cinema**, the **Cinémathèque Française**, **filmology** and the *Nouvelle Vague*.

Meanwhile, another key aspect of the planning of the dictionary was the building of a database, called a *headword tracker*, provided by the publisher and modified on an ongoing basis by us to form a listing of entry titles (or headwords) to be included, or considered for inclusion, in the dictionary.[5] This was used (and is in continuing use) to keep track of data, information, cross-references, feedback, word counts and so on. By the time the dictionary's first edition was ready for publication the database included nearly a thousand headwords. Alongside this, we compiled a list of publications using the bibliographic software Endnote, using searchable key words and entry headwords: this enabled us to efficiently compile the 'further reading' suggestions at the end of each entry.

As the project entered its second and third year and writing was well underway, each headword and entry was reviewed in light of its place in the discipline's overall architecture and, where appropriate, in relation to its past and current usages and/or prominence within film studies. Figure 5.2 shows some of these informal 'workings'.

The objective – a Borgesian one in miniature if you like – was to produce an armature for individual entries, a picture or map of interconnections between, and of fluctuations in the status of, various areas of enquiry. We wanted to set

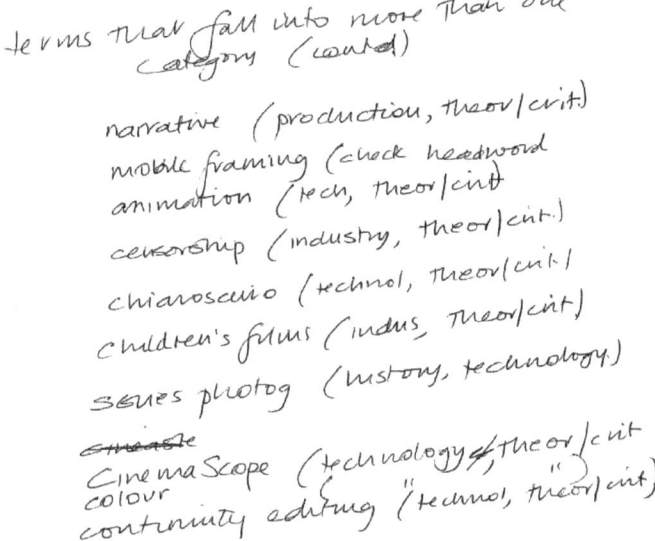

Figure 5.2 Thinking through category overlap. Permission: authors' own.

things up so that users could happen upon and follow their own paths, forking and otherwise, through the dictionary, making discoveries of their own about the discipline – including perhaps ones that we had not ourselves foreseen.

In the **costume** entry, for example, the reader is aided in their navigation through, and exploration of, the topic by some simple controls, which display differently in the print and the online versions of the dictionary. In the print version, an *asterisk* indicates that there is a separate entry for the indicated term; in the online version, blue type stands in for the asterisk, and works as a hyperlink. In the first sentence, the highlighting of (or the asterisks against) **production design** and **mise-en-scene** alert the reader to the dictionary's entries for these terms. Later in the entry it is noted that costume has been of interest to feminist film scholars, and here the reader is directed to the **feminist film theory** entry. At the end of the entry, the reader is invited to *see also* the discussion of the role of costume in the **heritage film**. By following these signposts and cross-references, the reader will gain a broader sense of the study of costume across several areas of film studies, while also being offered an invitation to take a wander through the discipline.

Our mind maps, templates, bibliography and headword list allowed us to marshal what was in effect a 'rolling' and recursive mapping of (as well, importantly, as an enquiry into *how* to map) the *discipline* of film studies. It was our hope that this apparatus would prove robust and flexible enough to ensure

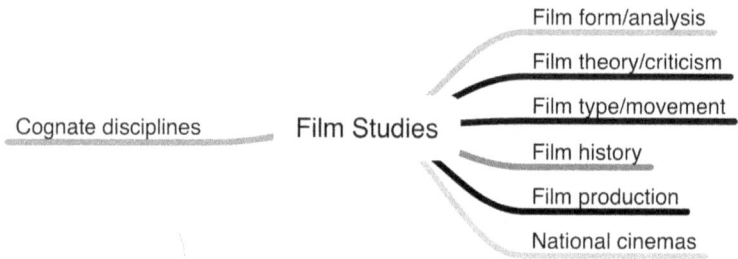

Figure 5.3 Mind map showing main sub-areas of film studies. Permission: authors' own.

that the mapping process would permit attention to changes in the discipline and provide a structure for incorporating any changes, and for refining and developing the map for future editions of the dictionary. The main sub-areas of film studies that emerged in our disciplinary enquiry are set out in Figure 5.3.

Each of the six sub-areas in turn can be broken down into further subfields, and so on. For example, if **film history** is looked at in terms of periodization, this sub-area takes in the study of **early cinema,** which in turn includes such film studies topics as **actualities, cinema of attractions, ride films, trick films** and so on; while considered historiographically, **film history** embraces a range of foci for the historical study of cinema. These might include histories of **film form,** film **aesthetics** and **film movements**; historical studies of film industries; and social and cultural histories of cinema and cinemagoing, including historical reception histories and audience studies.

Film theory/criticism

For present purposes, it may be helpful to take a closer look at the film studies sub-area-denoted film theory/criticism. Embracing both film-theoretical debates and film-critical terms (see Figure 5.4), this sub-area produces some seventy entries in all. The broad definition which opens the **film theory** entry reads as follows (the dictionary includes a separate entry on **film criticism**):

> A discourse that seeks to establish general principles concerning *film as a distinct art form or to set out general concepts underlying all films and *cinema: This might include the moving image *screen or screens, what is exhibited on these screens, and the nature of the viewer's encounter with the cinema screen and its contents. Theory provides conceptual and methodological tools for

thinking about, understanding, and explaining the objects with which a body of knowledge concerns itself – in the present instance film, films, and cinema – and ideally also takes on board any shifts or changes in disciplinary objects. At its most illuminating, theory measures its generalizations against its objects; and at its most grounded, theory derives its generalizations from its objects. Although the two terms are often used interchangeably and the two practices do overlap, film theory may be held in distinction from *film criticism, in that it is concerned mainly with general ideas relating to films and cinema as opposed to commentary on particular films or filmmakers. (Kuhn and Westwell 2012: 180)

Some of the film-theoretical topics that we identified, along with some subsidiary fields related to an important area of film theory, **psychoanalytic film theory**, are set out in Figure 5.4.

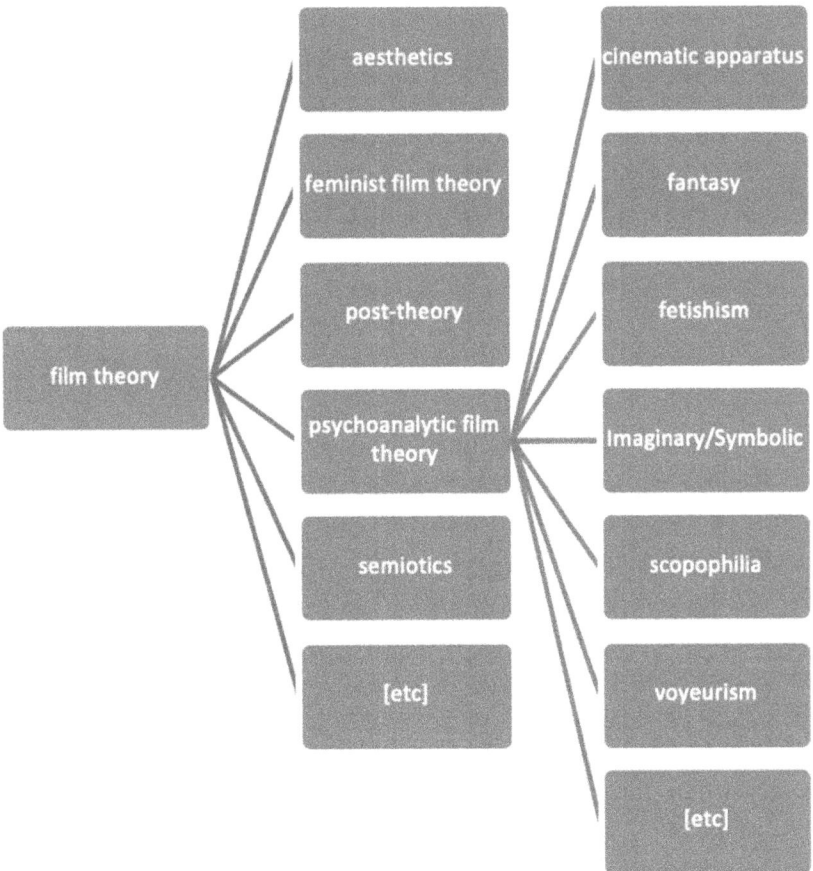

Figure 5.4 Film theory and some of its subsidiary fields. Permission: authors' own.

The template devised for formulating entries on topics within the film theory/criticism sub-area calls, inter alia, for a broad critical/theoretical definition (as in the opening of the passage quoted earlier) and a summary of current points of concern or development within the area. In the **film theory** entry, some of these issues are identified as follows:

> The current preoccupation with filmic engagement is being directed into a phenomenological concern with the lived experience of cinema, including questions about tactile and bodily engagements and forms of immersion (see **haptic visuality; phenomenology and film; philosophy and film**). Addressing the idea of the filmic experience may indeed help in thinking through the implications of today's multifaceted screen experience. And this in turn takes film theory back to one of its oldest concerns, the ontology of film: What is (digital) cinema? (Kuhn and Westwell 2012: 182)

In this passage, there are pointers to entries on *phenomenology and film* and *philosophy and film*, as well as a mention of the ontology of film, all of which reference film studies' engagement with external bodies of knowledge – with what we call *cognate disciplines*. At this point, we are called upon to consider how film and film theory can rethink and redraw the terrain of traditional disciplines. The dictionary speaks from inside film studies: and so cognate disciplines appear literally out on a limb on the disciplinary 'map' in Figure 5.3. If our first task was to survey and chart the discipline of film studies, you might say that at this point we were approaching the edges of our map and looking out onto less familiar territory.

The *film theory* entry notes that 'A conspicuous feature of contemporary film theory is its tendency to borrow concepts and approaches from other bodies of knowledge' (Kuhn and Westwell 2012: 181). Accordingly, we decided to explicitly address the issue of the instrumentality not just within film theory, but across film studies as a whole, of certain other disciplines. The 2012 edition of the dictionary includes as cognate disciplines: area studies, cultural studies, media studies, memory studies, phenomenology, philosophy, politics, psychology and sociology. There are obviously 'issues' with some of these disciplines, particularly in cases where the interchange with film studies is contested, or in flux. There are also disciplines that do not appear in this list and perhaps should. Not surprisingly, then, cognate disciplines was a feature of the dictionary that demanded considerable attention in planning for the second edition.

Headword	
Filename	
Alternative terms	
Crossreferences	
General definition of discipline	
Discipline in relation to film studies	
Key proponents	
History of usage in film studies	
Commentary/key debates on use in FS	
Current concerns/issues	
Reading	

Figure 5.5 Template used for cognate discipline entries. Permission: authors' own.

The template devised for the cognate disciplines entries (Figure 5.5) includes a reminder to discuss the discipline in its interaction with, or in relation to, film studies.

Film and philosophy

It is instructive to look at this interaction in the case of two cognate disciples: one of them – philosophy – features in the dictionary's first edition; the other – modern language studies – does not. As pointed out in the *philosophy and film* entry (Kuhn and Westwell 2012: 311–12), philosophers have written about films and cinema since the very earliest years of the medium. But it is really only since the 1990s that philosophy has begun to be widely taken on board within Anglophone film studies (consequent to an extent on the publication in English of Gilles Deleuze's books on the *movement image* and the *time image* (Deleuze 1986, 1989)). By the early 2000s, 'film-philosophy' had firmly established itself as a growth area for film studies scholarship, with regular conferences, academic monographs, anthologies and dedicated journals. But it did not come up in our early survey of the field, and so did not feature in our mappings of the core discipline. Therefore, after some debate, we decided to treat philosophy as a cognate discipline rather than as, say, a sub-area of film studies or a subset of film theory/criticism. That is, we took our cue from our map of the discipline at the time rather than adopting a vanguardist stance towards its future development: we do not consider this to be part of our remit. This may be justified in light of the different ways in which philosophy and film studies have intersected, four of which are noted in the 2012 entry:

> Film and philosophy intersect in several, sometimes overlapping, areas of inquiry. Firstly, films about philosophy: philosophy, philosophizing, or ethical dilemmas as themes or topics, as for example in Ma nuit chez Maude/My Night With Maud (France, 1969), one of Eric Rohmer's fêted 'moral tales' series. Some film studies inquiry in the area of film and ethics draws on this approach. Secondly, films as a vehicle for philosophizing: looking at films as illustrations or demonstrations of philosophical questions can be an effective way of making philosophy accessible to non-philosophers. Indeed this is a fairly common practice among teachers of philosophy, for whom certain films (The Matrix (US, 1999); Total Recall (US, 1990); Being John Malkovich (US, 1999); Memento (US, 2000)) and genres (*horror and *science fiction) exert a particularly powerful philosophical appeal. This approach may be characterised as belonging to philosophy rather than to film studies. Thirdly, films as philosophy or 'doing philosophy': film as philosophy takes seriously the idea that film is less an illustration of ideas and theory and more a form of reflection in itself, i.e. a form specific to the medium of cinema. [Stanley] Cavell, for example, sees mainstream and popular films as sites of philosophical reflection. Fourthly, philosophy in film theory: philosophy as providing a model for theorizing on film, by clarifying concepts and rooting out conceptual confusion. (Kuhn and Westwell 2012: 312–13)

While we acknowledge a role for philosophy in film theorizing here, we see it as just one of a number of points in its intersection with film studies. Moreover, this is arguably not the most significant concern for, or objective of, film-philosophy in its current form.

We could have sliced it in a different way, perhaps, with a headword such as philosophical film theory on the model of *psychoanalytic film theory*. But while this might offer some sort of logical consistency, it would undermine the spirit and the objective of our exercise in mapping the field of film studies itself. Psychoanalytic film theory has claimed a place in the core discipline of film studies for decades, during which time it has produced many offshoots that have more to do with the study of film than with psychoanalysis or psychoanalytic theory (the influential visual pleasure debate being a case in point), while the term **psychoanalytic film theory** and its variants is in widespread use in film studies textbooks and scholarly literature.

On the other hand, the term 'philosophical film theory' does not appear to exist in film studies. Even if one could conceive of such a thing, it could be seen as referencing only one of the areas where film studies and philosophy intersect: philosophy as providing a model for theorizing on film. Also, significantly, few practitioners of film-philosophy would regard what they do as film theory. What is clear, though, is that film-philosophy has moved on in the few years since the dictionary was first published, and it therefore needed to be looked at carefully for the revised edition. Perhaps the most obvious change made for the new edition is the entry headword: instead of **philosophy and film**, following what has become the firmly established usage in the field and its increasing visibility in teaching curricula, this is now **film-philosophy**. And the new entry's closing 'current concerns and issues' raise some questions that film-philosophy is posing for film studies now:

> The past few years have seen a continued outpouring of publications on numerous aspects of philosophy and film. These include overviews and introductory texts aimed at a film studies readership, and engagements with philosophical issues on the part of film scholars. These developments raise a number of questions for film studies: What distinguishes film-philosophy from film theory? Are there points of overlap? Does an understanding of film-philosophical issues require philosophical training? How can a philosophical approach bring to light hitherto unexamined aspects of film and cinema? (Kuhn and Westwell 2020: 203)

It is perhaps also worth giving some consideration to sub-areas or aspects of philosophical enquiry as they figure in film studies. The dictionary's first edition includes entries on **aesthetics**, **realism** and **phenomenology**, each of which can claim, in its own right, a history in and a relationship with film studies – a body of film studies literature and a curricular presence – that predates the rise of film-philosophy. The revised edition also includes a new entry on **ethics**, an area of significant growth in film studies in the last few years. But questions remain. Does an area like **phenomenology and film** belong in film theory alongside work on, say, embodied spectatorship? Or does it belong among the cognate disciplines? You might say that this is not important as long as the topics are covered. On the other hand, our mapping of the field forms the basis of the architecture of signposts and cross-references throughout the dictionary, and we do have a responsibility to point the user in helpful directions. In this particular instance, cross-referencing has been designed to enable readers to pursue either option, or both.

In considering the future relationship between philosophy and film studies, we might ask whether anything is likely to change in any of the areas in which film studies and philosophical enquiry meet – especially perhaps in the role of philosophy as providing a model for theorizing on film. The first is a question for film studies; the second is for philosophy and is of particular relevance in the present context. Is 'cinematic thinking' finding its way into philosophy? And if so, where, how and with what outcomes?

Film and modern languages

For the revised edition of the dictionary, we decided to add **modern language studies** to the cognate disciplines. The film studies programme in our own university and school (essentially of modern languages) was established in 2004; and film studies courses were taught initially by language specialists. This development was far from unique, and there is little doubt that the discipline of film studies has been affected by its embrace by modern language studies – most obviously at an institutional level, but possibly also in terms of overall trends in film studies curricula, teaching and scholarship. And so for the new edition we undertook to inquire whether and how the film studies map is being redrawn in light of inputs from modern languages teaching and scholarship. Relatedly, **area studies** was included in the first edition:

> Area studies is an umbrella term covering various interdisciplinary scholarly studies of the languages, peoples, societies, and cultures of a definable geographical area (as for example Latin American studies, Oriental and African studies, Scandinavian studies, Slavonic and Eastern European studies, etc.). (Kuhn and Westwell 2012: 16–17)

Among the national cinemas entries, we also include **Europe**; and this broad definition of area studies could encompass European 'languages, peoples, societies, and cultures' (Kuhn and Westwell 2012: 16). However, in terms of the histories of the various cognate disciplines and their relationship with film studies, this would not be right. The **area studies** entry in the dictionary follows the logic of our surveying and mapping of the field, in that its content and contextualization are guided by our map – in other words by the architecture of the discipline of film studies. We noted a marked rise in the presence of non-Anglophone and non-European cinemas in film studies curricula, textbooks and scholarship from around the mid-1990s. Much of this was pioneered by area studies specialists working on the films or film cultures of their territories of specialization, but it rapidly gave rise to what has become, since the turn of the millennium, a significant body of film studies teaching and scholarship on **World cinema**.

In its conclusion, the **Europe, film in** entry in the revised edition of the dictionary takes on board both this development and the emergent encounter between film studies and modern language studies:

> Outside *film history and historiography, the study of European cinema once tended to focus mainly on art cinema and its auteurs, with a partly related attention to the question of national differences in films and cinema cultures (see **authorship**). These concerns remain, but have lately been augmented by increased attention to histories of popular and 'middlebrow' European cinemas and genres, and more fundamentally – under worldwide trends towards globalization and with the borders of Europe and its constituent nations becoming more permeable – a re-examination of questions around national identity and cinema, alongside a rise of interest in *diasporic and *transnational cinemas within Europe. Recent years have also seen a surge of interest in European cinema cultures within the disciplines of *modern languages and *area studies. (Kuhn and Westwell 2020: 170–1)

At the same time, given the particular qualities and histories of these cinemas, any encounter with modern language studies will have different resonances across the various national cinemas of Europe. France, with its century and more of intellectual engagement with cinema, is once again an obvious case in point. Indeed, work on French cinema and cinema culture by French specialists has been highly formative of Anglophone film studies since the 1970s, and perhaps before.

But something different is going on in today's encounter between modern/European languages and film studies, where the direction of travel tends on the whole to be film studies towards modern language studies rather than vice versa. It is unfair to generalize, but one telling indicator is the extent to which courses on film are taught, and/or research disseminated, in language studies as opposed to film studies contexts. It would certainly be interesting to see if this particular encounter helps us in assessing how film and film theory can rethink and redraw the terrain of traditional disciplines, enabling different modes of thought and practice within them.

Identity

Another area in which there has been a clear shift of interest since we began work on the dictionary is that of identity. Identity has been a major preoccupation of Western popular culture in the last decade, via specific issues such as the Me Too Movement (#MeToo) and Black Lives Matter in the United States, alongside wider concerns about identity politics, political correctness, immigration and the rise of nationalism. As a consequence, discussion of identity has been increasingly present within film studies, shaping both teaching and research.

The 2012 edition of the dictionary had no standalone entry on identity, but its mapping of the discipline already contained a plethora of entries in which identity was a central element. Film studies has since its inception considered identity as a key element of the study of **narrative**, via the examination of plots, themes and character types in films. In relation to this, much work has also been undertaken on how prejudicial representation of specific identity characteristics has played a role in the subordination of minority groups, especially in relation to gender and race. Reception studies have considered how identity has been an important element in bringing together select interpretive communities around specific films; as for instance, in the consumption of mainstream Hollywood by certain marginalized ethnic groups. Film-theoretical approaches in relation to **feminist film theory**, **post-structuralism** and **queer theory** have also challenged notions of fixed identity, with identity instead figuring as performative, fluid, hybrid and decentred.

In order to reflect the greater emphasis being placed on identity within the discipline, we sought ways to enhance the prominence of this pre-existing content. We began by gathering all existing entries deemed relevant to identity, and then dividing these in relation to specific identity characteristics. It was immediately apparent, for example, that the dictionary already contained around a dozen entries relevant to the identity characteristic of race. Figure 5.6 shows a detail of this mapping process and indicates how some relevant headwords already existed (**gender**, national identity (covered under **national cinema**)), while others needed to be added (race, sexuality, social class, disability, religion). The chosen headwords also approximate the special characteristics identified in the UK Equality Act 2010, which forms a key point of orientation for scholars working in this area (National Archives). These new 'linking' entries (marked in Figure 5.6 with an asterisk) permitted access to a range of pre-existing entries, which themselves were updated in light of the new identity architecture. Finally, a new entry on **intersectionality** flagged the multifaceted nature of identity.

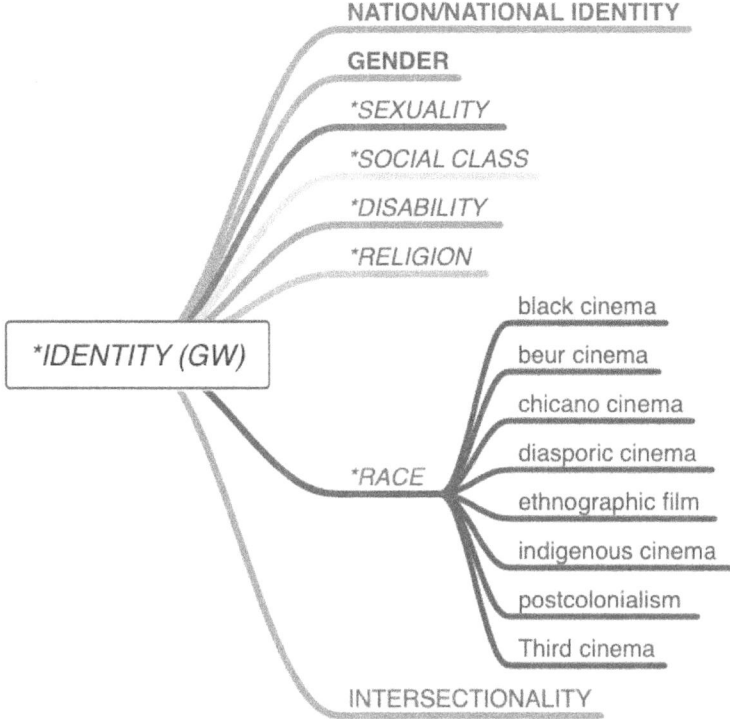

Figure 5.6 Retrofitting identity. Permission: authors' own.

As the entries related to **film theory, film criticism, film-philosophy, modern language studies and film**, and **identity** indicate, the dictionary provides an overview of film studies; and also an enactment of interconnections between, and fluctuations in the status of, various areas of enquiry within the discipline. The apparatus we have built is designed to be robust and flexible enough to accommodate shifts and developments in the discipline and to reflect these changes in future editions of the dictionary. The recent appearance of histories of the field, the publication of our dictionary and indeed the present volume, all point to a moment of disciplinary self-awareness that marks film studies' maturity. As confirmation, we might also cite current debates within the British Academy about what film studies is, where it belongs in the traditional disciplines, and which, if any, aspects of it ought to be embraced in the Academy's mission as 'the UK's expert body that supports and speaks for the humanities and social sciences' (British Academy).

This activity is perhaps also a sign of anxiety: the wider climate – funding councils seeking impact and interdisciplinary work, and thus requiring shifts in working practices and objects of study; the categorization used by Research Excellence Framework (REF) panels, with film studies betwixt and between; the shifting paradigms at play within the discipline; the rising number of courses on film put on by non-film studies specialists in other disciplines; general concerns about the interchange between film studies and more 'traditional' disciplines; even the dispersal across media forms of what was once readily identifiable as 'cinema'. All these anxieties are arguably contributing to considerable flux within and beyond a discipline whose distinctiveness derives from its unique and rich history, and especially from its focus on medium specificity as well as its encounters with a range of other disciplines.

Notes

1 The dictionary is also available online at https://www.oxfordreference.com/ (subscription required).
2 The use of bold in this sentence, and where it appears in the remainder of this chapter, signals that there is a corresponding entry in the dictionary.
3 As the bibliography for this chapter indicates, many of these texts have been published in a number of editions. This process of revision and renewal is indicative of the centrality of these works to the discipline over a considerable period of time.
4 While researching the second edition of the dictionary we also consulted, inter alia, Beaver 2015; Bordwell and Thompson 2016; D. O. Cook 2016; Hayward 2017; Katz, Klein and Nolen, 2012; Thomson 2014; as well as the relevant Cinema and Media Studies entries available in the Oxford Bibliographies online database; see https://www.oxfordbibliographies.com/ (subscription required).
5 A copy of the headword list used for the second edition can be viewed here: https://tinyurl.com/tm5qfyc

References

About the British Academy (n.d.), British Academy. Available online: https://www.thebritishacademy.ac.uk/about (accessed 23 December 2019).

Andrew, D. (2010), *What Cinema Is! Bazin's Quest and Its Charge*, Oxford: Wiley-Blackwell.

Beaver, F. E. (2015), *Dictionary of Film Terms the Aesthetic Companion to Film Art*, 5th edn, New York: Peter Lang.

Blandford, S., B. K. Grant and J. Hillier (2001), *The Film Studies Dictionary*, London: Arnold.

Bolas, T. (2009), *Screen Education: From Film Education to Media Studies*, Bristol: Intellect.
Bordwell, D. and K. Thompson (2004), *Film Art: An Introduction*, 7th edn, New York: McGraw-Hill Education.
Bordwell, D. and K. Thompson (2016), *Film Art: An Introduction*, 11th edn, New York: McGraw-Hill Education.
Cook, D. O. (2016), *A History of Narrative Film*, 5th edn, New York: W. W. Norton & Company.
Cook, P. (2007), *The Cinema Book*, 3rd edn, London: British Film Institute.
Deleuze, G. (1986), *Cinema 1: The Movement-Image*, London: Athlone.
Deleuze, G. (1989), *Cinema 2: The Time Image*, London: Athlone.
Dick, B. F. (2010), *Anatomy of Film*, 6th edn, Bedford: St. Martin's.
Equality Act, 2010 (n.d.), National Archives. Available online: http://www.legislation.gov.uk/ukpga/2010/15/contents (accessed 23 December 2019).
Grieveson, L. and H. Wasson (2008), *Inventing Film Studies*, Durham: Duke University Press.
Hayward, S. (2006), *Cinema Studies: The Key Concepts*, 3rd edn, London: Routledge.
Hayward, S. (2017), *Key Concepts in Cinema Studies*, 5th edn, London: Routledge.
Hill, J. and P. C. Gibson, eds (1998), *The Oxford Guide to Film Studies*, 1st edn, Oxford: Oxford University Press.
Katz, E., F. Klein and R. D. Nolen (2005), *The Film Encyclopedia: The Complete Guide to Film and the Film Industry*, 5th edn, New York: Collins Reference.
Katz, E., F. Klein and R. D. Nolen (2012), *The Film Encyclopedia: The Complete Guide to Film and the Film Industry*, 7th edn, New York: Collins Reference.
Konigsberg, I. (1997), *The Complete Film Dictionary*, 2nd edn, London: Bloomsbury.
Kuhn, A. (2009), '*Screen* and Screen Theorizing Today', *Screen*, 50 (1): 1–12.
Kuhn, A. and G. Westwell (2012), *A Dictionary of Film Studies*, 1st edn, Oxford: Oxford University Press.
Kuhn, A. and G. Westwell (2020), *A Dictionary of Film Studies*, 2nd edn, Oxford: Oxford University Press.
Monaco, J. (2009), *How to Read a Film: The Art, Technology, Language, History, and Theory of Film and Media*, 4th edn, New York: Oxford University Press.
Nelmes, J., ed. (2011), *An Introduction to Film Studies*, 5th edn, London: Routledge.
Nowell-Smith, G. (1996), *The Oxford History of World Cinema*, 1st edn, Oxford: Oxford University Press.
Polan, D. (2007), *Scenes of Instruction: The Beginnings of the US Study of Film*, Oakland: University of California Press.
Thomson, D. (2010), *The New Biographical Dictionary of Film*, 5th edn, London: Penguin.
Thomson, D. (2014), *The New Biographical Dictionary of Film*, 6th edn, London: Penguin.

6

A cinematic aided design approach and the need for (in)-disciplinarity

François Penz and Janina Schupp

We have been integrating cinematic modes of thinking in the University of Cambridge Department of Architecture for over twenty years. Central to our approach has always been that, while we borrow from film studies and other disciplines, ultimately the use of cinema is always aimed at enriching architectural education, research and practice. The first part of this chapter summarizes key hypotheses pertaining to this stance, while the second part highlights major research findings of an Arts and Humanities Research Council (AHRC)-funded research project, *CineMuseSpace:* A Cinematic *Musée Imaginaire of Spatial Cultural Differences* (2017–20), that expands many of the ideas developed in the first part to other cultures – China and Japan in particular.[1] *CineMuseSpace* is the first large-scale cross-cultural study of the cinematic everyday, led by François Penz, with Janina Schupp as the main researcher, and in international collaboration with Andong Lu at Nanjing University. In essence, *CineMuseSpace* proposes that in a globalized world spatial thinking is key to answering important, complex questions about cultural differences, which can inform the future of the built environment, while building new intercultural understandings. *CineMuseSpace* further hypothesizes that cinema is the ideal cultural form through which to examine global spatial practices.

Film as a site of post-occupancy studies

One of the perennial issues confronting the architecture profession is the lack of information concerning how buildings are occupied after completion, referred to as 'post-occupancy studies'. The vast majority of effort goes into designing buildings, while little research is carried out after a building has been handed over to the client. There is little incentive for architects to find out how their work is received by people inhabiting or using the buildings, as professional fees rarely include the post-occupancy phase. Little progress has been made since Cooper (2001) interrogated the profession in his article *Post-Occupancy Evaluation – Where Are You?*, despite post-occupancy evaluations having since been identified as a key method to improve design quality (Fraser 2014: 3). There are too few incentives for the profession to change, resulting in most finished buildings remaining 'mute objects', as architects fail to interrogate them.

However, filmmakers, on the contrary, are always on the lookout for interesting buildings and locations. In other words, as soon as architects have completed a building, filmmakers may move in. A good case in point is the Rolex building in Lausanne, by SANAA architects, used as a location by Wim Wenders in *If Buildings Could Talk . . .* (2010) (Penz 2018: 140). In this way, over the last 125 years, filmmakers have archived, expressed, characterized, interpreted and portrayed hundreds of thousands of buildings. These films make up an unintentional archive that makes visible how we live, love, work and sleep in buildings – a comprehensive encyclopaedia of architectural spaces and building elements and their use, which constitutes an extraordinary record of lived and practised spaces – a formidable reservoir of post-occupancy studies. In other words, films have accumulated the most comprehensive lived-in building data in existence – a largely ignored and untapped resource which can be mined in many different ways (Penz 2018: 4).

Understanding everyday life through cinema

As a source of post-occupancy studies, films have primarily exposed precious everyday gestures and large fragments of our daily life. Not just the buildings have been archived and preserved, but, for us more importantly, the lives they contain. Of course, in fiction films, these lives have been dramatized: but large segments correspond faithfully to a form of observation of the quotidian from which drama will unavoidably erupt. The seemingly quiet daily routine depicted at the start of many films is the necessary fertile ground from which disruptions will materialize. In fact, most films contain nuggets of everyday lives well worth studying. Clearly, some films respond more fruitfully to post-occupancy analysis than others. Eric Rohmer's cinema depicts pure everyday life within very ordinary location-based settings. Jean-Luc Godard employs a similar technique, using actual, often domestic, locations as the ground for his drama, and so do Jim Jarmusch, Yasujirō Ozu, Michelangelo Antonioni, Ken Loach, Mike Leigh and many others who follow the dictates of naturalism in their choice of settings.

If one had to single out one film that depends for its drama on the particular resonance with the domestic interior, it would probably have to be *Jeanne Dielman, 23, quai du commerce, 1080 Bruxelles* (Akerman 1975), which carefully depicts the life of a middle-aged woman living in a flat in Brussels with her son. Over three hours – and three days – the film offers an extraordinary, slow-moving account of domesticity – which eventually culminates in a murder on the third day. This is a moving account of a life unravelling, in all its painstakingly observed details. *Jeanne Dielman* holds a mirror up to our own daily routine, making us notice what we have long ignored: our own everyday life.

The key assumption here is that the everyday on film helps us to rediscover what should be obvious to architects. Indeed, Perec rightly stated that 'everydayness is not evidence but opacity: a form of blindness, a mode of anaesthesia' (Perec 1974: np). While we may be blind to our own quotidian activities, we enjoy observing other people's everyday lives on the screen. Films defamiliarize the automatic: they present architects with a novel way of examining everyday life through the lens of cinema and the moving image.

Data mining the filmic archive

The filmic archive built for the *CineMuseSpace* project concentrates on the domestic environment, as this is the ideal vehicle for revealing spatial cultural differences; it best reflects on 'how profound is everything involving the house, the "home" and domesticity, and thus everyday life . . . the loftiest values of art, ethics and culture' (Lefebvre 2014: 516). Data mining in our case consists of turning cinematic scenes into data and information to compile statistics out of cinematic drama, for the purpose of analysing the everyday: we exploit the content of film towards an end for which it was not primarily intended. As agent, product and source of history, film need not be left to be mere entertainment – it offers a wealth of material that can be judiciously used to improve our architecture and our lives. The film *Salmer fra kjøkkenet* (Kitchen Stories) (Hamer 2003) is the perfect metaphor to illustrate this data mining process, as we witness a Swedish efficiency-researcher seated on a high chair, observing,

Figure 6.1 Data mining in *Kitchen Stories* (Bent Hamar, Sweden 2003).

noting and drawing meticulously the everyday life pattern of a Norwegian man in his own home (Figure 6.1).

Much less explicitly, we have observed and annotated hundreds of scenes from films to derive a comprehensive architectural user manual of lived space.

Through this process of observation, we noted that numerous film scenes have portrayed everyday lives in such a systematic way that the tropes present clear similarities with *Architects' Data* (Neufert 1936), a catalogue of prototypical home layouts, which include human figures in many of the drawings to communicate scale, proportion and activities.

An architectonics of cinema

While our work is the latest offering in a long line of efforts to architectural standardization, there have been others: in particular, Rem Koolhaas's

Elements of Architecture (Koolhaas 2014), developed for the Venice Biennale of 2014. Koolhaas's classifications have enabled us to extend our cinematic encyclopaedia of lived domestic situations based on Neufert, to the different basic components of architecture – such as doors, windows, stairs and other elements. Our 'architectonics of cinema' studied how key building elements have been cinematically realized and their complex connotations in usage revealed in staged dramatic scenes, so as to throw new light on building components often taken for granted by architects or engineers who might perceive them as purely utilitarian elements. This approach proved very fruitful. Instead of regarding the architectural elements as passive nouns – doors, windows, corridors – we viewed them as verbs and actions that embody affects and carry emotion; as Pallasmaa stated, 'The act of passing through a door is an authentic architectural experience, not the door itself. Looking through the window is an authentic architectural experience, not the window itself as a visual unit' (Pallasmaa 2000: 08).

To understand architectural elements in action, we need to add time to space – and only cinema gives us access to both dimensions simultaneously. For example, doors in films are not just a convenient way to transition from one space to another: a door can be not only the expression of passage, a revelator, a threshold, a contested space and a place of rejection, but also one of expectation and hope. Conceiving of architectural elements as active and connotative also allows us to read films differently. For example, *L'Eclisse* (Antonioni 1962) (Figure 6.2) can be construed as a film about windows: as communication; for

Figure 6.2 A multitude of windows in *L'Eclisse* (Michelangelo Antonioni, Italy 1962)

dreaming; that separate or that unite; that interrogate; that hide. It reveals that windows are not just to let light in, prevent heat from escaping, or a means of ventilation, but present us with a myriad of functions that often go unnoticed, but that cinema reveals.

Revealing such a multitude of facets make us look at the humble door and window in new and unexpected ways, becoming aware of the emotional dimensions that are part of their function, but are usually not investigated or taught in schools of architecture (though they could and perhaps should be). A similar cinematic reading for stairs, corridors, walls and corners has also been performed (Penz 2018: 123).

Detecting cinematic cultural differences: Descola's ontologies

An initial analysis of the architectonics of windows from different cultures will here form the point of departure for the second part. In Figure 6.3, on the left, in *Tokyo Twilight* (Yasujirō Ozu, Japan 1957), the window is treated as a site for contemplation, as both father-in-law and son-in-law stop their conversation to observe the snow falling outside; the outdoor surroundings can be construed as an extension of themselves, expressing a characteristically Japanese feeling for the harmony and connection between humans and nature. By contrast, in the image on the right, we witness James Stewart in Hitchcock's *Rear Window* (USA 1953) observing his neighbours through binoculars, in a typical voyeuristic activity central to the theme of the film.

Figure 6.3 The contemplative window in Ozu's *Tokyo Twilight* (Japan 1957) versus Hitchcock's voyeuristic approach in *Rear Window* (USA 1953).

In these contrasting examples lies our central thesis: the use of the same building element – in this case the window – in a dramatic situation expressing emotions, can potentially start to reveal different attitudes and connotations in different cultures, which may be important to the design of a building, but may also be interesting in themselves. In this case, the act of looking from inside to outside may have a bearing on cultural attitudes to nature and to other people. James Stewart and his binoculars in *Rear Window* are a typical anthropocentric way of looking at the world, while the two men sitting together in *Tokyo Twilight* have a communality of vision in relation to the outdoors. Hitchcock dramatizes a very active use of the window, while Ozu makes it a vehicle for a contemplative moment. This simple comparative exercise hints at different cultural sensibilities.

Our project has probed this issue through the structuralist approach of French anthropologist Philippe Descola, deployed in his exhibition at the Musée du Quai Branly in Paris, *La Fabrique des Images* (Descola 2010). Descola proposes a novel way of analysing iconic images from other cultures by dividing them into four ontologies, or sets of classifications, according to qualities detected in objects and paintings. Succinctly put, the four ontologies are the animated world of *animism*, the objective world of *naturalism*, the subdivided world of *totemism* and the entangled world of *analogism*.

Inspired by Descola's approach, we extended his categorization of images to cinematic spaces, with a view to constructing a cinematic ontology of spatial cultural differences. We identified and analysed fifty significant fiction films from the Western tradition of naturalism typically represented by European and American films, and an equivalent number from the Eastern tradition of analogism typically represented by Chinese and Japanese films. The construction of a cinematic spatial cultural classification was central to *CineMuseSpace*'s research.

A new digital methodology to analyse filmic data

In order to identify the traces of the everyday running through the cinematic fabric of films, we developed a new system of qualitative and quantitative moving image analysis using new software frameworks. We needed to set up a very large central database to contain and make manageable one hundred full-length feature films to which we could apply detailed time-based annotation in order to extract and organize the information we required. We devised and developed the core digital tool in collaboration with Jan Gerber and Sebastian Lütgert, based on their 2011 *Pan.do/ra* database technology.[2] The *CineMuseSpace* approach analyses raw cinematic data into clips and tags them with agreed keywords. We produced and shared an exhaustive lexicon of keywords deriving from the ontological categories to enable a team of researchers to work in different locations using the same database, to create a pool of consistently metadata-labelled items.

The primary criteria for selecting fiction films were the following: release after 1950 and up to the present; the action being set at the time of production; and over 15 per cent of total running time depicting everyday activities. Ideally, we chose films made by a director from the culture portrayed, critically acclaimed through the festival circuit and/or by film scholars, and shot in the country depicted. The films in the database were then analysed and their everyday sequences digitally annotated. This computer-aided analysis of the content of film could be seen as a new incarnation of 1970s computer-aided statistical film analysis, such as Cinemetrics, pioneered by Vlada Petric (1974) and Barry Salt.

The keyword ontology for the *CineMuseSpace* project relates the practices of the everyday to the domestic built environment across different cultural contexts, and it could be applied within any cultural matrix. It also registers the manner of representation, reflecting Descola's structuralist approach to image analysis through the various mise en scène and cinematic strategies employed to represent these slices of everyday lives. To facilitate and record both the analysis of content and the analysis of cinematics, the project deploys an overall dual categorization: the varied rhythms of occupancy of the spaces depicted and their cinematic framing.

The first main branch of the keyword ontology extracts circadian rhythms, paying attention to seasons, time of the day, weather and the bodily rhythms of the characters in the film. This analysis identifies repeated patterns and divergences in daily activities – such as the way rooms are used according to the time of day, or how everyday life varies season by season. In this branch, the environment of the action is also categorized, from the geographical location of the dwelling and its building structure and occupancy as a whole, down to individual architectural components and their varied uses – for example, the way windows are opened to facilitate communication with neighbours. A core element of the analysis is the classification of the type of domestic activity, who performs it and where in the building depicted. General practices identified include, for example, 'cooking', 'talking', 'reading', 'switching on an appliance', as well as more culturally specific activities such as 'playing mah-jong'. We also note the age and gender of the characters carrying out these daily activities. Lived spaces such as the kitchen, bathroom or bedroom are marked up with information on practices performed there. Communal and outdoor spaces are tagged so the way everyday life moves across particular rooms, or how it flows from private to public spaces can be followed, which proved especially important in Chinese culture. Items down to the smallest most handled units of everyday practice are annotated, from crockery, clothing and furniture, to personal transport.

Our ontology classifies the cinematic framing of domestic life under its second main branch, which includes both the mise en scène and mise-en-cadre of the ordinary. Keywords identify the shot type, camera height, camera angle and direction of filming, plus a curated selection of principal visual components – as defined by Bruce Block in *The Visual Story* (2008) – such as shape, line and space. The mise en scène ontology also employs a valence and arousal model for emotion classification transposed from the field of psychology (see Lang 1980). The entire lexicon comprises over 3,000 keywords.

Thousands of film clips with attached metadata, searchable by combinations of keywords, were made available in a malleable repository, so that differences in spatial practices across diverse cultures could be analysed and immediately compared. As all the filmic information extracted can be combined in new juxtapositions, the data on domestic occupancy can be mined for both quantitative and qualitative examination. The novel connections between filmic fragments and their analytic metadata forged in the process yield insights into patterns of everyday life in domestic interiors, highlighting recurrences as well as variations in daily activities, gender balance and interaction between inhabitants and architectural elements.

Systematic analysis of spatial cultural differences

The everyday, as Lefebvre noted, is the 'sole surviving common (. . .) point of reference' (Lefebvre 1987: 9), constituting shared ground between people and across cultures. Comparing and contrasting daily practices performed around the globe reveals everyday domestic life's spatial cultural commonalities and differences. The cinematic everyday also reveals the range of ways in which we perceive and represent our reality, depending on cultural context. *CineMuseSpace* focused its data mining on retrieving correlations between everyday activities in different cultures.

Our analysis of spatial cultural differences used three areas of comparison: the space; the social structures and modes of living; and the use of the camera apparatus and approaches to filming the everyday. Analysis of a scene featuring eating from *Good Morning* (Ozu, Japan 1959) compared with a parallel scene from *Boyhood* (Linklater, USA 2014) provides an example of this structured revelation of spatial cultural differences. In Ozu's traditional Japanese multipurpose room, *shoji* (mobile partitions) create a layering of space, while solid walls delimit Linklater's typical American dining room. The staging of each scene shows the difference between modes of family eating in the Japanese and American environment, such as the level of the activity: seated on zabuton cushions at floor level in Japan and on raised dining chairs in typical Western culture. Juxtaposing these two scenes draws attention not only to the differences in domestic architecture but also to the diverging design of furniture like dining tables, domestic accessories such as lamps, as well as decoration. Ingredients in the food itself, cutlery and even condiments in the two scenes vary significantly: variations in the small objects constituting the environments of everyday life and facilitating activities highlight cultural difference.

The framing of the sequences also differs significantly in the use of cinematic language and tools. After an establishing shot, Linklater frames his characters at eye level and proceeds to cut between shot and reverse shot of individuals, revealing their immediate emotions and inner life, in the clear tradition of naturalist representation. In contrast, Ozu's camera is at the primary low level of the activity, capturing the floor, an architectural element directly involved in the act of eating. By comparing many scenes containing parallel elements, *CineMuseSpace* found that in Japanese films condiments are often spread out on the floor, making it an extension of the dining table.

The static framing of the characters in *Good Morning* emphasizes family relationships in analogist fashion, representing their position in the microcosm of the dwelling and including in a single frame the spatial relationship of individuals to all other elements. The symmetry within the frame is the foil for the architectural spatial layering of the mise en scène, from the sliding doors opening on the foreground to the entrance, and other rooms in the background framed by further sliding doors.

This three-level analysis, juxtaposing portrayals of the same activity from different cultures, can reveal spatial cultural differences on a global scale, not only offering potentially interesting ethnographical clues but also enabling a more profound understanding of local idiom in how people occupy their dwelling space. In an age of digital design strongly influenced by standardized CAD software (see Penz 2018: 220–1), we hope this can lead to more appropriate, culturally specific architectures.

Comparison of actions associated with a range of architectural elements in films from different countries reveals the manifold functions of stairs, doors and windows – practical and symbolic. For example, the window as it is used in films, exposes various permutations in the activities of observing, communicating, escaping and throwing objects through to the outside. Cinema reveals both conscious and unconscious actions, illustrating, beyond the explicit architectural function of ventilation and lighting, how windows can be a channel for communication, a metaphor for emotion, act as passage or transition area, and, when characters sit inside the window frame or on the sill, can become a space of their own. Spatial cultural differences are revealed by, for example, the demarcation of personal space represented by a window. While in films embodying a Western, naturalism-dominated outlook, windows typically seem to extend the private space of the owner and are often encountered at a distance, in films apparently underpinned by the fluid aesthetic of analogism, such as the Chinese examples analysed, windows are a public access point to be approached, looked into and knocked on, without reference to ownership.

In a second step, the *CineMuseSpace* project built on the core findings on spatial cultural differences revealed by the database of annotated clips. We catalogued and published the activity and architectural-usage data as a functional aid to architectural design (somewhat in the manner of Neufert) and as a contribution to broader cultural knowledge overall. The resulting *Catalogue Raisonné of Everyday Life Activities* (Penz and Schupp 2019) unites core everyday domestic activities and the range of fundamental building elements defined by the project.

Loosely based on Georges Perec's provocative re-imagining of the characteristics of an apartment according to 'heptadian' rhythms, which 'would give us apartments of seven rooms known respectively as the Mondayery, Tuesdayery, Wednesdayery, Thursdayery, Fridayery, Saturdayery and Sundayery' (Perec 1974: 32), the first section of the catalogue is organized around ordinary activities, to each of which is allocated a day of the week: Monday for maintenance – washing and cleaning of bodies and domestic spaces; Tuesday for food-related activities – cooking, eating and drinking; Wednesday for creativity – painting, making music and drawing; Thursday for rest – sleeping, relaxing and waking up; Friday for intellectual activity – studying, working, calculating and thinking; Saturday for recreation – gardening, partying and playing games; and Sunday is for technology-related activities – using computers, mobile phones and domestic appliances.

The second section of the catalogue focuses on five key building elements pertaining to architecture, to create an 'architectonics of cinema': walls, doors, corridors, stairs and windows. It records the way the diverse functions of these elements are cinematically practised and revealed, to generate new insights and defamiliarize building components often taken for granted, throwing new light on their potentials.

Practice-based approaches to spatial cultural differences

The *CineMuseSpace* project combined real-world observations through practice-based fieldwork with its digital film analysis to generate an embodied understanding of spatial practices. Since the collaboration with Andong Lu at Nanjing University was fundamental to the cross-cultural comparison between naturalist and analogist portrayals of spatial practices, the practice-based research took place in China. In 2018, the University of Nanjing hosted our digital filmmaking workshop 'Cinematic Interpretation of Spatiality: A Workshop and Seminar on Cinematic Architecture', to explore a range of spatial concepts through moving image media (see Schupp, Lu and Penz 2019). Architects, scholars from the fields of architecture studies and film studies, and filmmakers from China and Japan, came together to explore through practice-based filmmaking a chosen concept of space. We designed the brief to emphasize the relationship between architecture and the moving image, requiring participants to identify and express the special qualities of public building interiors and exteriors and particular urban environments in digital audiovisual form. The 100 participants together produced ten short films in total, which revealed a multitude of spatial experiences and understandings in Chinese culture, from spatial structuring and illusions, to the everyday interaction, usage and memories associated with built spaces and public gardens in the city.

One film, *Garden Stroll: Illusive Realm* (Chen 2018), aimed to deconstruct the natural and spatial artifice of the public garden and to explore what remains once the illusion is shattered. It depicts a visitor (played by Wei Deng) strolling through the garden and pouring himself a cup of tea, while around him the environment is slowly removed from sight by invisible hands, to expose the illusory creation of nature. The camera follows the stroll in close-up, before pulling out slowly to reveal the actual spatial context. To create and deconstruct this garden illusion, the team designed a set made of layered planes printed with images, where each plane represented a characteristic element of the Chinese garden. A moon gate in the first layer was cut out to reveal the next layer of the artificial environment. The second layer presented a lattice window in a wall framed by bamboo plants. Only when these illusory spatial elements are removed does the view onto the real world – here symbolized by an urban street – become accessible to the viewer as the illusion of the garden is shattered. The camera finally withdraws, leaving the main character in the distance as he rejoins the real cityscape around him. The film was recorded as a single shot using drone technology. Through this gradual removal of spatial layers, the film generates an analytical view of the cultural construction of illusory spaces in public gardens.

The ten short films which came out of the workshop demonstrated the premise of *CineMuseSpace*: the medium of film can function to reveal aspects of our everyday spaces and their ordinary use that cannot be grasped in architectural diagrams or other kinds of documentation.[3] These practice-based research findings serve to validate the hypothesis that the medium of film captures the everyday experience of lived spaces in a unique way.

Conclusion

A reappraisal of daily gestures though film enables us to see the home with fresh eyes, renewing our interest in architectural domestic design. As a result of changes in patterns of everyday life, the way we live changes through time, necessitating a rethinking of our homes. Defamiliarizing what Lefebvre referred to as the 'minor magic of everyday life' opens up a vista of a more human-centred approach to architecture. Film facilitates this approach, enabling us to explore the spaces of the past in order to better anticipate the requirements and spaces of the future. In an increasingly globalized world, the *CineMuseSpace* project proposes a greater level of understanding and engagement between different cultures.

Our similarities and differences have to be acknowledged, revealed and celebrated. Narrative cinema opens up the path to innovative reflection on the complexity of architecture as experience, and the need to take full account of everyday activities both big and small, determined by needs, desires, seasons or time of day, in designing domestic dwellings.

Acknowledgements

This work is supported by the Arts and Humanities Research Council (AHRC, UK) Research Grant: A Cinematic *Musée Imaginaire* of Spatial Cultural Differences (*CineMuseSpace*), which took place at the Department of Architecture, University of Cambridge, between 2017 and 2020.

Notes

1   See online at: https://www.cinemusespace.com (accessed 1 March 2020).
2   See online at: https://www.pan.do/ra (accessed 1 March 2020).
3   The ten short films were exhibited at 'Architecture of Two', Nextmixing Gallery, Shanghai, 2018.

References

Block, B. A. (2008), *The Visual Story: Seeing the Structure of Film, TV, and New Media*, Boston: Focal Press.
Boyhood (2014), [Film] Dir. Richard Linklater, USA: IFC Productions; Detour Filmproduction.
Cooper, I. (2001), 'Post-occupancy Evaluation – Where Are You?' *Building Research & Information*, [Online], 29 (2): 158–63.
Descola, P. and Collectif (2010), *La Fabrique des images: Visions du monde et formes de la représentation*, Paris: Somogy éditions d'art.
Fraser, M. (2014), *Architects and Research-Based Knowledge: A Literature Review*, Royal Institute of British Architects.
Garden Stroll: Illusive Realm (2018), [Film] Dir. Jie Chen, China: CineMuseSpace 'Cinematic Interpretation of Spatiality: A Workshop and Seminar on Cinematic Architecture'.

If Buildings Could Talk... (2010), [Film]. Dir. Wim Wenders, Germany: Neue Road Movies.
Jeanne Dielman, 23, quai du commerce, 1080 Bruxelles (1975), [Film] Dir. Chantal Akerman, France/Belgium: Paradise Films.
Kitchen Stories (2003), [Film] Dir. Bent Hamar, Sweden: BOB Film Sweden AB.
Koolhaas, R., J. Westcott, I. Boom, Harvard University Graduate School of Design and AMO. (2014), *Elements of architecture*, Venice: Marsilio Editori Spa.
Lang, P. J. (1980), 'Behavioral Treatment and Bio-Behavioral Assessment: Computer Applications', in J. B. Sidowski, J. H. Johnson and T. A. Williams, *Technology in Mental Health Care Delivery Systems*, 119–37, Norwood: Ablex.
L'Eclisse (The Eclipse) (1962), [Film] Dir. Michelangelo Antonioni, Italy: Cineriz.
Lefebvre, H. (1987), 'The Everyday and Everydayness', *Yale French Studies*, 73: 7–11.
Lefebvre, H. (2014), *Critique of Everyday Life*, The three-volume text, London: Verso.
Neufert, E. (1936), *Bauentwurfslehre [Architects' Data]*, Berlin: Bauwelt-Verlag.
Ohayō (Good Morning) (1959), [Film] Dir. Yasujirô Ozu, Japan: Shochiku.
Pallasmaa, J. (2000), 'From Frame to Framing', *Oz*, 22 (1), [online]. Available from: http://newprairiepress.org/oz/vol22/iss1/2 (accessed 26 September 2016).
Penz, F. (2018), *Cinematic Aided Design: An Everyday Life Approach to Architecture*, New York: Routledge.
Penz, F. and J. Schupp (2019), *A Catalogue Raisonné of Everyday Life Activities*, Shanghai and Cambridge: CineMuseSpace Project.
Perec, G. (1974), *Espèces d'espaces*, Espace critique, Paris: Galilée.
Petric, V. (1974), 'A Visual/Analytic History of the Silent Cinema (1895–1930)', 30th Congress *of the International Federation of Film Archives*, 25–27 May [online]. Available online at http://files.eric.ed.gov/fulltext/ED098639.pdf (accessed 30 May 2019).
Rear Window (1953), [Film] Dir. Alfred Hitchcock, USA: Alfred J Hitchcock Productions.
Schupp, J., A. Lu and F. Penz (2019), 'Cinematic Interpretation of Spatiality', *Cambridge Journal of China Studies*, 13 (4): 24–52.
Tokyo Twilight (1957), [Film] Dir. Yasujiro Ozu, Japan: Shochiku.

7

Microcinematography and biomedical science

Brian Stramer

The motion picture originated in the biological laboratory.
Rosenberger 1929a: 343–52

I am an experimental scientist specializing in cell biology who makes short films. As surprising as it might sound, these skills absolutely rely on each other: I make films through the lens of a microscope – what is called 'microcinematography' or 'cinemicroscopy' – as part of the scientific discovery process, and as a vital educational tool. There is no sound to be acquired in these films and everything is visual. This type of filmmaking is remarkably ubiquitous in virtually all biological disciplines, from cell biology and embryology (Wallingford 2019; Wellmann 2018), to more clinically associated disciplines such as immunology (Pittet et al. 2018) and cancer biology (Condeelis and Weissleder 2010). I have previously given a brief history for scientists of two key early cinemicroscopists (see Stramer and Dunn 2015); in this chapter, I will examine the broader contexts, nature and potentials of microcinematography in the biomedical sciences.

The most obvious use of film in biomedical sciences is as an educational tool. We have all watched scientific documentaries that show a time-lapse film of cells in action viewed under a microscope, whether it is embryos undergoing early stages of development, or cancer cells rapidly proliferating in a dish. I also use films in my undergraduate lectures to highlight critically important concepts. For example, one lecture I give to first-year undergraduates is on the histology of blood cells. This is a pretty dry topic. Students are asked to examine smears of blood on a slide beneath a microscope and then recognize the difference between red blood cells and the variety of different white blood cell types; importantly, they must also understand their different functions in the body. One type of white blood cell that I teach about is the neutrophil, whose function is almost exclusively to hunt down and kill bacteria. By the time I get to the neutrophil in my lecture, after having systematically described the different blood cells one cell type at a time, the students are half asleep. To fight their stupor, I attempt to add some colour to the lecture and explain that neutrophils are analogous to any predator in the animal kingdom: much like a lion hunting antelope on the African savannah, these cells really can hunt down their microscopic prey. Of course, this elicits eye rolls as a result of this seemingly melodramatic analogy. It is far better to illustrate neutrophil function by displaying a live movie of their activity.

One of the most famous films in cell biology is the anecdotally named *The Chase* (c. 1950) made by the scientist Dr David Rogers at Vanderbilt University (Figure 7.1). In this microscope film, the neutrophil chases a bacterium within a field of red blood cells with the bacteria attempting to evade its predator: the neutrophil is incredibly focused on its prey, pushing the red blood cells out of the way to finally catch the bacteria, despite its valiant effort to escape. The drama would not be out of place in a wildlife documentary. As a teaching tool, *The Chase* is extremely effective: students suddenly wake from their mid-lecture snooze to cheer on the poor bacteria; and importantly, they now understand the function of neutrophils. What is clear is that the film aided their learning process.

The Chase is far more than simply an educational tool; biologists learn all kinds of important things from watching such films that we are still trying to

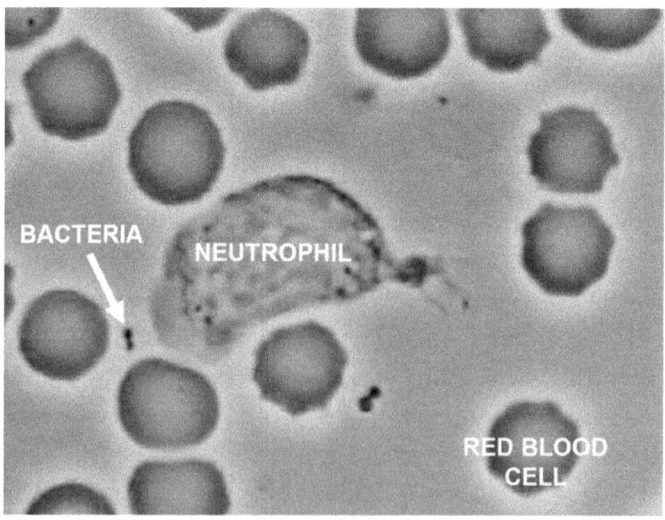

Figure 7.1 Still from David Rogers' *The Chase* (c. 1950).

understand to this day. For instance, somehow, the neutrophil 'smells' some unknown substance from the bacteria that allows it to lock on to its prey. This allows the neutrophil to discriminate friend from foe, and differentiate the bacteria from other cells in the blood smear (like red blood cells). Through watching the film, scientists also realized that neutrophils (and indeed all migrating cells) have some kind of internal migration machinery that tells the cell to have a specific orientation: a specialized front, which seems to be involved in steering the cell's motion, and a cell rear. This polarized shape is essential for neutrophils (and all migrating cells) to navigate their complex environment and sense extracellular cues. These are issues that cell biologists are still trying to understand and would not have arisen without filming. There is hidden information in film due to the fact that this medium inherently deals with time as a variable.

Cinemicroscopy is key to my laboratory's study of the role and regulation of cell migration during embryonic development. These are very broad topics that extend from understanding the intracellular protein machinery that drives cell motility, to the wider effects that cell movements have on organ development in embryos. Making movies is absolutely essential to understand these processes due to their dynamic nature. For example, how does the intracellular machinery generate forces required for cells to change shape and subsequently move in a directed fashion? How do tissues – and the cells that make up these tissues – bend and twist themselves into the correct organization? Time-lapse imaging allows us to track the movement of whole cells during embryonic development to determine how cellular reorganization leads to tissue sculpting; similarly, it allows us to track the movement of individual protein machines inside cells in order to understand how these machines translate into cell movements.

Performing these experiments requires choosing an appropriate microscope (depending on the frame rate, resolution and magnification required to see the relevant biological process) and an appropriate 'labelling' (i.e. highlighting) of the cell type – or intracellular protein – of interest. The 'label' of choice for these experiments is most often a special protein from jellyfish called green fluorescent protein (GFP) – or some chemical derivative of GFP – as it glows a bright green colour when exposed to a particular wavelength of light, thereby allowing individual cells – or proteins inside cells – to be clearly observed (Mavrakis, Pourquie and Lecuit 2010). Since its discovery in the 1960s, scientists have altered the GFP protein to fluoresce in a variety of different colours, increasing our colour palette, thus allowing us to label multiple different proteins or cells simultaneously in our experiments. For obvious reasons, this has revolutionized biomedical science and led to three scientists sharing a Nobel Prize for the discovery of GFP in 2008.[1] We now can track the interaction of different cell types and proteins simultaneously in our experiments, which allows us to examine complex biological ecosystems.

To properly perform these cinemicroscopy experiments requires some basic knowledge of the underlying process in question. How long does the process take? How quickly are the cells moving? How large are the cells or proteins that we need to image? This basic understanding – or 'guesstimates' – allows us to choose the right type of microscope, magnification and frame rate (among many other parameters) that allows us to visualize the process at sufficient spatial and temporal detail to test our hypotheses. Once the imaging is deemed sufficient, we will then acquire multiple retakes using a defined set of imaging parameters (frame rate, magnification, etc.) so that we can directly compare our films to make sure cellular behaviours are consistent – or to compare the norm to situations where we perturb the system, by treating with chemical inhibitors, for example. Like a real film we may display our best 'take' in order to describe the process to an audience (or in a manuscript). However, unlike real films, we will use all of our takes to generate enough data to allow for statistical analysis. Additionally, our microscopic takes are never spliced in sequence like a real film in order to create a broader narrative in a scientific manuscript.

Once our biological films are generated, we edit them through the use of computer software that is capable of reconstructing the microscopic images. For example, the images are often acquired using microscopes that can remove out of focus light and thus collect images at very precise (and thin) planes within the cell or tissue; the microscope acquires images in the x, y and z plane, so images can be reconstructed into a three-dimensional time-lapse projection. At this stage, the analysis has only just begun: the next step is to turn the film into something quantifiable.

It is no longer sufficient to simply use biological films as a descriptive tool. We use computational approaches to measure time-dependent variables from our films (e.g. cell speed, cell shape changes, tissue remodelling and protein motion), which is essential to statistically analyse the data and test if our hypotheses are correct. The film is turned into numeric data and then archived for possible future analysis, often never to be viewed again. This is where the analogy with mainstream cinematography falls apart. While scientists are using their films to create a scientific narrative much like a real cinematographer, the story is in the numbers that are extracted from the film. The modern experimental film is not simply a qualitative, visual description of a microscopic process, but a way to gather data and confirm – or refute – experimental hypotheses. In this respect, microcinematography is very much rooted in the origins of the moving image itself.

Many biological processes have been discovered by simple observation. In order to better understand a *process*, it helps to methodically characterize it by carefully sequencing static images of its dynamics. For example, in the late nineteenth century the zoologist Ilya Metchnikoff discovered that when he wounded a starfish larva with a thorn, he could observe cells 'rush' (movement over a number of days) to the wound site. Through a basic sequencing of images from his experiment (without the use of time-lapse filmmaking) he discovered innate immunity, for which he received a Nobel Prize in 1908.[2] Although this was not a 'moving image' per se, it was based on the principles that underlie it: instead of creating a sensation of change over time through filming, Metchnikoff created a better understanding of his process by fragmenting that change over time into static images.

Scientists and scientific questions drove some of the most significant early moving image experiments. For example, the late nineteenth-century chronophotographic experiments of the French scientist and physiologist Étienne-Jules Marey captured human and animal movement in time with unprecedented accuracy and speed using high-speed static image cameras; this work opened up new understandings of these movements, developed new technologies for capturing images at speed and progressed the development of early scientific moving image work more generally (Braun 1995). The concurrent and the less-scientific chronophotographic work of the photographer Eadweard Muybridge in California started with the *scientific* question of whether horses have all their feet off the ground at any one time during running; his sequenced imaging of this animal movement was essential not only to answer this question affirmatively but also to prove the result to others (Solnit 2003). For those who doubt that this was a true scientific discovery, this experiment was highlighted on the cover of *Scientific American* ('A Horse's Motion Scientifically Determined', *Scientific American*, 1878).

By the early twentieth century, the role of the moving image as scientific device, educational tool and entertainment medium became even more blurred in the biology laboratory. As cameras started to be attached to microscopes, what was seen under the microscope by only scientists could now be witnessed by the public in the thousands: the new scale of the world opened up by microcinematography enabled a hybrid of scientifically educational entertainment. For example, the naturalist documentary filmmakers Martin Duncan and Charles Urban created *The Unseen World* film series in 1903. In the now-infamous short *Cheese Mites* (1903) from that series, a man sits down to eat a piece of cheese to discover, after turning his magnifying glass on his dish, microscopic cheese mites scurrying about.

Many prominent still photographers also delved into the microscopic world using the moving image. Roman Vishniac imaged a variety of bacterial and cellular specimens throughout his career, although his focus remained largely the static image (Radzyner and Barker 2018). John Ott on the other hand spent his career using time-lapse microscopy to entertain and educate audiences about the natural world; he teamed up with the Walt Disney Corporation to make popular science films, and also with an American university to develop time-lapse techniques to understand a variety of disease-related processes, from cancer cell growth to the spread of tuberculosis (Williamson 2019).

Microcinematography remained an important tool for many scientists in the early twentieth century. For example, Jean Comandon at the Pasteur Institute in Paris famously made some short microcinematographic films to examine spirochetes (the organisms that cause syphilis) in *Ultramicroscope Time-Lapse of Syphilis Parasite* (1910). His microscopic movies garnered much international attention, including an article in the *New York Times* in 1909 which stated that 'Physiological questions of the greatest importance, impossible of elucidation in the past, can probably be solved by this new method' of microscopic live imaging ('Microbes Caught in Action' 1909). Despite its obvious use for public education, it is arguable whether his movies were ever really scientific research tools. Revealingly, Comandon moved on to become a cinematographer working for the French film equipment and production company Pathé.

Microcinematography became a much more viable scientific research tool with the invention of the 'cell culture' experimental technique in 1906 by the scientist Ross Harrison (Harrison 1906). This technique enabled the live imaging of animal cells in a dish and the ability to grow cells outside of the body, so cell-scale biological processes could now be easily observed, filmed and later projected to scientific audiences. For example, Alexis Carrel, a pioneer of mammalian cell culture, used a microcinematographic apparatus to study the movement of fibroblasts and macrophages in the 1920s (Carrel and Ebeling 1926). His work generated much interest in the scientific community, and so to assist others in making such movies his assistant Heinz Rosenberger published a methods article in the journal *Science* on the use of the microcinematographic apparatus; his stated goal was to convince scientists 'who have not yet realized the great possibilities of the motion-picture camera in research laboratories' (Rosenberger 1929b: 672).

Some of the earliest and most important experiments involving the live imaging of cells and embryos were performed at the Strangeways Research Laboratory (an institution funded by the prominent Medical Research Council in the UK), especially the development and use of time-lapse techniques (see Stramer and Dunn 2015). For example, Strangeways pathologist Ronald Canti made *The Cultivation of Living Tissue* (1925) film to show a variety of different cell types undergoing migration in a petri dish, along with developing embryos and whole tissues from a variety of animals. To illustrate the passing of time, Canti positioned a clock in the corner of the film so that the audience could see the minute and hour hands frantically spinning around in order to highlight how slow these various biological processes were. The film had a clear educational and public appeal. Indeed, the film was converted from its original 35 mm format to the more economical and mainstream 16 mm format in 1927, only a couple of years after its completion and only four years after Eastman Kodak invented the 16 mm format.

The Cultivation of Living Tissue is especially significant in its use of microcinematography as a *scientific* tool to address a hypothesis-driven question. As a pathologist, Canti was best known for studying the effects of radiation on

Figure 7.2 Still from Ronald Canti's *The Cultivation of Living Tissue* (1928) showing the microcinematographic apparatus developed by Dr Ronald Canti, including the microscope and cell culture incubator, along with the cine-camera and actuating clock that turned the camera into a time-lapse apparatus.

cells, and he used film to ask a simple question: What were X-rays really doing to affect cells? This was a timely question as radiation was beginning to be used to treat cancers with some success, but scientists had no idea why this treatment was effective. In this experiment, we see a movie of cancer cells moving around in culture and subsequently being exposed to radiation from a source of radium. The cells go from being highly motile and active to suddenly ceasing their movement and starting to die. Canti's obituary in the journal *Nature* highlighted the significance of this work in helping convince 'more people of the efficacy of the radiation treatment of cancer than any other' ('Obituary: Dr R. G. Canti' 1936). His film work was funded by the prominent British Empire Cancer Campaign (a predecessor of Cancer Research UK), a clear hallmark of scientific legitimacy of the time. Time-lapse imaging is a now a standard technique used by numerous researchers studying various aspects of cancer development and treatment.

The importance of Canti's film is further evidenced by its wide distribution throughout the world during his time as a scientist at the Strangeways Laboratory. It was displayed not only at scientific conferences but also to lay audiences – from a Friday Evening Discourse at The Royal Institution, to students in the United States, and even a private screening to the UK prime minister James Ramsay MacDonald ('Cultivation of Living Tissue Cells' 1932; 'Biology Movie Coming' 1930; and 'Cinematographic Demonstration of Living Tissue Cells' 1933). Canti's death in 1936 was widely covered in eminent scientific journals, such as *Nature*, as well as news outlets around the world (The Cinema Has Helped Science (1936).

Not all press regarding the work of Canti and colleagues was positive. While many may assume that fears of human cloning arose from modern research in stem cells and human genome sequencing, news periodicals in Canti's time aired similar concerns of work at the Strangeways Laboratory with articles such as 'Could You Love a Chemical Baby?' (Burke 1938). Canti's filmwork both enabled new scientific understandings and brought those understandings to new public audiences. However, the visceral power of these visual images no doubt also drove some of the public concerns with the thorny moral issues that surround the creation and modification of life.

The use of microcinematography in research was often criticized by scientists for not completely dissimilar reasons. For example, the Nobel Prize-winning scientist Peter Medawar (1915–87) questioned if films could solve biological problems, as he thought biologists were 'distracted and beguiled by the sheer beauty' of these movies (see Medawar 1986, and Landecker 2009). To be fair to Peter Medawar, most, if not all, of the movies that were being generated in the biological laboratory during this time were being analysed solely from a visual perspective, without any effort to quantify their results and thus show that their 'experiments' were reproducible. Peter Medawar was questioning the use of movies as a rigorous experimental tool: movies were often a one-off recording that simply described a process – watching a biological process is not good enough if we want to gain mechanistic insight.

Michael Abercrombie (1912–79), the pioneering cell biologist and one-time director of the Strangeways Research Laboratory, showed how movies can give us meaningful mechanistic insight in biological research. He spent his career studying the underlying mechanisms that allowed cells to generate movement, and he created the terminology that scientists of numerous disciplines – from cancer biology to immunology and basic cell biology – still use to this day. Furthermore, he provided a foundation for how we think cells generate motion that we still teach to students. It was not just his groundbreaking qualitative descriptions of migrating cells that he is known for; Abercrombie was one of the first to use cinemicroscopy as a rigorous quantitative tool. In a series of publications in the 1950s, he spent significant effort quantifying the actual speed of moving cells. This subsequently allowed him to highlight subtle effects of cells interacting with one another in cell culture that only a rigorous statistical analysis could reveal. This led to scientists describing Abercrombie as a 'cellular ethologist', as he showed the scientific community that movie making could indeed be a quantitative tool that is capable of revealing hidden detail behind cellular behaviours (see Dunn and Jones 1998). Indeed, there is now a regular scientific meeting in Abercrombie's name, which brings together international researchers with nearly all quantifying various cellular behaviours through microcinematography.[3]

Abercrombie's quantitative approach required painstaking work. For example, quantifying cell speed necessitated clever analysis of his time-lapse movies, which involved making a series of enlarged prints of individual frames and then manually tracking each individual cell by hand through each successive frame of the film. Today microscopic movies are recorded digitally rather than with analogue film, so scientists can take advantage of the computational power of modern computing to automatically highlight features from their microscopic movies and easily track the motion of cells and intracellular features as well. Think about ubiquitous computer vision algorithms such as those used in digital cameras to automatically recognize faces: analogous approaches are now being applied to biomedical movies.

It is no longer a few cells that are being tracked using film, but hundreds or even thousands of cells; this tracking of entire cell populations has been given the name '*in toto* imaging' (McDole et al. 2018). With this information scientists are beginning to understand how entire populations of cells within an embryo coordinate with each other in order to form functioning tissues; or allowing pharmaceutical companies to perform high-throughput screens to elucidate drug compounds that may affect cancer metastasis. Furthermore, it is no longer just time-lapse movies that are being generated, but also high-speed imaging that is providing additional details in experiments. As one obituary of Ronald Canti highlighted: 'cinema has provided scientists with a new time machine . . . that enables time to be accelerated or retarded at will' (The Cinema Has Helped Science (1936)). The experiments that I have described thus far – such as movies of moving cells in culture – involve processes that evolve very slowly, and so real time must be accelerated so that these processes can be viewed and analysed effectively. However, biologists are increasingly examining subcellular processes, such as the movement of individual molecular machines that are moving at great speeds, and in this case the process requires live imaging at very high frame rates, which are subsequently slowed down in order to quantify the movement. These techniques are allowing scientists to infer a biochemical level of detail from their films that was previously impossible.

These new imaging approaches to biomedical movies have spawned a new sub-discipline of cell biology – Quantitative Cell Biology – that is, allowing scientists to quantify their data and subsequently mathematically model their underlying process, or infer biophysical properties (Lippincott-Schwartz 2014: 3427). This is also creating issues related to Big Data as biologists struggle to handle the associated data deluge that comes with tracking thousands of cellular features within an individual experiment. Films really can now provide mechanistic insight that sceptics such as Peter Medawar would clearly appreciate.

From a microcinematography perspective, there are now also many different choices of microscope that are at a scientist's disposal. Not only can we change the microscope objective to alter the magnification, but we can also change the microscope itself depending on the sample or biological process in question. If a scientist needs a wider view of their organism – for example, if they are studying the development of whole embryos – they may choose one type of microscope that images from multiple angles, thus allowing for better three-dimensional resolution. Alternatively, their process may involve studying small molecules moving very rapidly, which would change their choice of microscope and camera set-up to allow for higher frame rates. Textbooks on basic techniques in video microscopy (see Inoue and Spring 1997) are almost obsolete as new microscope modalities and imaging methods are advancing at such a great pace.

Some journals, such as *The Journal of Visualized Experiments* (*Jove*), publish videos of scientific experiments involving microscopic live imaging, along with precise details on how to logistically carry out each experiment and subsequently analyse the associated data.[4] A number of other scientific journals have also started publishing video podcasts that allow scientists to explain the key insights from their work and display the multimedia associated with the manuscript.[5] Furthermore, many publications now have supplementary information associated with the manuscript that contains video files of their microscopic movies. These supplemental video files are essential to help the scientist explain their biological process of interest and convey their scientific narrative in the manuscript.

The journal podcasts and supplemental video files are films created by scientists, for scientists. However, scientists are starting to use movies as a direct public engagement tool as well. For example, the American Society of Cell Biology (ASCB), which sponsors large scientific conferences every year, have a new competition called 'Celldance' for scientists to generate edited films of their work with the help of ASCB funds (for post-production support, including soundtracks from Hollywood composers).[6] One of the 2014 winners, entitled *Killing Cancer – Cytotoxic T-Cells On Patrol* (2014), included a soundtrack from Hollywood composer Ted Masur; it was described by the director of the National Institutes of Health Francis Collins as a 'microscopic blockbuster' (Fleischman 2015). This was not an animation: it was live action sequences of innate immune cells hunting for abnormal cancerous cells, and subsequently destroying them. As explained by Collins, capturing this drama is not easy as the cells are incredibly small: 'Actor Brad Pitt stands 5 feet 11 inches, while a cytotoxic T cell measures only about 10 microns – roughly 1/10th the width of a human hair' (Fleischman 2015). The line between entertainment, education and experimentation is as blurred as ever.

Most scientists today turn their films into data and numbers, but the films themselves are visually powerful objects in their own right, capturing the beauty of biological processes in an array of colours. While films from scientific experiments are not explicitly created with a narrative structure, and have no sound, we are increasingly seeing them being edited to provide an additional sense of drama and broader narrative, as the 'Celldance' entries show. Furthermore, grant funding bodies always want academics to engage more actively with the public about their research questions; these microscopic films are an accessible resource to educate and engage wider audiences about biology.

Stories are being told under the microscope every day in the biological laboratory. Films now allow scientists to capture dynamics of tissues, cells and proteins, and subsequently measure time-dependent variables (e.g. cell speed, tissue strains and protein activity) like no other experimental modality in the biological laboratory. Additionally, with the help of computer vision algorithms these films can help us 'see' things and quantify subtle behaviours that are often not obvious to the naked eye. As with the very origins of filmmaking in the work of Marey and Muybridge in the late nineteenth century, microcinematography is fundamental to making and communicating scientific discoveries: it continues to be a distinct form of the cinematic as both a scientific and an educational tool. From its origins, it has been a form of entertainment. While the initial development and subsequent proliferation of microcinematography by filmmakers such as Comandon and Ott were largely driven by public curiosity, microcinematographic films are now even more striking with the advent of glowing protein labels and high-resolution microscopy. Despite Peter Medawar's criticism noted earlier, there is nothing wrong with being 'beguiled by the sheer beauty' of these films. Perhaps it is time for traditional filmmakers to team up with scientists in order to create an entirely new form of the cinematic?

Acknowledgements

I would like to thank the Wellcome Library, and, in particular, Angela Saward, the curator of their Moving Image and Sound Collection, for help with restoration and digitization of some of the films discussed in this chapter. To see more scientific films from the Wellcome Library, please visit their website (https://wellcomelibrary.org/collections/about-the-collections/moving-image-and-sound-collection/). I would also like to thank the Wellcome Trust for research funding (grant number 107859/Z/15/Z).

Notes

1 See online at: https://www.nobelprize.org/prizes/chemistry/2008/press-release/ (accessed 1 March 2020).
2 See online at: https://www.nobelprize.org/prizes/medicine/1908/mechnikov/biographical/ (accessed 1 March 2020).
3 See online at: https://www.rms.org.uk/discover-engage/event-calendar/abercrombie-meeting-2017.html (accessed 1 March 2020).
4 See online at: http://www.jove.com/ (accessed 1 March 2020).
5 See online at: http://www.cell.com/video and http://jcb.rupress.org/biosights (accessed 1 March 2020).
6 See online at: https://www.ascb.org/tag/celldance/ (accessed 01 March 2020).

References

'A Horse's Motion Scientifically Determined' (1878), *Scientific American*, 39 (16): 241.
'Biology Movie Coming' (1930), *The Oberlin Review*, 14 October, 58 (1): 1.
Braun, M. (1995), *Picturing Time: The Work of Etienne-Jules Marey (1830–1904)*, Chicago: University of Chicago Press.
Burke, N. (1938), 'Could You Love a Chemical Baby?', *Tit-Bits*, 16 April.
Carrel, A. and A. Ebeling (1926), 'The Fundamental Properties of the Fibroblast and the Macrophage: II. The Macrophage', *The Journal of Experimental Medicine*, 44 (3): 285–305.
Cheese Mites (1903), [Film] Dir. Charles Urban and Martin Duncan, UK. Available online: https://player.bfi.org.uk/free/film/watch-cheese-mites-1903-online (accessed 01 January 2020).
'Cinematographic Demonstration of Living Tissue Cells' (1933), *British Medical Journal*, 25 February, 1: 333.
Condeelis, J. and R. Weissleder (2010), 'In Vivo Imaging in Cancer', *Cold Spring Harbor Perspectives in Biology*, 2 (12): a003848.
Davis, J. R., C. Huang, J. Zanet, S. Harrison, E. Rosten, S. Cox, D. Soong, G. Dunn and B. Stramer (2012), 'Emergence of Embryonic Pattern through Contact Inhibition of Locomotion', *Development*, 139 (24): 4555–60.
Dunn, G. and G. Jones (1998), 'Michael Abercrombie: The Pioneer Ethologist of Cells', *Trends in Cell Biology*, 8: 124–6.
Fleischman, J. (2015), 'NIH Director Collins Hails ASCB's Celldance Video As "Microscopic Blockbuster"', 29 January. Available online: https://www.ascb.org/careers/nih-director-collins-hails-ascbs-celldance-video-as-microscopic-blockbuster/ (accessed 01 January 2020).

Harrison, R. (1906), 'Observations on the Living Developing Nerve Fiber', *Proceedings of the Society for Experimental Biology and Medicine*, 01 August, 4 (1): 140–3.

Inoue, S. and K. Spring (1997), *Video Microscopy, The Fundamentals*, New York: Springer.

Killing Cancer – Cytotoxic T-Cells On Patrol (2014), [Film] Dir. Alex Ritter, USA.

Landecker, H. (2009), 'Seeing Things: From Microcinematography to Live Cell Imaging', *Nature Methods*, 6 (10): 707–9.

Lippincott-Schwartz, J. (2014), 'Quantitative Cell Biology: Transforming the Conceptual, Theoretical, Instrumental, and Methodological Approaches to Cell Biology', *Molecular Biology of the Cell*, 25 (22): 3437.

Matsubayashi, Y., A. Louani, A. Dragu, B. Sanchez-Sanchez, E. Serna-Morales, L. Yolland, A. Gyoergy, G. Vizcay, R. Fleck, J. Heddleston, T. Chew, D. Siekhaus and B. Stramer (2017), 'A Moving Source of Matrix Components Is Essential for De Novo Basement Membrane Formation', *Current Biology*, 27 (22): 3526–34.

Mavrakis, M., O. Pourquie and T. Lecuit (2010), 'Lighting up Developmental Mechanisms: How Fluorescence Imaging Heralded a New Era', *Development*, 137 (3): 373–87.

McDole, K., Katie McDole, Léo Guignard, Fernando Amat, Andrew Berger, Grégoire Malandain, Loïc A. Royer, Srinivas C. Turaga, Kristin Branson, Philipp J. Keller (2018), 'In Toto Imaging and Reconstruction of Post-Implantation Mouse Development at the Single-Cell Level', *Cell*, 175 (3): 859–76.

Medawar, P. (1986), *Memoirs of a Thinking Radish*, Oxford: Oxford University Press.

'Microbes Caught in Action' (1909), *New York Times*, 31 October: 3.

'Obituary: Dr R. G. Canti' (1936), *Nature*, 137: 262–3.

Pittet, M. J., Mikael J. Pittet, Christopher S. Garris, Sean P. Arlauckas and Ralph Weissleder (2018), 'Recording the Wild Lives of Immune Cells', *Science Immunology*, 3 (27).

Radzyner, H. and N. Barker (2018), 'Illuminating Roman Vishniac: A Career in Biological Photography and Cinematography', *The Journal of Biocommunication*, 42 (1). https://journals.uic.edu/ojs/index.php/jbc/article/view/9201.

Rosenberger, H. (1929a), 'Micro-Cinematography in Medical Research', *Journal of Dental Research*, 01 June, 9 (3): 343–52.

Rosenberger, H. (1929b), 'A Standard Microcinematographic Apparatus', *Science*, 28 June, 69 (1800): 672–4.

Solnit, R. (2003), *Motion Studies: Time, Space and Eadweard Muybridge*, London: Bloomsbury Press.

Stramer, B. M. and G. A. Dunn (2015), 'Cells on Film – The Past and Future of Cinemicroscopy', *Journal of Cell Science*, 128 (1): 9–13.

The Chase (*c.* 1950), [Film] Dir. David Rogers, USA: Vanderbuilt University. Available online: https://www.youtube.com/watch?v=Kb-m1uDoWfU (accessed 01 January 2020).

'The Cinema Has Helped Science' (1936), *The Straits Times*, 1 February: 17.

The Cultivation of Living Tissue (1928), [Film], Dir. Robert Canti, UK: Strangeways Research Laboratory. Available online at: https://www.youtube.com/watch?v=ln_R-_V6Rns [Part 1]; https://www.youtube.com/watch?v=vOd9QFkFqpw [Part 2]; and https://www.youtube.com/watch?v=OIhaaNeFgdE [Part 3] (accessed 01 January 2020).

'The Cultivation of Living Tissue Cells' (1932), *Nature*, (130): 805.

Ultramicroscope Time-Lapse of Syphilis Parasite (1910), [Film], Dir. Jean Comandon, Fr. Available online at: https://commons.wikimedia.org/wiki/File:Ultramicroscope_time-lapse_of_syphilis_parasite-Comandon-1910.ogv (accessed 01 January 2020).

Wallingford, J. B. (2019), 'The 200-year Effort to See the Embryo', *Science*, 23 August, 365 (6455): 758–9.

Wellmann, J. (2018), 'Model and Movement: Studying Cell Movement in Early Morphogenesis, 1900 to the Present', *History and Philosophy of the Life Sciences*, 11 September, 40 (3): 59.

Williamson, C. (2019), 'Nature and the Wonders of the Moving Image: John Ott's Postwar Popular Science Filmmaking', *Film History*, 31 (3): 27–54.

Yolland, L., M. Burki, S. Marcotti, A. Luchici, F. Kenny, J. Davis, E. Serna-Morales, J. Muller, M. Sixt, A. Davidson, W. Wood, L. Schumacher, R. Endres, M. Miodownik and B. Stramer (2019), 'Persistent and Polarised Global Actin Flow Is Essential for Directionality during Cell Migration', *Nature Cell Biology*, 11: 1370–81.

Zanet, J., B. Stramer, T. Millard, P. Martin, F. Payre and S. Plaza (2009), 'Fascin Is Required for Blood Cell Migration during Drosophila Embryogenesis', *Development*, 136 (15): 2557–65.

8

Cinematic forms and cultural heritage

Maureen Thomas

In June 2019, in Oslo, Viking Planet opened: a purpose-designed digital immersive cinematic space, offering a fresh experience of the Viking Age (800–1050 CE). In March 1913, in Berlin, the Ufa-Pavillon am Nollendorfplatz cinematograph playhouse opened with Guazzoni's film, *Quo Vadis?* offering access to the Emperor Nero's Rome (50–4 CE). Inside the 700-seater auditorium, with daylight projection and a roof that opened to the stars, as well as a twenty-five-piece orchestra and sound effects, the show featured live actors (Marconi 1913: 4). The line between theatre, concert and film was undrawn: immersive cinematograph heralded twenty-first-century digitally enabled audiovisual experience.

Olden times

The term 'cultural heritage' was not current at the time to describe early picture palaces, or content about ancient Rome, but the twenty-first-century definition includes both:

> As part of human activity, Cultural Heritage produces tangible representations of value systems, beliefs, traditions and lifestyles. As an essential part of culture as a whole, Cultural Heritage contains these visible and tangible traces from antiquity to the recent past. Cultural Heritage can be expressed as Intangible or Tangible (ICOMOS 2002: 21).

> Intangible Cultural Heritage . . . include(s) oral traditions, customs, languages, music, dance, rituals, festivals. (ICOMOS 2002: 23)

> Cultural heritage does not end at monuments and collections of objects. It also includes traditions or living expressions inherited from our ancestors and passed

on to our descendants, such as oral traditions, performing arts, social practices, rituals, festive events, knowledge and practices. (ICH UNESCO)

Cinema at the beginning of the twentieth century may be said to have fulfilled the functions of oral traditions, performing arts, social practices, rituals and festive events of earlier ages, both in the tangible (picture-palace, film-reels) and intangible (cultural content, values) sense. In *Quo Vadis?* Christian hostage Lycia is rescued from the spectacular circus – surely a Roman festive social practice. Film, especially in an immersive setting such as Kaufmann's Ufa-Pavillon, is surely a performing art. Thea von Harbou and Fritz Lang's *Siegfrieds Tod* (Death of Siegfried) and *Kriemhild's Rache* (Kriemhild's Revenge), together known as the *Nibelungenlied* (1924), which also premiered in Berlin, did not merely adapt the Middle High German epic *Nibelungenlied* of c. 1200 (Whobrey 2018), but incorporated related material (Hauer 1990), itself drawing on intertwining tale-tellings (Shippey 2018: 63–82), to create a spectacular Northern drama of power, politics, passion and betrayal rivalling ancient Greek tragedy.

Just as in the early days of cinema, in the twenty-first century much of the cultural heritage of myth and legend comes through audiovisual depictions, which, like their predecessors in rhyme and prose text, mould written, oral and visual sources into coherent stories for the audience of the day. Ian Hislop (2014) characterizes our legendarized past as the 'olden days' – culturally meaningful, as much as, or more than, historical: promoting legendary figures like King Arthur, who operate in an idealized world, over documented historical ones like King Alfred, whose real actions may not carry such symbolic weight.

Von Harbou and Lang's *Die Nibelungen* brings to the screen legendary heroic deeds, values and power struggles as significant to the 1920s as to earlier days, while Fleischer's *The Vikings* (1958) depicts the legendary pagan Ragnar Lodbrok and his sons clashing with Christian England and its values. Both evoke the olden days of Northern European culture. Ragnar also inspires the television series, *The Vikings* (Hirst 2013–20), popular worldwide (Tecxipio 2018).

In Fleischer's film, Kirk Douglas as Einar Ragnarsson thrills by 'running the oars' of a longship, a feat attributed, by Icelandic writer Snorri Sturluson in his 1225 *Heimskringla* (Kristjansson 1988b: 166–75), to Olaf Tryggvason, king of Norway from 995 to 1000, on his renowned 'Long Serpent': 'King Olaf was the greatest athlete in Norway'; he 'went along the oars outside the ship while his men rowed the Serpent'[1] (Ólasson 1946: 231, trans Thomas). Snorri writes 300 years after Olaf's time – this intangible olden-day Viking prowess no doubt fascinated his contemporary readers as much as modern audiences, for whom Douglas, himself performing the stunt, makes it screen-tangible (Douglas 1988: 271–6).

When the 'Avengers' *Thor* superhero movies (Thor: The Dark World (2013); Thor: Ragnarok (2017); Thor: Love and Thunder (forthcoming)), like Lang's film, invite audiences into the realm of Northern European mythology, now played out in modern America, they follow the example of Snorri's prose *Edda* (Sturluson 2008), written two centuries after Christianity had spread across the Northern world (Faulkes 1982: x), where pagan gods interact with humans and influence events with their superpowers (Faulkes 1982). Medieval manuscripts chronicling pre-Christian gods and mythical heroes like Siegfried, or founding forebears like Ragnar or Arthur, who lived, if at all, centuries before the time of their authors, are, like these films, imaginative backward-looking depictions of long-ago olden times.

Beyond cinema: Simulation and immersion

From the 1990s, interactive games take up the challenge of cultural heritage, and, in 2020, virtual reality (VR) experience and 270-degree screen format revisit the Viking Age (Graham 2019). Viking Planet describes itself as 'a 1600-square meter digital museum', a 'portal to the Viking Age'.[2] It does not exhibit physical artefacts but contains five beyond-cinema components:

1. A VR experience: *Virtual Viking – The Ambush* (Gustavson 2019)
2. A 270-degree cinema ('SagaScope'): *Fjorðr – The Viking Life*, inviting the audience 'to step into the Viking Age'
3. 'Hologram theatre': life-size figures 'beamed . . . back in time' displaying 'Viking fashion . . . on a catwalk'
4. 'Viking windows': Interactive audio, images, animations and text about the Viking Age
5. 'Selfie zone': Visitors pose in front of Viking Age stills

For the twelve-minute VR experience *Ambush*, the audience, wearing head-mounted VR displays, sit in rows of '4D chairs' which roll and jerk as the action unfolds, to join the crew of a ninth-century longship as it is ambushed at sea. 'Based on thousands of still images from Norway, actors and stunt performers are captured live with more than a hundred cameras programmed inside a game engine' to create 'the first Virtual Reality experience of its kind in the world'.[3] The audience enjoys a theme park–like ride – a return to the early roots of cinema in fairground entertainment.

In the VR scenario frame story, an elderly Viking recalls a youthful raid (Graham 2019). This narrative stance is intrinsically male-centred, and the ship is crewed by men; but since the visitor is wearing a headset, the point of view inside the experience itself is non-gendered. Nonetheless, it demonstrates the process by which, for many years, women readers, audience-members and gamers have been obliged to adopt a masculine perspective towards the drama world in order to identify with the main (heroic) protagonists – Einar Ragnarsson dancing on the oars – rather than the often-victimized female characters – Lycia persecuted by Nero (Mulvey 2020: 18–24).

In SagaScope, 'inside a Viking-helmet-shaped theatre', scenes of *Viking Life* unfold, 'as full 270^0 cinematic immersion or with multiple cinema images playing simultaneously, accompanied by a soundtrack and atmospheric soundscapes'. This 'fact-based account' 'places the Viking Age in the context of European history', taking 'a time travel leap from the Futhark alphabet and the times of the Viking runes into the digital age and the resurgence of Viking culture and storytelling in contemporary entertainment'.[4] In the dramatized film scenario, a group of Viking men embark on a seafaring journey, gathering their gear while the women take care of children, mind cooking pots and wave goodbye. The costumes and props are meticulously researched following archaeological and historical evidence; the cinematography brings sea and mountain into the theatre. This view of the Viking everyday and male and female roles is still conjectural; but the documentary footage of preserved artefacts and sites with commentary, which alternates with the staged scenario, leaves room for interpretation.

The digital museum immersive visit ends at a 'wall-mounted screen', where, 'if visitors enter an e-mail address from a mobile device', they can

> select whatever Viking universe visual setting they prefer. . . . The user's image can be shown integrated into a battle, among Vikings at the farmstead, or in any of the other optional locations; and the picture will be taken automatically. The Selfie is sent straight back to the visitor's mobile device, but printouts can also be ordered for collection at the Viking Planet gift shop.[5]

Visitors are invited to assimilate themselves into the simulated Viking culture.

The Ufa-Pavillon, a purpose-built picture palace, represented tangible cultural heritage at the beginning of cinema history; Viking Planet, a physical exhibition space designed for digitally enhanced, generated and supported audiovisual media, represents twenty-first century-tangible cultural heritage. Both aim for immersion. Cinema has long reached out from the screen, for example with 3D (Ross 2015) and at the turn of the 1950s and 1960s, Hollywood's 'Smell-o-Vision', 'Percepto' (mild electric shock), 'Illusion-o' (screen ghosts visible through infrared glasses) and the audience voting for alternative endings (Cook 1990: 532–6). In the twenty-first century, cinematic forms have entered the museum, as cultural heritage both tangible (architecture, film, projectors) and intangible (content/social practices/ values).

Interpretation

Saxo Grammaticus described Ragnar Lodbrok and Lagertha, his wife, in his Latin *Gesta Danorum* (History of the Danes) (Book IX, 4.1–4.11) – written, like the *Nibelungenlied*, in about 1200, three centuries after the time of the legendary characters portrayed. Since then, perspectives have changed. The *Vikings* television series amplifies Lagertha's role, her strength of character, agency and strategy, creating a *dramatis persona* akin to Dragon Queen Daenarys Targaryen in the *Game of Thrones* television series (2013–19) (adapted from George R. R. Martin's *Song of Ice and Fire* novels (2013)). Joan Bergin, costume designer on *The Vikings*, claims, of real-life Vikings: 'They were a very advanced culture'; 'women could rule . . . they were warriors . . . Lagertha embodies this' (Snead 2013).

Saxo's Lagertha indeed leads a group of women who, forced into a brothel by the Swedish king Frø after his victory over Siward, king of Norway, dress as men and join Ragnar, Siward's grandson, when he seeks vengeance (Saxo: IX, 4.1.). Saxo describes Lagertha: 'a skilled female fighter, who bore a man's temper in a girl's body; with locks flowing loose over her shoulders she would do battle in the forefront of the most valiant warriors' (Saxo IX, 4.2; trans Jesch 2001: 176).

In Saxo's account, Ragnar marries Lagertha and has a son and two daughters with her. Back to wars in Scania (constantly in dispute between Danes and Swedes), Ragnar repudiates Lagertha in favour of a political union with Thora, princess of the Swedes (Saxo IX, 4.4). But when Ragnar is in desperate need, Lagertha brings a fleet of 120 ships from Norway to his aid and, 'with a measure of vitality at odds with her tender frame, roused the mettle of the faltering soldiery by a splendid exhibition of bravery. She flew round the rear of the unprepared enemy in a circling manoeuvre and carried the panic which had been felt by the allies into the camp of their adversaries' (Saxo IX, 4.11 trans Jesch 2001: 180). Saxo writes 'circumvolans', literally 'flew round', giving Lagertha impressive superpower. Bergin's twenty-first-century view may seem to be supported by Saxo's text, but his Lagertha finally appears to be something more than human, rather than a typical Viking woman; she has been associated with the Valkyries of Norse mythology, like Lang's Brünhild (Jesch 2001: 180).

It is hard to separate tale-telling from history in the account of pagan Viking 'olden days' given by Saxo (b. c.1160, d. 1220), which he contrasts with the orderly Christian culture in which he himself lives (Jesch 2001: 176–8) – where the church has brought into line heathen Scandinavia, presumably including flying women. The art of writing and making books came with Christianity and Saxo wields his pen some 300 years after the events he records; sixty years after the publication of Geoffrey of Monmouth's tales of King Arthur in his Latin *History of the Kings of Britain* (Reeve and Wright 2009), which had rapidly become the talk of Europe, including Scandinavia (Kalinka 2015). Geoffrey credits Arthur with conquering Ireland, Iceland, the Orkneys, Gotland, Norway and Denmark (Reeve, ed. 2009: 205), of which there is no evidence elsewhere, though these areas all came under Scandinavian domination in the centuries before Saxo and Geoffrey lived. Arthur and Ragnar are both olden-day heroes who spearhead the unification of the Northern European world.

All purveyors of myth, legend and distant history include contemporary views and insights in their storyworlds. Jesch (2001: 176–208) argues that fighting females and Valkyries, found only in Saxo or legendary sagas written long after the periods they evoke, can be seen as literary types rather than a reflection of actual society. Lawbooks and chronicles suggest that though women enjoyed considerable social status, they were subject to men and man-made laws (Foote and Wilson 1970: 108–11), much as they have been since. Gotland Law, from shortly after 1200, stipulates fines for inappropriate behaviour (Foote and Wilson 1970: xix):

> Take her wrist or ankle, pay four ounces; touch her elbow or her leg between knee and calf, pay two and two-thirds ounces; take hold of her shoulder or just above the knee, pay one- and two-thirds ounces; touch her breast, pay one ounce; but if you touch her higher still above the knee, 'that is the touch dishonourable and is called the fool's clasp; no money is payable for that – most women put up with it when it gets that far'. (Foote and Wilson 1970: 112)

Some cultural behaviours and judgements seem not to have changed much. But Danish Saxo, a Christian cleric, unlike Bergin, appears not to admire the pre-Christian warrior women he records:

> There were once women in Denmark who dressed themselves to look like men and spent almost every minute cultivating soldiers' skills; they did not want the sinews of their valour to lose tautness and be infected by self-indulgence. Loathing a dainty style of living, they would harden body and mind with toil and endurance, rejecting the fickle pliancy of girls and compelling their womanish spirits to act with a virile ruthlessness. They courted military celebrity so earnestly that you would have guessed they had unsexed themselves. Those especially who had forceful personalities or were tall and elegant embarked on this way of life. As if they were forgetful of their true selves they put toughness before allure, aimed at conflicts instead of kisses, tasted blood, not lips, sought the clash of arms rather than the arm's embrace, fitted to weapons hands which should have been weaving, desired not the couch but the kill, and those they could have appeased with looks they attacked with lances. (Jesch 2001: 176)

Allure, kisses, lips, embraces, weaving, the couch, appeasing looks – these, not toughness, weapons and ruthlessness, are appropriate to medieval Christian women.

History, myth, cultural heritage and audiovisual media: Focusing on women

From the seeds planted by Saxo, the Lagertha of television series *Vikings* grows to a prominent player, tough and ruthless, with various suitors, would-be rapists and one rapee (King Harald Finehair). Essentially, Lagertha's story is fabricated to interconnect the imaginative dramatization of value conflicts as well as political conflicts between Christian Anglo-Saxons and heathen Vikings, also highlighted by the film *The Vikings*. Motifs of honour, deceit and wounded pride are borrowed from other sources than Saxo, such as the *Nibelungenlied* and the thirteenth-century Old Norse *Saga of the Völsungs* (Crawford 2017; Finch 1965), which tells a Scandinavian version of the tragic Nibelung story. These tales of a heroic age are transmitted through texts written down in the Middle Ages, where Viking past and medieval present are conflated into legendary 'olden times'. Hirst's *Vikings* continues the tradition, adding a spice of the twenty-first century to Lagertha.

These hybrid olden days are similar to Martin's fictional Westeros in *Game of Thrones*, with its Viking-sounding name, where the warring dynasties of Lannisters and Starks evoke the fifteenth-century English Wars of the Roses – the television set and costumes are an appropriate visual cross between Viking and Medieval. This alluring 'olden time' amalgam was popularized by Oxford University professor of Anglo-Saxon and English Literature, J. R. R. Tolkien, in his *Lord of the Rings* novels (1955) (ranked sixth in *The Times* (2008) list of the '50 greatest British Writers since 1945'), faithfully filmed by Peter Jackson (2001–3) to international delight. Jackson's storyworld location, a New Zealand landscape *doré* lost to Europe, is filtered through a long tradition of poetry, tale-making and literature remediated in the twenty-first-century present as film. Tolkien's Middle Earth, where hobbits, elves, dwarves and humans mingle as in the Old Norse cosmos (O'Donahue 2010: 17–18), may not be twentieth-century evidence-based 'history', but it is based on scholarship and represents an influential incarnation of cultural heritage, carrying on a living tradition of mythopoeia. Small hobbits prefer cosy rural homes, good food, firesides and slippers, but rise when attacked by greedy, ruthless powers to perform deeds of heroism inspired by decent values. Judging by its worldwide appeal (Watson 2019), twenty-first-century audiences identify with this mythic screen olden time, where a diverse culture able to overcome evil and remain faithful to its decent values offers hope to the modern world.

Contrariwise, a modern perspective can unwittingly impose inappropriate cultural norms on archaeological evidence. A rich burial excavated in the nineteenth century at Birka, Sweden, whose grave goods confirmed hitherto speculative visions of high-status Viking warriors, was shown, when Stockholm University bioarchaeologist Anna Kjellström analysed DNA in 2014, to be that of a woman leader (Price et al. 2019). Perhaps Saxo's martial women dressed as men were not just a legend – but the nineteenth century assumed that swords meant men, while the twenty-first century is eager to see women on an equal martial footing.

In 2001–3,[6] I created an interactive video installation, *Vala* (Thomas 2005) which dramatizes the 'Edda' poem, *Völuspá* (The Seeress's Prophecy), thought to have been orally composed by around 1000 and a vital source of knowledge of Northern mythology (Dronke 1999: 3–153). The installation experimented with Viking-age imagery, aesthetics and techniques derived – as is the poem itself – from the oral singing of tales, where pre-composed elements are combined in real time to suit a particular subject, moment and audience (Lord [1960]

2016). *Völuspá*, written down *c.* 1270 (Dronke 1969: xi–xiii), is spoken by a seeress, consulted by the god Odin for her knowledge of the gods, the origins of the world and humankind, and their fates (Kristjánsson 1988: 40–4). Though scholars have generally assumed that the poet was male, there seems no intrinsic reason why she should not have been a woman, as I have suggested elsewhere (Thomas 1988) – indeed, the fluid associational style can be regarded as a type of *écriture féminine* (female scriptive space) (Aneja 2008); and the poem ends with fields sprouting anew in the wake of dire conflicts and natural catastrophe.

When I adapted and expanded the material for smartphone as *RuneCast* (2007) (Thomas 2009a), Norwegian 3D digital artist, conservator and Viking-art expert Marianne Selsjord created a navigable, interactive 3D-mythworld as the interface to access video, music and audio, all embodying the aesthetic of the poem. The work uses navigable media, like oral composition unbound by printed page or screen frame, to integrate intangible cultural heritage into the experience of form as well as content (Prager, Thomas and Selsjord 2015).

This female take, based on a Viking-age poem spoken by a wisewoman, highlights a Viking-age woman's role rarely represented in films and fantasies (Thomas 2009b). Though in Fleischer's 1958 *The Vikings*, a seeress, Kitala, has a decisive effect on the action, she is characterized as a witchy fortune-teller rather than a guardian of intangible cultural heritage like Vala. That dignified role is, though, possibly supported by the ninth-century Oseberg ship burial, Norway, of two high-status women – once, because of location and extraordinary richness, originally speculatively identified as Queen Åsa of the Ynglings and her handmaid (Christensen, Ingstad and Myhre 1992), but who, according to more recent scholarship, judging by their grave goods, may both have been wisewomen or seeresses (Nordström 2006: 399–403) evidently highly esteemed.

The 2017 television miniseries *Historien om Danmark* (History of Denmark) takes a less speculative approach to kings and queens, shooting on locations where significant events actually occurred, with a presenter, expert interviews and voice-over commentary. Silent dramatized scenarios set in castles are atmospherically lit but shot as the buildings are today – bare-walled and unfurnished except for strictly necessary props: writing desk, throne, table. Avoiding constructed dialogue and accidental anachronisms, the form emphasizes that history is interpretation; however, the austere impression the empty, unheated castles give is at odds with preserved artefacts and contemporary representations and descriptions, which suggest they were warmly, often opulently, furnished, luxuriating in colour (Brindle 2012).

Episode 5 (of 10) of the series, '*Sen midelalder*' (Late Middle Ages), includes, among the battles and conquests of her father, King Valdemar Atterdag of Denmark, a few brief scenes featuring Queen Margrete I of Denmark, Norway and Sweden (1353–1412), a genuine medieval ruler. Newborn Margrete cries in the arms of her warlike father; at eleven, she dines in silence opposite her 24-year-old husband, King Håkon VI of Norway; seventeen years old, she caresses her pregnant belly; at twenty-two, she plays, like any young mother, with her small son in a summer field; aged twenty-seven, she confers with advisers after the death of her husband and is appointed Regent for her (only) son, now ten; then at thirty-four, at his tomb, she mourns his death as a seventeen-year old. Margrete selects a new young heir (her sister's grandson) and, aged forty-four, looks on as, just of age at fifteen, he dons the triple crown of the Kalmar Union between Denmark, Norway and Sweden, which Margrete orchestrated; finally, Margrete's tomb effigy shows her dead, aged fifty-nine.

Though Margrete, recorded not in legendary history written centuries after her death, but in contemporary chronicles and documents, ruled for forty-four years, in 2017 she is not shown as a strong strategic queen, but as the daughter of her father, the mother of her son and the supporter of her male heir, who did not in fact rule until after her death. In 2020, a feature film, *Margrete – Queen of the North* (Charlotte Sieling) commenced production supported by the film institutes and public broadcasters of the Scandinavian countries (Mitchell 2020); however, the advance press from Danish Broadcasting focuses more on sensation than strategy: 'New film on the way about Denmark's first female ruler: burnt her false son and hired a pirate' (Rosenkvist Dam 2020 trans Thomas). Historian Etting uses more measured terms: when Margrete's right to rule is challenged by an imposter, her advisers invoke the law to protect her (Etting 2004: 135–8). Burning at the stake makes spectacular film and television, but is hardly representative of Queen Margrete's achievements; and Queen Elizabeth I of England is respected for her use of privateers. It seems that the cultural heritage of strong, proactive olden-day Scandinavian female leaders glimpsed by Bergin and maybe represented by the Birka warrior does not necessarily carry forward to twenty-first-century depictions of Margrete, their heir in real life.

In 2011, in an attempt to communicate in a contemporary way what it might have been like to be medieval girl-queen Margrete, I devised, supported by the Norwegian Film Institute's Script Fund, an interactive drama, *Queens of the North*. This was before Viking Planet: business models and exhibition environments lagged far behind emerging technologies and dramaturgies for interactive storytelling. In 2019–21, as senior artistic researcher at the Norwegian National Film School, I am realizing the project with Snow Castle Games, Oslo. The computer game is intended to form the basis of a locative Augmented Reality experience at Margrete's home, Akershus Fortress, Oslo.

Few facts are available about Margrete's early years (Haug 2000). But *Queens Game* is a 'HiStoryGame', not a lesson, imagining, from research into social and cultural practices, what the life of a child queen might have been like. It integrates expressive animated (non-motion capture) characters and in-game drama with challenging, non-violent gameplay, where players can explore and affect the storyworld without losing control of their character. The rich and enduring 'olden realm' of King Arthur and Queen Guinevere, entered by Margrete through an enchanted chess set, provides a way-in for modern players as well as a contrast to Margrete's life at Akershus Fortress in the fourteenth century.

Danish princess Margrete, just married, aged ten, to King Håkon of Norway (aged twenty-three), cementing an alliance between their fathers (Etting 2004: 6), arrives at her future home (Figure 8.1); her new husband is off fighting beside her father Valdemar of Denmark and her father-in-law Magnus of Sweden. But lively music-loving Margrete makes friends with rebellious bookworm Ingegerd, the same age as herself (Figure 8.2), whose mother is Margrete's new head of household. The girls, in reality, became lifelong friends: Margrete destined to rule one of the largest states in Europe and Ingegerd to become Abbess of Vadstena Cloister, where Margrete often stayed in later life – founded

Figure 8.1 *Queens Game* pre-production 3D dramatic atmosphere test, 2019. Courtesy of Snow Castle Games Oslo.

Figure 8.2 *Queens Game* Margrete and Ingegerd concept art, 2020. By kind permission of the artist, Wenche Hellekås.

by Ingegerd's strong-minded and politically active grandmother, Saint Birgitta of Sweden (d. 1373) (Beskow and Landen 2003).

Queens Game uses the mechanisms of role-playing games to create a spatially organized, immersive dramatic experience on the model of medieval storytellers such as Thomas Malory (Cooper 2008), dramatists like Adam de la Halle (Cartier 1971) and the creators of the Corpus Christi Mystery Plays (Kolve 1966) to immerse players in an environment, visuals, music and sound inspired by the authentic aesthetics and poetics of the time – intrinsic intangible cultural heritage.

Keeping up with the times

As we adapt to new technologies, our lives are becoming increasingly fragmented, multifaceted, interactive. Linear novels and films are less relevant now for reflecting our realities. What forms of art and entertainment are most relevant now? . . . Video games. Interactive entertainment. Yet, many people don't like video games. . . . I'm not remotely interested in shockingly good graphics, in murder simulators, in guns and knives and swords. I'm not that interested in adrenaline. . . . I'm interested in care, in characters, in creation, in finding a path forward inside games that helps me find my path forward in life. . . . At my studio we are making games with people who don't like video games because we want to break out of established paradigms.

Code, 2016

Overtly historical computer games, since the early days of 'edutainment' in the 1990s, have been driven by war, combat and strategy, featuring male protagonists.[7] Medieval adventure designed for people who do like video games, swords, personal combat and epic battles fought by motion-captured characters in meticulously researched historical costume and environments does well: *Kingdom Come, Deliverance* (2018) sold over two million copies in its first year (Jones 2019). There are no noticeable women, excepting Lady Stephanie, a hostage, but its DownLoadable Content (DLC) addition, *A Woman's Lot* (2019) offers a female playable character, Teresa. Although she wears female costume and at the start is feeding hens, Teresa soon becomes a fighter, wielding the skills of original protagonist, Henry 'as well as you would expect of an ordinary milkmaid' (Official Introduction Video 2019). Records show medieval women warriors did exist, though usually as leaders rather than fighters, and as the exception rather than the rule (McLaughlin 1990; Eads 2012) – but the game assumes that fighting is intrinsically the most interesting activity, so an interesting woman character has to fight, though of course not as well as hero Henry.

As game designer Brie Code recognizes, too few games attract women. Far too few feature girls as active protagonists, not dressed up as boys or playing damsels in distress in male adventures (Sarkeesian 2013). However, some twenty-first-century titles do address social history. Set, like *Queens Game*, in the Middle Ages, these include *Medieval Defenders* (2016), *The Plague* (2015), *The Black Death* (2016) and *A Plague Tale: Innocence* (2019) – which features a female protagonist (though dressed as a boy and acting like one) battling rats in a realistic, devastated, medieval European landscape.

Nonetheless, history games directed towards girls still mostly offer disappointing female roles. *Little Big Planet 3: Women In History Costume Pack* (2016) suggests celebrating Women's Day by 'dressing Sackgirl® up as four of the most famous and influential women from the pages of history': Cleopatra, Elizabeth I of England, Joan of Arc and Wu Zetian; while *A Princess Tale* (2016) breezily avers: 'Life's good when you're the Princess; no responsibilities, nobody telling you what to do or where to go, just running around, having fun and flirting your life away. So what happens when the fate of the world falls into the hands of the most irresponsible bubble head to ever trip over royal birth?' (STEAM 2016). When not dressed as boys doing boy-things, girls are period fashion models, clumsy swordswomen or comic bubblehead royals. Margrete I of Norway was none of these things: she grew up to rule effectively, avoiding war by diplomacy and strategy (see Etting 2004).

In *Queens Game*, Margrete, supported and teased by her best friend, is a real-life royal child hero, in contrast to Disney's spun-sugar princesses. Her story, that of a girl who has to forge her own way in a challenging world not designed for female leadership, is as modern as it is medieval – the kind of non-adrenaline-driven, non-violent, character- and experience-based story for which Code pleads (Code 2016). Girls, like Grete Thunberg (2019) or Malala Yousafzai (2014), can tackle important real-world issues effectively: Margrete did exactly that. This child-bride – of whom there are still many, some within European communities – uses well the skills she learns at chess.

According to Joseph Campbell, whose *Hero with a Thousand Faces* (1949) inspired filmmakers George Lucas and Stephen Spielberg in the 1970s, 'The rise and fall of civilisations in the long, broad course of history can be seen to have been largely a function of the integrity and cogency of their supporting canons of myth; for not authority but aspiration is the motivator, builder and transformer of civilization' (Campbell 1982: 5). Enduring 'myths offer life models', but in every new telling 'moral order has to catch up with the moral necessities of actual life in time, here and now' (Campbell and Moyers [1988] 1991: 16). It seems *Game of Thrones* reflects contemporary moral necessities, enabling strong female leaders to identify with the myths of olden times, which depict their kind as natural rather than anomalous. Likewise, the image of self-actuating Lagertha in *Vikings* replaces the hapless, plump, bound Viking woman, whose flaxen plaits are severed by her elderly husband in a circus-like axe-throwing display for the entertainment of his feasting companions, in Fleischer's 1958 box office smash, *The Vikings*. The axe-thrower's public humiliation of his wife (for suspected infidelity) tells us more about Hollywood in 1958 than Vikings a thousand years earlier.

In the twenty-first century, cinematic forms and mythopoeia have stepped, together, via interactive computer games, into the museum, to stage simulated action, virtually and interactively, at locations where, in the past, the olden days could be filmed, but not experienced. From the Ufa-Pavillon to Viking Planet and beyond, like their oral and literary storytelling predecessors, cinematic forms carry forward important cultural heritage, constructing new exhibition environments to absorb and entertain their audiences with fresh takes on olden times. They offer a vibrant way of preserving and updating our heritage both tangible and intangible, supporting a living sense of the moral order, continuity and cultural identity.

Notes

1 'Óláfr konungr var mestr íþróttamaðr í Nóregi . . . Óláfr konungr gekk eptir árum útbyrðis, er menn hans röru á Orminum.' Ólasson 1946: 231.
2 See online at: https://thevikingplanet.com/ (accessed 1 March 2020).
3 See online at: https://thevikingplanet.com/ (accessed 1 March 2020).
4 See online at: https://thevikingplanet.com/ (accessed 1 March 2020).
5 See online at: https://thevikingplanet.com/ (accessed 1 March 2020).
6 As a senior creative research fellow at the Interactive Institute, Malmö, Sweden.
7 See, for example, *The Great War: 1914-1918* (1992) (Game) Blue Byte Studio GmbH; *Historion* (1992) (Game) Ruske & Pühretmajer Edutainment GmbH/HEURIKA-Klett Softwareverlag GmbH; *Napoleon: Total War* (2010) (Game) Creative Assembly; *Ways of History* (2017) (Game) Glyph Worlds.

References

Aneja, A. ([1992] 2008), 'The Medusa's Slip: Hélène Cisoux and the Underpinnings of écriture feminine', *Lit: Literature Interpretation Theory*, 4 (1): 17–27.
A Plague Tale: Innocence (2019), [Game] Asobo Studios SARL/ Focus Home Interactive SAS.
A Princess Tale (2016), [Game] Warfare Studios/Adorlea.
A Woman's Lot, Kingdom Come: Deliverance DLC (2019), [Game] Warhorse Studios S.R.O; (2019) 'Kingdom Come: Deliverance – A Woman's Lot Introduction', [official introduction video], Warhorse Studios. Available online: https://www.youtube.com/watch?v=BB-Pei7i0Xg&vl=en-GB (accessed 01 March 2020).
Beskow, P. and A. Landen, eds (2003), *Birgitta af Vadstena*, Stockholm: Natur og Kultur.
Brindle, S. (2012), *Dover Castle*, English Heritage/Historic England.
Campbell, J. (1949), *The Hero with a Thousand Faces*, New York: Bollingen Foundation/Pantheon Press.
Campbell, J. (1982), *Creative Mythology*, New York: Penguin.

Campbell, J. and B. Moyers ([1988] 1991), *The Power of Myth*, New York: Anchor Books.
Cartier, N. (1971), *Le Bossu Desenchante: Etude Sur Le Jeu De La Feuillee*, Paris: Librairie Droz.
Christensen, A., A.-S. Ingstad and B. Myhre (1992), *Oseberg dronningens grav*, Oslo: Schibsted.
Code, B. (2016), 'Video Games Are Boring', *Biz*, 07 December 2016. Available online: https://www.gamesindustry.biz/articles/2016-11-07-video-games-are-boring (accessed 01 March 2020).
Cook, D. (1990), *A History of Narrative Film*, New York and London: W.W. Norton & Co.
Cooper, H., ed. (2008), *Sir Thomas Malory: Le Morte D'Arthur*, Oxford: Oxford University Press.
Crawford, J. (2017), *The Saga of the Volsungs with the Saga of Ragnar Lothbrok*, Cambridge, MA: Hackett.
Die Nibelungen – Siegfrieds Tod (Death of Siegfried) and *Kriemhild's Rache* (Kriemhild's Revenge) (1924), [Film] Dir. Fritz Lang, Germany: Decla Bioscop AG, Universum Film (UFA).
Douglas, K. (1988), *The Ragman's Son*, New York: Simon and Schuster.
Dronke, U. (1969), *The Poetic Edda, Volume I: Heroic Poems*, Oxford: Clarendon/Oxford University.
Dronke, U. (1999), *The Poetic Edda, Volume II: Mythological Poems*, Oxford: Clarenden Press.
Eads, V. (2012), 'Means, Motive, Opportunity: Medieval Women and the Recourse to Arms', *De Re Militari*. Available online: https://deremilitari.org/2012/09/eads-means-motive-opportunity/ (accessed 01 March 2020).
Etting, V. (2004), *Queen Margrete I (1353–1412) and the Founding of the Nordic Union*, Leiden and Boston: Brill.
Faulkes, A. (1982), *Snorri Sturluson: Edda*, Oxford: Clarendon Press.
Finch, R. G. (1965), *The Saga of the Volsungs*, London: Nelson.
Foote, P. and D. Wilson (1970), *The Viking Achievement*, London: Sidgwick & Jackson.
Game of Thrones (2013–2019), [TV programme] Dir. D. Benioff and D. Weiss, USA: HBO and others.
Graham, P. (2019), 'Hammerhead Talks Vikings and VR', *VR Focus*, June. Available online: https://www.vrfocus.com/2019/06/hammerhead-talks-vikings-and-vr/ (accessed 01 March 2020).
Hauer, S. (1990), 'The Sources of Fritz Lang's "Die Nibelungen"', *Literature/Film Quarterly*, 18 (2): 103–10, Salisbury University. Available online: https://www.jstor.org/stable/43797589 (accessed 01 March 2020).
Haug, E. (2000), *Margrete – den siste dronning i Sverreaetten*, Oslo: Cappellen Damm.
Hislop, I. (2014), [TV programme] *Ian Hislop's Olden Days*, BBC2.

Historien om Danmark (History of Denmark) (2017), [TV programme] Denmark: DR Danish Broadcasting Co.

Homo Novus (2018), [Film], Dir. Anna Viduleja, Latvia: Film Angels.

ICH (Intangible Cultural Heritage) UNESCO 'What is Intangible Heritage?'. Available online: https://ich.unesco.org/en/what-is-intangible-heritage-00003 (accessed 01 March 2020).

ICOMO (International Committee on Cultural Tourism International Committee on Monuments and Sites) (2002), *International Cultural Tourism Charter: Principles and Guidelines for Managing Tourism at Places of Cultural and Heritage Significance*, International Council on Monuments and Sites, ICOMOS International Cultural Tourism Committee.

Jesch, J. (2001), *Women in the Viking Age*, Woodbridge: Boydell Press.

Jones, A. (2019), 'Kingdom Come: Deliverance has Sold Two Million Copies', *PCgamesN*. Available online: https://www.pcgamesn.com/kingdom-come-deliverance/kingdom-come-deliverance-sales-numbers (accessed 01 March 2020).

Kalinke, M., ed. (2015), *The Arthur of the North*, Cardiff: University of Wales Press.

Kingdom Come, Deliverance (2018), [Game] Warhorse Studios s.r.o.

Kolve, A. (1966), *The Play Called Corpus Christi*, Stanford: Stanford University Press.

Kristjánsson J, (1988), *Eddas and Sagas*, trans. P. Foote, Reykjavik: Hið Íslenska bókmenntafélag.

Kristjánsson, J. (1988), 'Snorri Sturlusson', in *Eddas and Sagas*, 166–75, Reykjavik: Hið íslenska bókmenntafélag.

Little Big Planet 3: Women in History Costume Pack (2016), [Game] Sony Interactive Entertainment Europe.

Lord, A. ([1960] 2016), *The Singer of Tales: Third Edition*, Cambridge, MA: Harvard University Press.

Marconi Transatlantic Wireless Telegraph (1913), 'Berlin Crazy on Film Shows; Americans Open Finest Moving Picture Theatre in City', *New York Times*, 14 March: Editorial 04. Available online: https://timesmachine.nytimes.com/timesmachine/1913/03/23/100258007.html (accessed 01 March 2020). See also https://timesmachine.nytimes.com/timesmachine/1912/12/15/100600161.pdf

Margrete – Queen of the North (forthcoming), [Film] Dir. Charlotte Sieling, Sweden: SF Studios, Norway: Filmkameratene, Czech Republic: Sirena Film.

Martin, G. R. R. (2013), *Song of Ice and Fire*, London: Bantam Box Edition.

McLaughlin, M. (1990), 'The Woman Warrior: Gender, Warfare and Society in Medieval Europe', *Women's Studies*, 17: 193–209. Available online: https://doi.org/10.1080/00497878.1990.9978805 (accessed 01 March 2020).

Medieval Defenders (2016), [Game] Creobit/8floor.

Mitchell, W. (2020), 'Trine Dyrholm to star in Charlotte Sieling's historical epic "Margrete – Queen Of The North"', *Screen Daily*, 14 February 2020. Available online:

https://www.screendaily.com/news/trine-dyrholm-to-star-in-charlotte-sielings-historical-epic-margrete-queen-of-the-north/5147154.article (accessed 01 March 2020).

Mulvey, L. (2020), *Afterimages*, London: Reaktion Books.

Nordström, N. (2006), 'From Queen to Sorcerer', in C. Raudvere, A. Andrén and K. Jennbert (eds), *Old Norse Religion in Long-term Perspectives: Origins, Changes, and Interactions*, 399–403, Lund: Nordic Academic Press.

O'Donahue, H. (2010), *From Asgard to Valhalla*, London and New York: I.B. Tauris.

Ólasson, P. E., ed. (1946), Chapter 85, 'Frá Íþróttum Óláfs Konungs', in *Heimskringla*, 231, Reykjavík: Menntamálaráð og þjóðvinafélag.

Prager, P., M. Thomas and M. Selsjord (2015), 'Transposing, Transforming and Transcending Tradition in Creative Digital Media', in D. Harrison (ed.), *Handbook of Research on Digital Media and Creative Technologies*, 141–9, Hershey: IGI Global.

Price, N., C. Hedenstierna-Jonson, T. Zachrisson, A. Kjellström, J. Storå, M. Krzewińska, T. Günther, V. Sobrado, M. Jakobsson and A. Götherström (2019), 'Viking warrior women? Reassessing Birka chamber grave Bj.581', *Antiquity*, 93 (367): 181–98. Available online: https://www.cambridge.org/core/journals/antiquity/article/viking-warrior-women-reassessing-birka-chamber-grave-bj581/7CC691F69FAE51DDE905D27E049FADCD (accessed 01 March 2020).

Queens Game (forthcoming), Oslo: Snow Castle Games.

Quo Vadis? (1913), [Film] Dir. Enrico Guazzoni, Italy: Società Italiana Cines.

Reeve M., ed., Neil Wright, trans. (2009), *Geoffrey of Monmouth: The History of the Kings of Britain, an Edition and Translation of 'De gestis Britonum [Historia Regum Britanniæ]'*, Woodbridge: Boydell Press.

Rosenkvist Dam, C. (2020), 'Ny film på vej om Danmarks første kvindelige regent: Brændte sin falske søn og hyrede en pirat', *DRDK News*, 14 February 2020. Available online: https://www.dr.dk/nyheder/kultur/historie/ny-film-paa-vej-om-danmarks-foerste-kvindelige-regent (accessed 01 March 2020).

Ross, M. (2015), *3D Cinema: Optical Illusions and Tactile Experiences*, London: Palgrave Macmillan.

Sarkeesian, A. (2013), *Tropes vs Women in Video Games*. [Online 3-part video series]: Feminist Frequency. Available online: https://feministfrequency.com/series/tropes-vs-women-in-video-games/ and https://www.youtube.com/watch?v=X6p5AZp7r_Q (accessed 01 March 2020).

Saxo Grammaticus (1200), *Gesta Danorum*. Available online: http://wayback-01.kb.dk/wayback/20100504153455/; and http://www2.kb.dk/elib/lit/dan/saxo/lat/or.dsr/9/4/index.htm (accessed 01 March 2020).

Shippey, T. (2018), *Laughing Shall I Die*, London: Reaktion Books.

Snead, E. (2013), 'The Vikings' Costume Designer Joan Bergin Dispels Norse Myths', *Hollywood Reporter*, 26 April 2013. Available online: https://www.hollywoodrepo

rter.com/news/vikings-costume-designer-joan-bergin-dispels-norse-myths-446667 (accessed 01 March 2020).

Sturluson, S. (2008), *Edda*, trans. A. Faulkes, London: J.M. Dent, Everyman.

Tecxipio (2018), 'TV Show Viewership: Vikings'. Available online: https://www.tecxipio.com/single-post/television-show-viewership-vikings (accessed 01 March 2020).

The Black Death (2016), [Game] Small Impact Games&Syrin Studios/Green Man Loaded.

The Lord of the Rings (2001–2003), [Film trilogy] Dir. Peter Jackson, New Zealand, USA: New Line Cinema, WingNut Films, The Saul Zaentz Company.

The Plague (2015), [Game] Serious Games Interactive.

The Vikings (1958), [Film] Dir. Richard Fleischer, USA: Brynaprod S.A, Bavaria Film, Cutleigh Productions.

'The 50 greatest British writers since 1945' (2008), *The Times*, 05 January. Available online: https://www.thetimes.co.uk/article/the-50-greatest-british-writers-since-1945-ws3g69xrf90 (accessed 01 March 2020).

Thomas, M. (1988), 'Gunnlaðarsaga og kvenröddin í íslenskri bókmenntahefð', *Skírnir*, Vor, Reykjavik: Hið íslenska bókmenntafélag.

Thomas, M. (2005), 'Playing with Chance and Choice – Orality, Narrativity and Cinematic Media', in B. Bushoff (ed.), *Developing Interactive Narrative Content: sagas/sagasnet*, 371–442, Munich: High Text.

Thomas, M. (2009a), 'Digitality and Immaterial Culture: What did Viking Women Think?' *International Journal of Digital Cultural Heritage and Electronic Tourism*, 1: 2, 177–99.

Thomas, M. (2009b), 'Taking a Chance on Losing Yourself in the Game' (Special Issue: 'Women in Games'). *Digital Creativity*, 20 (4): 211–34.

Thor (2011), [Film] Dir. Kenneth Branagh, USA: Paramount Picture, Marvel Entertainment, Marvel Studios.

Thor: Love and Thunder (forthcoming), [Film] Dir. Taika Waititi, USA: Marvel Studios, Walt Disney Pictures.

Thor: Ragnarok (2017), [Film] Dir. Taika Waititi, USA: Marvel Studios, Walt Disney Pictures, Government of Australia.

Thor: The Dark World (2013), [Film] Dir. Alan Taylor, USA: Marvel Studios, Walt Disney Pictures.

Thunberg, G. (2019), *No-One Is Too Small To Make a Difference*, New York: Penguin.

Tolkien, J. R. R. (1955), *The Lord of the Rings*, London: Allen and Unwin.

Viking Planet, Oslo. Available online: https://thevikingplanet.com/ (accessed 01 March 2020).

Vikings (2013–2020), [TV programme] Dir. Michael Hirst, Ireland: Octagon Films, Canada: Unit 5 Productions.

Virtual Viking – The Ambush (2019), [VR movie] Dir Erik Gustavson, Norway/UK: The Viking Planet, Ridley Scott Creative Group, Hammerhead and Dimension.

Watson, A. (2019), 'Lord of the Rings Films, Production Costs and Box Office Revenue', *Statista*, 09 August. Available online: https://www.statista.com/statistics/323463/lord-of-the-rings-films-production-costs-box-office-revenue/ (accessed 01 March 2020).

Whobrey, W. (2018), *The Nibelungenlied: Eith The Klage*, Indianapolis: Hackett Publishing Company, Inc.

Yousafszai, M. and C. Lamb (2014), *I Am Malala: The Story of the Girl Who Stood Up for Education and was Shot by the Taliban*, London: Weidenfeld and Nicolson.

Part Three

Reconstructing: from Writing to Architecture

9

The modulation of emphasis

Screenwriting as a literary art

Clare L. E. Foster

Screenwriting is not an end in itself but a means to an end. It is a form of writing that suggests, models, tests, accompanies and participates in an extended, multiple and collaborative 'writing' process. Because its goal is to deliver exactly what we see and hear on the screen, for exactly as long as we get to absorb it, in no other art form is the reader's attention directed so completely. In terms of language, this means that word length, sentence length and choice of punctuation are critical. But at the same time, despite being exactly and deliberately chosen, screenwriting language does not command the fixed status of the words of a play, or novel, but is an instrumental bid for experiential affect, an experiment, a temporary gesture, metonymic for the 'kind of thing'. This condition of detailed yet contingent fixity, of perfected suggestion, defines the practice. Its literary mastery consists in the intensely controlled modulation of emphasis. In this, time and timing are key. As in music, the art of film depends on duration and sequence: the meaning of an image is a function of how much, and when, we get to look at it.

The digital era has radically changed the creative and commercial environment for 'films'. Screenplays correspondingly have both more and less status. They are increasingly enjoyed as a literature in their own right, separate entities from the end product for which they are functionally a tool; while others are no longer storytelling in the conventional sense at all, but 'content' that is endlessly transferable across as many media and platforms as possible. This chapter reflects on that changed status. It asks what screenwriting, as a kind of writing, has in common with other kinds of written texts. Its observations are based on my experience as a screenwriter for hire in a US studio-distributor market niche that arguably no longer exists: the character-driven narrative theatrical feature film (then called the 'Oscar prestige' or 'art house' film).[1] I specialized in adapting historical events or books into films for filmmakers such as Mike Newell, Geena Davis and Kristin Scott Thomas and for companies such as Fox Searchlight, New Line Cinema, Film 4, Sony Pictures Classics and Disney. In other words, I worked in development, as opposed to speculatively writing a script and then selling it (a 'spec'). Development is a distinct screenwriting experience because creative decisions have to be explicitly argued, detailed choices on the page verbally fought for, defended and explained. These vigorous debates over exact choice of words – how often to remind us of something, how hard to hit a note – expose principles that belong to all screenwriting, some of which are discussed in this chapter.

This practitioner experience belongs to the branch of the industry making so-called 'execution-dependent' films: that is, films that will or will not make a profit based on what they are actually like to watch. Such films are now a minor revenue stream. Since the early 2000s, when ancillary revenues (primarily from computer games, but also from music, merchandise, amusement rides, theatre, and other kinds of remakes) began to outstrip theatrical receipts, most high-budget theatrically released films have been marketing events driving the exploitation of rights and content in as many other platforms, markets and media as possible: loss-leading investments in brand penetration. Opening weekend theatrical grosses (income from out-of-home screenings) are designed to create 'eventhood', aimed less at this particular film's theatrical future than at the branching network of related revenue streams, and the future 'franchise'. A significant opening weekend – often the result of enforced block-booked screen space via extortionate deals with exhibitors – supports a film's wider multimedia rights 'world', even if audiences and critics reject this particular narrative instance of it. So box office charts are somewhat cheeky relics from a previous era when who actually showed up to see an individual film mattered. Most profits today depend not on the empirical effectiveness of individual films, but on ownership of channels of distribution, control of market share, and the monetising of intellectual property rights. This points to the first respect in which a screenplay is distinct from other kinds of creative written texts: it is never only bounded, defined by, or constituted in its own words. It is always also its adaptive potentials.

To write a screenplay is simultaneously to create *both* a text *and* a set of theoretical 'underlying rights', for which the protected (temporarily fixed words) of that particular draft act as a legal claim, or security. The reciprocal relationship between any full-draft screenplay and these underlying rights is an issue in law that is constantly arbitrated. The relevant union (in my case, the Writers Guild of America) offers fellow writers who are full members to determine exactly where, when, and by whom a particular character or set of characters, sequence of events, beginning, middle and end, or quality of climax came into sufficient being to be available to ownership. Sometimes, but not always, this is called 'story' and is separately contracted and credited. This characteristic status of screenplays as more than their present literal instance or current fixed form – as a putative set of as yet unrealized potentials – has a huge impact not only on the kinds of scripts that get written and made but also on the way they are written. It deepens on the sense of contingency, liveness and suggestion that belongs already to screenplays as changeable 'blueprints' for a final product. Even in its finest, published, Oscar-winning form, screenwriting still exists in the propositional, proleptic mode of an instance; it has the existential status of 'the draft'.

An expanded notion of 'writing'

Screenwriting is neither the only, nor the final, form of writing that gives rise to a 'film'. It is part of a constant, uninterrupted multi-stage creative process that involves written language in a variety of degrees of summary. Directing, cinematography, acting, editing and test screenings of first cuts are all crucial moments when films are written. The distinction between writing and rewriting disappears. Test screenings of the first cut of a finished film can be a crucial 'writing' moment: in response sometimes half a film might be re-shot, or endings completely changed. I was in the audience for a test screening for Fox Searchlight's 1997 British comedy *The Full Monty* (written by Simon Beaufoy), which the Searchlight executives wanted substantially re-shot because they did not find the first cut funny. They were astonished when the invited audience of Writers Guild of America and perhaps crucially BAFTA members roared with laughter and gave the film positive scores. The version of the film released was almost unchanged from the version shown that night, and it was later nominated for an Academy Award.

Various 'others' who intervene to shape films are effectively 'writers' too, in a way not true of theatre, novels or poetry. Gatekeepers exist at every stage, often imposing personal wishes with a heavy hand: the anticipation of such pressures frames a screenplay before a word is written, and after the screenplay is finished. For talent themselves (whether writer, director, actor or producer) to have any degree of creative control, they need personal leverage based on past successes. As Kevin West described Danny Boyle's battle to use Hindi-speaking actors in *Slumdog Millionaire* with Warner Independent:

> Although Boyle had raised money on the basis of an English-language script, he told his producers... that he wanted to film the children's scenes in Hindi. Boyle admits the idea must have struck them as crazy, but because only $13 million was at stake *he had just enough personal leverage* [author's italics] to squeak the major changes past the moneymen. 'I've had a couple of hits,' Boyle says with the good cheer of a director looking at his next. 'They gritted their teeth and went, "Okay".' (West 2009)

Films are 'greenlit' (approved for production) based on precedent. The 'breakthrough' moment for the likes of a Beaufoy or Boyle is to start a new line of precedent, to sneak a 'first' unexpectedly successful creatively-controlled film past the gatekeepers to create their own personal leverage. Films are often discussed in terms of oppositions such as business versus art, or studio versus independent: for me as a screenwriter, the key distinction that meaningfully separates types of films is whether they seek to satisfy or buck the constraints of pre-existing expectations. In other words, whether or not they are trying to do the most difficult, but also most rewarding and politically-important thing in a risk-averse industry driven by precedent: deliver an audience experience not already prefigured. A film's identity is a function of its relationship to its contexts of expectation.

Audiences: The screenplay as time-specific address

In contrast to commercial principles elsewhere, the film industry is driven by tradition. Perceptions about audiences are constantly analysed based on past films. This is another respect in which a screenplay not only consists of its words: a film – or a script – *is* the audiences it implies. A point about the industry often popularly misunderstood is that these audiences are by definition always *mixed*. In the film industry, discussion is less of texts per se, than of their potential to appeal in different ways to different audiences. Producers will always want their films to appeal to more than one audience: a priority in the case of adaptations of literature or history. An adapted screenplay simultaneously addresses at least two very different audiences: those who know the original material and those who do not. The former will enjoy the way the material is being reread/rewritten (to 'adapt' is to do both at once, in public); the latter will need the adaptation to work like an original film, containing within it all the information needed to understand and enjoy it. The trick is to make the new creation equally enjoyable for both. The culminating self-referential scenes in Greta Gerwig's *Little Women* (2020) deftly allude to this challenge. If, as in this film, the work being adapted also belongs to a distant time or place, different levels of audience knowledge about its wider historical context become a further consideration. Many different types and levels of assumed knowledge might need to be catered for in a single film.

Mass audiences, then, should not be seen as homogenous unities with the *same* capacities to appreciate, enjoy, recognize or understand. Rather, they are artful aggregates and odd bedfellows: unlikely combinations of constituencies. A screenplay inscribes these different audiences, each with different degrees of priority, through its choice of words, its pace, how explicit or obvious it makes things, and how much it invites the audience to observe for themselves rather than 'telling' them the point: in short, through the way it reflects, expresses and contests sets of expectations about cinematic style, narrative and generic context. An example of this is the subtle difference between two Jane Austen film adaptations made in the same year (1995) using similar UK talent (even some of the same below-the-line talent) and with similar UK locations: but with subtly different audience priorities. The primary target audience for *Sense and Sensibility* (1995) was the theatrical US 'Oscar prestige' market, with UK broadcast as secondary; in contrast, *Persuasion* (1995) was aimed primarily at the UK audiences (*Screen Two*, for the BBC), with, if successful, a critic- and festival-led US theatrical release as a secondary target audience. Emma Thompson's screenplay for *Sense and Sensibility* was perfectly aimed at the US theatrical prestige market: its wry observations, realizations, twists and quips occur rhythmically one scene after another, reflecting the screenwriting axiom I was taught at UCLA film school of every beat being essential and moving the story forward. It is no surprise it won the Oscar for Best Adapted Screenplay. In contrast, Nick Dear's screenplay for *Persuasion* permits itself occasional detours and extended moments of reflection. For example, a dinner party scene (a setting US screenwriting teaching says to always avoid, like phone calls) continues for several minutes of thoughtful conversation, utterly realistic in the way it meanders seemingly with no hurry to get to the scene's 'point'; and ends not with a punch, beat or scenic objective, but an afterthought, a tangential observation by Fiona Shaw (as Mrs Croft) about the curtailed nature of women's lives – an incidental detail that delivers the felt texture of the period as a whole, beyond this particular novel. Both films are consummately crafted, the result of detailed artistic deliberation across like-minded teams of writer, director, performers and editor: they differ because of the different relative priority of their primary and secondary target audiences – a difference that begins with the screenplay. Script changes in the assignments I was hired to write, even the choice of single words, were argued over in terms of the relative priority of different target audiences.

The erroneous idea that 'mass appeal' indicates mass sameness perhaps derives from seeing audiences for film and television like the consumers of material products. But films are not made speculatively, that is, in the hope they will find an audience who might like them enough to buy them: they are made responsively, in the light of what already has proven traction in the marketplace. Audiences precede, rather than follow, the act of creation: entertainment programmes deal pre-eminently in 'recognition capital' they themselves create (Foster, forthcoming). This circularity is key to understanding screenwriting. For while there is no act of cultural creation that is not to some degree driven by perceptions about existing audience expectations, screenwriting's meanings are made out of collective expectations as its primary *material*. Audience expectations, not only words, are screenwriting's substance, its matter, coded in the above-all traditional contexts in which films are green-lit and consumed. A screenplay is a calculated act of address, on both a macro and a micro level, whether its actual audiences correspond to these imagined targets or not. It produces as well as reflects a particular public – and must do so coherently to be successful for *actual* audiences of any kind. This seems to me well understood by artists and audiences in practice: part of the appeal of deliberately 'viewing together' today (however technically achieved) is often the extent to which actual audiences take a perverse or parodic pleasure in their role as *not* the intended audience for a film, but rather as unintended or uninscribed viewers.

These dynamics of protended audiences belong to some extent to all literature: all writing implicitly declares 'who it is for' to some extent through the language in which it is written. But perceptions of audiences are a determining logic in screenwriting. Words in screenplays are changed based on what someone – often a team of people – believes different audiences will or will not be able to 'get'. For example, ten minutes was spent in a development meeting arguing about the date of the slugline on the first page of my screenplay for Sebastian Faulk's *Birdsong*. Despite an image of a cyclist riding over the bridge of a peaceful river past a sign saying 'The Somme', the US producer wanted the date '1914' to be included on screen to prompt US audiences to recognize the imminence of the First World War. The UK producers thought it should be 1910, the same as in the novel. The producer who divided his time between Los Angeles and London got the team to agree to 1912, as a compromise. It was often my job as a writer for hire to preserve the coherence and consistency of the film in the midst of such disputes. Because it engages so specifically with audiences, a screenplay also engages with a specific moment in time. As such, films are valuable historical evidence of highly located perceptions about certain audiences' assumed knowledge and cultural values: a 'snapshot' of a zeitgeist less marked in other types of writing (fiction, drama, poetry) that are freer to address *both* their moment *and* an ongoing, unknown future reception.

The audience-centred nature of screenwriting makes its art a kind of dance with predictability. Predictability is characteristic of the kind of big-budget films John Logan is often hired to write: a punch(line) is regularly delivered, preferably more than one per page (i.e. per minute). In this word-association dialogue from *Skyfall* (2012), predictability is literally the game:

> **BOND**
> Swim.
> **DOCTOR HALL**
> Moonlight
> **BOND**
> Dance.
> **DOCTOR HALL**
> Murder.
> **BOND**
> . . . Employment.
> **DOCTOR HALL**
> Country
> **BOND**
> England.
> **DOCTOR HALL**
> . . . Skyfall
> Bond stops.
> His eyes freeze over. He does not respond.

> BOND
> <u>Skyfall</u>.
> DOCTOR HALL
> Done.

He stands. And walks out.

Behind the mirror:

> MALLORY
> This is going well.

Here, Logan's signature ping-pong dialogue, with its laconic smash ('Done') and baseline pick up of sarcastic commentary ('This is going well'), is explicitly about audience expectations: self-referential wit apposite in a revived franchise like the Bond films. All film genres depend on such anticipatory processes, suspense films overtly so. We never only look *at* a motion picture: we are always also in it.

Other films seek to unfold by defying generic expectations, instead of creating their own sets of narrative expectations internally, within themselves, as stories well told. The first few seconds of a screenplay will tell you whether a film belongs to the former or latter group. Take the opening lines of Tom McCarthy's *Win Win* (2011), for example:

> **EXT. WATCHUNG RESERVATION – DAWN**
>
> It's a bitter cold January morning. The woods are quiet. Desolate. In the far off distance a man is jogging. He banks around the end of a small pond and runs right at us. This is **MIKE FLAHERTY, FORTY-TWO**. He is running hard. Or at least as hard as he can.
>
> Suddenly **TWO JOGGERS** blow past him.

A man is running, is running to get fit, is running to get fit with difficulty, is overtaken by 'real' runners: the verb 'blow', positioned at the end of this sequence as a mini-culmination, underwritten by the flicker of hope in the wry 'at least', has the conclusive quality of an epitome. A lot of work is done by this monosyllable: it gives the impression of the runners' wind-creating wake, suggesting that this is something Mike himself experiences; it very slightly takes us by surprise (it's not 'run') in the way that Mike is taken by surprise, performing the realization prompted by the previous images for him as for us; and thereby acknowledges (while trying not to admit) failure. The basic idea of this opening – someone making themselves jog, although they find it hard and are no good at it – is itself metonymic for a whole life, as would be expected in this programmatic position. But it is also programming the reader/viewer to draw their own conclusions, to view interpretatively and above all to attend to detail as significant. Unpredictable, it sets up an invitation to observe and deduce as the basic relationship between screenwriter and audience, acknowledging this relationship with tone: the wry 'at least'.

Affect: The screenplay as empirical experience

You can't analyze [a film]. It's not an intellectual art form, really. It's an emotional art form . . . [and] if you start dissecting it, you start doing things for the wrong reasons, rather than [trusting] that first impression.

Eastwood, 2011: 20

The primary goal of all screenwriting is experience in the receiver. As with musical composition, the purpose of the words on the page is the orchestration of specific, intended emotion. As musicologist Daniel Leech-Wilkinson says, music itself doesn't exist, it happens: *to* somebody. This instrumentality is a further respect in which screenwriting doesn't only consist in its written words. It is a performative, empirical phenomenon, attempting to replicate for its reader what they would emotionally experience while watching the film play out second by second. This affective purpose makes the screenwriter a paradoxical figure: temporarily making all the detailed creative decisions of director, actor, editor, composer and production designer, in order to attract those collaborators who will then change those same carefully imagined details.

Screenwriting is thus a kind of anti-writing: writing that succeeds by writing itself out of the game, and by avoiding attracting attention to itself. Anything that distracts the reader from experiencing the moment as it unfolds in real time must be avoided. Shot descriptions, for example, are usually encoded in description: rather than 'CLOSE UP', a screenplay might describe motes of dust stirred in the air from the tip of a fine brush, for example; or instead of 'WIDE SHOT', describe a helicopter as a tiny insect above a sea of green. Not only can there be no beautiful, striking, complex or abstract language, but verbal economy – the degree of generality used – is also crucial, because the *time* to read and understand must match the speed with which we would take things in on the screen. So not saying things is as important as saying them. A screenplay must be read through, to time, in a single sitting, and should take as long to read as the film to watch: about a page a minute is the rule of thumb. Otherwise it is impossible to tell if a tiny detail set up earlier is successfully recalled later, or if enough 'nails in the coffin' have been laid for a climactic moment to work. A screenplay's connections, timings, builds, set-ups and pay-offs are its mechanism of emotional delivery.

As the film critic Roger Ebert has stated,

> When we watch a film, the director is essentially standing behind us and saying, 'Look here', and 'Look there', 'Hear this', and 'Hear that', and 'Feel this', and 'Feel the way I want you to feel'. And we give up conscious control over our intelligence. We become voyeurs. We become people who are absorbed into the story, if the story is working. And it's an emotional experience. (Renée 2013: np)

Like music, film creates emotion by notes being played longer or shorter, harder or softer, and by their organization into patterns, builds, crescendos and interludes in which duration and sequence itself delivers meaning. To me, as a screenwriter for hire, the vocabulary of 'watching' or 'viewing' seems too passive, a reversal of the situation, in which filmmakers or the film are doing something *to* audiences: making them see, think, feel, realize. Myriad choices that deliberately and constantly direct the audience's attention are encoded in every second of screen time. When parts of films are discussed in excerpt, abstractly, or out of their original context, this understanding of films as characteristically affective instruments is sometimes forgotten: an affect that has as much to do with duration, sequence and set-up as it has to do with image.

Duration: The screenplay as a sequence of prompts of varying emphasis

While the medium of a screenplay is language, this relationship to duration-based emphasis – to time and timing – means its art lies less in the words themselves, than in the textures of emphasis they perform. Traditionally, film studies has viewed its subject matter as a medium, and as one defined by the image. This is understandable in a discipline that emerged in the 1960s in contradistinction to both literature and theatre. But the meaning of a cinematic image, like that of a musical note or phrase, is a function of exactly when, and for how long, we get to look at it. The time-limiting of images determines their significance; duration (both short and long) controls focal point as much as than depth of field or colour. It is the brevity with which Romeo glimpses Juliet's red dress, momentarily in sharp focus, that makes it powerful in Zeffirelli's 1968 *Romeo and Juliet*; as it is the length of time we are given to dwell on the child who stands out for their red coat in Spielberg's 1993 *Schindler's List*.

Control of emphasis belongs to all writing: but in screenwriting it becomes fundamental, because film, as a visual medium, cannot *not* represent. The words of a screenplay cannot *not* take a point of view, cannot *not* frame, each and every second.

In film, everything has to be chosen and specified – from the colour of a hat, to whether a telegraph pole should be included in the background or the frame shifted slightly to avoid it: the job of the director (and the screenwriter before them) is to make those choices actively, and purposefully. Every image, whether moving or still, is loaded for significance. This may seem an obvious point, but it is a crucial one, because film is not an art form that invites contemplation of its many levels of interpretation *at our leisure*: each unit of information moves the story forward in a continuous present moment, without time to stop and consider things from a different angle, or to reflect. It is not up to the audience to read or view a film: it is interpreted for them already.

This embedded interpretation, or loading for significance, can be seen as the content of screenwriting. It is what emphasis conveys *beyond* the surface of the words or the image. In this, duration is key. The main thing that gets adjusted as a screenplay becomes more and more polished is the blank space on the page: carriage returns, line spaces, full stops versus commas and parentheses are all used to control exactly how long the screenwriter gives the reader to make a connection, or for a beat to sink in.

Timing dominates the art form in part because a film is experienced in one sitting and in one direction: forwards. This linearity conditions the particular relationship to audience of screenwriting compared to other durational and embodied arts. What we are meant to notice and how much significance to attach to it has to be clear immediately, moment by moment. This is why screenwriting cannot be seen as only characteristically visual. The time-limiting of images is a structure of attention, a phrase Zoe Svendsen, Lecturer in English at the University of Cambridge, uses in her theorising of dramaturgy (Svendsen forthcoming). Sometimes a screenplay cannot 'afford' time for a necessary visual detail, and another moment must be found where it can be layered in. In each successive moment, if the focus of audience engagement is not clear, a reader/viewer might worry they have missed something, or cease to feel addressed, and be taken out of the experience.

A screenplay proceeds, then, by constantly modulating the precise degree of generality in language, and the corresponding amount of time we are given to notice something. A second more or less time held on a reaction shot, for example, can cause a diametrically opposite meaning. Say a husband and wife face each other in a restaurant; she is crying, he doesn't know why: a second longer on his bewildered face makes him appear thoughtful and concerned, the one in the right, and the problem lying with her; by contrast, if there is a quick cut to his bewildered face, the same expression can make him seem in the wrong, as if he doesn't understand. Screenplays are peppered with such looks, glances and cutaways to articulate such differences. The need to hold attention or let something occur to the audience created the screenplay convention to simply say 'beat'. Such calibrations of time guide the texture of emphasis in every script. A screenplay can be defined as a sequence of prompts which different audiences will or will not 'get' according to the emphasis placed upon them.

Conclusion: Screenwriting as a model for the performativity of all writing

People have forgotten how to tell stories today – they don't have an ending. They have a beginning that keeps on being a beginning.
Attr. Steven Spielberg – per Emily Caston

Screenwriting brings certain dynamics that belong to all written texts to the fore. The reciprocal, tradition-beholden and mutually-originary relationship between writing and audiences reminds us that all art is by definition a form of implicitly public statement, an act of communication between people (both imagined and actual) that performs their presence in its moment, both intentionally and not. This repositioning of writing as human interaction, rather than the creation of an object, has particular relevance in a digital era.

One of the aspects of character-driven narrative screenplays that has been most transformed by a digital, global environment is the centrality of time and timing that I have just described. The linearity, sequence and duration that characterized the art form as I practised it made 'the end' (in both senses) primary. But none of this matters as much if films are expected to be consumed in excerpt, piecemeal, in any order, and any number of times. Previously, films were out-of-home social events that were time-specific and scarce, and captive audiences could be expected to allow two hours to build towards a pay-off that would satisfyingly make sense of all that came before. Today, a recognizable set-piece, moment or character that can be excerpted, shared and made into a meme might be more important. The previous primacy of narrative structure – the modulation of emphasis and choice of sequence in *storytelling* – has given way to content worlds: characters, situations and relationships that can extend across multiple outings without closure, and do not depend on a particular sequence of detailed revelation.

In the late 2000s, many celebrated the transformation from what Lawrence Lessig called a 'read-only' culture to 'read-write' culture , as end-user-driven content creation of all kinds – interactive, immersive, virtually real, etc. – was in the ascendant (Lessig 2008). In 2006 Henry Jenkins coined the term 'convergence culture', to describe a digitally enabled intermediality that Frank Rose would five years later hail as a 'trans-media multi-verse' in which 'integral elements of a fiction [are] dispersed systematically across multiple delivery channels for the purpose of creating a unified and coordinated entertainment experience' (see Jenkins 2006 and Rose 2011). Rose and others anticipated an expansion of the power of storytelling through this transmedia revolution. But cautionary voices that then warned about a possible dystopic digitally-driven future – such as media theorist and producer Emily Caston, and novelist Jennifer Egan (2011) – have been proved right. The transmedia age has not seen film become the 'anchor medium' for 'deeper media' that increases the transporting power of narrative by giving 'additive comprehension', as Rose predicted (Jenkins 2006: 123). On the contrary, the desire to exploit rights in concepts and characters in as many media and platforms as possible has given rise to an idea of 'story' as a never-ending expandable medium whose business logic is to avoid an 'end'.

But a narrative without an end is also a narrative without a located storytelling point of view – de-emphasizing the human makers and audiences inscribed in and experienced through the work. The decentralized authorship co-determined by end-users offered by a transmedia environment is driven by a generalized recognizability. This is a very different relationship to audience than narrative films that seek to take audiences into new territory or show them something they didn't previously know. Transmedia, multimedia, franchising and on-demand consumption all give the *impression* of increased participation – as if it is all created for 'you', not 'us' – without delivering actual power. The ability to register a like or dislike is not tantamount to agency; nor is the ability to interactively influence what 'happens' in the event of a still highly prefigured plot. Multiplatform or franchisable content also appears to be produced with more audience-centredness than ever before, but this represents a move towards audience 'training' (in current industry parlance) rather than audience satisfaction. Both promise a chimerical empowerment that distracts attention from the limited degree of control of user experience on offer – a user experience that can be seen as far narrower, in fact, than the offer of open and various interpretation (reading, in the widest sense) made by a fixed work of art.

A character-driven narrative film would now run markedly against the grain of the current entertainment business environment, in which content-providers and advertising companies have largely merged. This is not an environment designed to deliver carefully curated experiences given by one set of persons to another, or new experiences *not* based on existing audience knowledge, experience or expectations. As Ross Berger has shown, computer games can't be emotional experiences for reasons intrinsic to the constraints of their medium (Berger 2020: 80–2). In this sense, while written, games are not literary. If screenwriting raises productive questions about the criteria of literature and the literary, it is in its characteristic focus on the deliberate, constant and detailed control of attention it literarily captures: the primacy, in storytelling, of *how* the story is told, not *what* the story is about. This direct link between human beings communicating with each other – a dance with expectations – has been replaced with a deracinated recognizability that operates as its own value or currency.

If a 'film' in such a data-driven environment – now seemingly infinitely reproducible, searchable, excerptable and shareable – is no longer a social event, time-specific and scarce, and, crucially, no longer a linear, durational 'experience', we might usefully reconsider the category of 'film' as defined not by its medium – what *isn't* visual, now? – but by its contexts of exhibition: a certain set of social and cultural conditions of reception. In this case, a 'film' might be understood as whatever happens in a movie theatre; or, if accessed online, whatever has an emotional effectiveness that depends on having an end (in both senses). In both cases, control of emphasis, sequence, duration and the arcs and crescendos they build – in other words, the art with which narrative expectations are played with – would still be important. So understood, 'film' would continue to imply and address particular audiences, and thus remain a political phenomenon, in the widest sense.

Certainly, in an era of algorithmic social control, the ability of a narrative to subvert its given frame of expectations has political implications. A screenplay, insofar as it is an opportunity to show audiences something that an algorithm didn't suggest, that they didn't know existed, and didn't search for, illuminates the political importance (in the widest sense) of all self-consciously public forms of storytelling. Playing with expectations in order to reveal them, directing attention to intended audiences, and making transparent instrumental emotional purposes, are important literary skills to unpack, and to model.

Note

1   Much of the talent involved in that bracket in the 1990s and early 2000s has relocated to subscriber-based global streaming services in the last few years, often called 'television' and created as miniseries, where creative control for above-the-line talent and the so-called originals are still highly valued in the economic equation.

References

Berger, R. (2020), *Dramatic Storytelling and Narrative Design: A Writer's Guide to Dramatic Storytelling and Transmedia*, Florida: Taylor and Francis.

Eastwood, C. (2011), 'A Conversation between Clint Eastwood and Dustin Lance Blank', conducted by Richard Stayton, *Written By: The Magazine of the Writers Guild of America*, November/December 2011.

Egan, J. (2011), *A Visit From the Goon Squad*, New York: Alfred A. Knopf.

Foster, Clare L. E. (forthcoming), *Recognition Capital*, Publisher in negotiation.

Jenkins, H. (2006), *Convergence Culture: Where Old and New Media Collide*, New York: New York University Press.

Lessig, L. (2008), *Remix: Making Art and Commerce Thrive in the Hybrid Economy*, London: Bloomsbury.

Persuasion (1995), [Film] Dir. Roger Michell, UK: BBC.

Renée, V. (2013), 'Roger Ebert on the Nature of Film: "A Movie is Not a Logical Art Form"', *No Film School*, 07 July. Available online: https://nofilmschool.com/2013/07/roger-ebert-movie-not-a-logical-art-form (accessed on 01 April 2020).

Rose, F. (2011), *The Art of Immersion: How the Digital Generation Is Remaking Hollywood, Madison Avenue and the Way We Tell Stories: Entertainment in a Connected World*, New York: W. W. Norton.

Sense and Sensibility (1995), [Film] Dir. Ang Lee, US: Columbia Pictures et al.
Svendsen, Z. (forthcoming), *Theatre & Dramaturgy*, London: Palgrave Macmillan.
West, K. (2009), 'Independent Spirits', *W Magazine*, 01 February. Available online: https://www.wmagazine.com/story/indie-directors/ (accessed 01 April 2020).

10

Mapping Andrei Tarkovsky's *Stalker*
An architectural exploration of the 'Zone'

Stavros Alifragkis

Introduction

Andrei Tarkovsky's cinema of contemplation, rather than embarking on a quest for realism or faithful reconstructions of physical spaces or historical events, constitutes a search for faith in humankind and requires of its audiences a corresponding leap of faith towards a Heideggerian *Gelassenheit* – a distancing from reality – which, according to Bird, translates into specific ethical action: 'a renewed belief in the potential for meaning in reality' (Bird 2004: 372–3). His movies can be construed as inner searches journeying towards self-discovery and awareness, whose dynamic and shifting landscapes reflect great profoundness and richness in an almost anthropomorphic manner; they are pulsating projections of tormented souls, as are most of Tarkovsky's protagonists.

Even in his historical/biographical movies, Tarkovsky appears to be less preoccupied with historical accuracy and the realistic representation of everyday life and more focused towards achieving a kind of poetic abstraction that generates the filmic ambience of mystagogy and spirituality that have been habitually associated with his artistic work, thus rendering his cinematic landscapes as extremely contemporary. In *Andrei Rublev* (1969 (1966)), for example, he utilizes history as an open-ended reference plane, which enables his personal, subjective, eclectic and extremely idiosyncratic cinematic narration to unwind, unobscured by the reality of early fifteenth-century Russia and the political complexities of his time. The cinematic landscapes that are generated in his creative interpretation of Russian iconographer Andrei Rublev's (Андрей Рублёв, *c*. 1365–1430) biography foster pockets of medieval quotidian life that evolve independently and somewhat unaware of Russia's religious and political contemporaneity. At the same time, they describe social micro-ecosystems that are extremely vulnerable to historical upheavals: a world that staggered between deep, genuine and sincere belief in a merciful god and demonic superstition. The coarse, whitewashed, vibrating walls of the church in Vladimir (Dormition Cathedral, twelfth century) that Rublev was commissioned to paint in 1408, the liturgical procession of rhythmical verticality in the beech forest where the builder's guild was ambushed, and the steep banks of clay or the textured pit where the casting of the new bell took place construct meaningful narrative spaces that underline the profoundness of his cinematic microcosmoses without anchoring them to specific locations. Tarkovsky plunges into Russian tradition to retrieve such universal elements as abstraction, elliptical narrative structure, symbolism and, occasionally, allegory, which elevate his work from a mere reconstruction of rural life to an experiential odyssey into the depths of the human soul. These filmic landscapes, dimmed in celestial mist or veiled behind finely woven curtains of rainfall, amplify the vagueness and abstraction of his storyworlds and force them to the periphery of realism, in a zone of undefined limits and limitations, where allegory, poetry and dream coexist in a state of creative agitation.

The aesthetic groundwork for this cinematic tradition may be traced back to the work of Eisenstein's (Сергей Эйзенштейн, 1898–1910) *Ivan the Terrible I and II* (Иван Грозный I, 1944 and Иван Грозный II, 1958) and was furthered in Parajanov's (Сергей Параджанов, 1924–90) *The Colour of Pomegranates* (Цвет граната, 1969), where historical events and biographical accounts have been effectively manipulated in a creative way to produce new, subjective but engaging stories and narrative expressive spaces (Nitsche et al. 2002). Rublev, Tsar Ivan IV (Иван Грозный, 1530–84) and Armenian poet and musician Sayat-Nova (Саят-Нова, 1712–95) are mere vessels, whose personal narratives construct subjective moving image portraits of different eras and corresponding sets of filmic landscapes that transcend their temporal and spatial connotations, thus becoming less localizable, free-floating constructs in space and time. Tarkovsky's landscapes seem to mimic the idiosyncratic behaviour of the Solarian 'plasmic ocean' (*Solaris*, 1972); mesmerizing in their mystical obscurity, bewildering in their continuous and resourceful formal rejuvenation, dense and impassable by the impertinent eye but crystal clear, friendly and accessible to the investigative gaze of the humble, such as the Stalker, the scouter, salvager and unaccredited guide to the Zone. Occasionally, they briefly assume the form of familiar environments, only to lure the outsiders deeper into their opaque, shifting and multilayered architectures. Solidifying temporarily their fluid constellations and gradually peeling each layer off for a telling instance, the Zone in *Stalker* (1979), loosely based on the 1971–2 science fiction novel Пикник на Обочине (*Roadside Picnic*) by the acclaimed Strugatsky brothers, Arkady (Аркадий Стругацкий, 1925–91) and Boris (Борис Стругацкий, 1933–2012), constitute the ambitious tasks tackled in the following sections.

This chapter puts forward a novel understanding of the Zone in *Stalker* that correlates different spatial categories – marked by spatio-temporal pleats – and Tarkovsky's itinerant camera – the choreographed procession through space – in an attempt to discuss his film poetics from a chiefly architectural point of view. Spatial categories – the Battlefield, the Dry Tunnel, the Meatgrinder, the Sand-dunes Shed and the Room that grants all wishes – and their corresponding spatial attributes describe a complex set of dynamic relations between natural, human-made and in-between cinematic environments. Drawing on architectural theories on space and placemaking, this chapter debates how Tarkovsky's disjointed film sets become meaningful narrative spaces as a monumental architecture of procession. The architectural mapping of the Zone introduced here, counterpointed by what lies beyond this mysterious fenced-off enclave, enables a better understanding of both the filmmaker's distinct screen language – mise en scène, mise en cadre and editing – and the construction of his personal and idiosyncratic filmic landscape. Finally, this analysis offers an alternative to the interpretation of the Zone as a post-apocalyptic industrial wasteland, one that waives its negative connotations and reverses the terms under which the Zone and its surrounding spaces are understood and decoded as a meaningful whole.

Locating the pro-filmic space

When it comes to reading cinematic spaces, the stress lies equally on the description of the actual three-dimensional elements of the natural or human-made terrain and their interrelation, as well as their continuously reassessed relation with the boundaries of the frame, the positioning of the protagonists and the space of the camera. Therefore, mise en scène and mise en cadre are two key elements utilized here to interpret the structure and the symbolic function of the filmic space of the Zone in *Stalker* (1979). Having said that, one should not dismiss the significance that lies in locating a suitable setting for the shoots. *Repérage* is a painstaking and time-consuming process that requires an experienced eye and presupposes a profound understanding of the place and its inner qualities. In the cinema of Tarkovsky, these locations are never mere backgrounds that strictly meet the prerequisites of the subject matter or film style.[1] Shooting locations for *Stalker* (1979) include the following: (i) a one-time distillery and mill south of the Tallinn's port (Rotermanni Kvartal, Rotermann Quarter), a nearby former power station (Kultuurikatel) and the adjacent Flora chemical works – which served as the natural sets for the Plague Quarter (Gamble 2019); (ii) both the abandoned Jägala-Joa hydropower plant on the river Jägala (Yagala) in Estonia and the nearby dam served as the background for the Battlefield and possibly the Dry Tunnel; (iii) the still-operating thermal power plant no. 20 on Вавилова (Vavilova) Street in the outskirts of Moscow, dominates the background of several shots (Bessmertny [1977] 2017), most memorably the one with the Stalker and his family walking back to their house; (iv) and the Мосфильм (Mosfilm) studios, at 1 Mosfilmovskaya street, Moscow, where the sets for the Stalker's house, the café-bar, the Meatgrinder, the Sand-dunes Shed and the Room were built. It is not possible to confirm other shooting locations mentioned in the relevant bibliography.

Tarkovsky's vast planes covered with lush vegetation have formulated the par excellence cinematic iconography of the great Soviet outdoors, although they were not the main focus of his movies. Furthermore, natural elements, such as the persistent presence of water (in the form of cleansing rainfall or purifying running streams) and mystical mist, recur in Tarkovsky's work and have contributed greatly to the articulation of a distinctive cinematic style that demonstrates eclectic affinities with the work of Greek filmmaker Angelopoulos (Θόδωρος Αγγελόπουλος, 1935–2012). One such analogy is the introduction of human-made spaces in the cinematic narration – mostly urban in the case of Angelopoulos, and rural in the case of Tarkovsky – that act as spatial, symbolic counterpoints to the varied representations of nature in their movies (Alifragkis 2017; Durgnat 1990: 46). Bird highlights the persistent presence of three distinct types of spaces in Tarkovsky's movies: nature, the fragile home/shelter and the shrine/cathedral with its vertical architectural elements (i.e. network of columns at regular intervals). Furthermore, he notes that these are often depicted in an agitated state of dynamic equilibrium, with nature invariably in the process of reclaiming human-made spaces (shelter and shrine), thus emphasizing our precarious presence in this world: '[n]ature is simply a flow that absorbs the human gaze, though sometimes it eerily seems to be returning it' (Bird 2008:

52–3). Tarkovsky appears to understand the natural-human-made environment diptych as a continuous but not uninterrupted flow, with architecture being the continuation of nature and with unexpected spatial folds, seams and framing regulating the transitions (Bird 2008: 54–5). One could maintain that the Zone in *Stalker* (1979), a visual fugue between natural and human-made landscapes that possess unique qualities, is the main driving force behind the development of the plot, as it constructs the narrative space within which the Stalker's story unfolds and acquires its essential meaning. However, the forest expanses near Tallinn, where parts of the movie were shot, bear no distinctive characteristics, as argued previously, other than loose references to what Norberg-Schulz terms as the archetypal 'romantic landscape' with reference to Central Europe and Scandinavia in particular (Norberg-Schulz 1979: 42–5), whose spatial ambiguities are resourcefully manipulated by Tarkovsky in order to stimulate the actions of his heroes. In this sense, the Zone in *Stalker* (1979) is a de-territorialized space generator that supplies the raw material for the myth via its architectural qualities. Furthermore, *Stalker* (1979) and *Solaris* (1972) mark a shift in Tarkovsky's value system, from an ethnocentric tradition, that is, Russophile and Christian Orthodox, towards a more global, humanitarian approach. This is probably why he refuses to 'geographically concretize' or localize many of the *topoi* that appear in these two movies (Deltcheva and Vlasov 1997: 539).

The choreography of the three-dimensional plateau

This research understands *Stalker* (1979) as a procession of visually distinct but interlinked natural, human-made and in-between settings that acquire their special meaning through movement in space. It could be the case that Tarkovsky's movie communicates with its audiences via what Le Corbusier (1887–1965) describes as a *promenade architecturale*, a potential reborrowing from the narrative arts and the Flaubertian *flâneur*, with reference to Villa Savoye (1929–30) in Poissy-sur-Seine, France: '[L'architecture arabe] s'apprécie "a la marche", avec le pied; c'est en marchant en se déplaçant que l'on voit se développer les ordonnances de l'architecture' (Le Corbusier and Jeanneret [1934] 1995: 24; see also Samuel 2010). Le Corbusier's architectural promenade contends that spaces become meaningful – or designers generate spatial meaning – through the construction of meticulously framed vistas and the careful manipulation of their succession for the travelling eye. This, however, implies that spatial meaning lies not only with the framed views per se but also with the visual *raccords*, the joints that stitch up the spatial experience or, alternatively, the Deleuzian fold (Deleuze 1993). Spatial folds are manifest throughout Tarkovsky's movie (Alifragkis, 2020). First, there exists the Heideggerian space of the boundary (see Heidegger [1950] 2002: 1–56), which mediates between the Zone and what lies beyond. Then, one has to acknowledge the subtle but unmistakable presence of multiple *plis* (pleats) inside the cinematic landscape of the Zone. These delineate the distinct spatial categories described in detail in the following text. Furthermore, according to Deleuze, the fold presupposes the unfold, 'the condition of its manifestation' (Deleuze 1993: 35–6) that regulates the enfilade of spatial categories inside the Zone. Contrary to what Le Corbusier professes, the latter reverberate the spatial qualities of the baroque architecture, insofar as the late baroque idiom is 'the art of planning each suite of rooms to meet the often conflicting requirements of display and comfort' (cited in el-Khoury 1996: 29). Deltcheva and Vlasov consider the introduction by Tarkovsky of dialectical opposites, for example, earthbound house *versus* space station, as the most prominent feature of the spatial organization of *Solaris* (1972). These perform two distinct functions: on a practical level they serve as visual counterpoints; and on a symbolic level they correspond to two Bakhtinian chronotopes, where the familiar and safe is juxtaposed against the alien and mysterious (Deltcheva and Vlasov 1997: 534). However, such crude binary oppositions as inside the Zone *versus* outside, indoors *versus* outdoors, human-made *versus* natural are rendered meaningless in the context of *Stalker*'s (1979) narrative universe. Many researchers point at the commonalities between settings that exist outside and inside the Zone, for example, the Stalker's house and the Room that grants all wishes share common architectural features (floor planks, textured walls, etc.), probably because both shoots took place at Mosfilm, Moscow (Dempsey 1981: 16; Johnson and Petrie 1994: 151). Similarly, many interiors are permeated by natural elements, such as rainfall and running water, while patches of built space in various degrees of decay speckle the movie's exterior shots. The boundary between inside and outside is porous, allowing for mutual recalibrations (Burns 2011: 114). The plot is dictated by a carefully choreographed succession of naturalized built environments, where nature reclaims human-made structures, and artificial landscapes, where machinery and factories – symptoms of the 'paleotechnic phase' of our technological development, according to Mumford (Mumford [1934] 1955: 151–211) – invade nature. These, for Bachelard, exist in a discursive opposition and not as demarcations of irreconcilable ontological categories (Bachelard 1994: 215). Such visual reconciliations can be witnessed in byzantine frescoes and icons, where the divine inhabits an abstract, metaphysical space with no physical or conceptual limits between earth and sky, interior and exterior, day and night (see della Dora 2016).

Despite the osmosis that develops through the various boundaries of the movie, certain Bakhtinian chronotopes (Bakhtin 1981: 84–258) emerge as distinct cinematic spaces, thus informing this cartographic expedition to the realm of *Stalker* (1979) with a series of observations about its dynamic geography. There exists, outside the Zone, a loosely defined area in visual terms that comprises the high-ceilinged, scarcely furnished, roomy but rundown flat or detached house, where the Stalker and his family live; the café-bar, where the Stalker meets up with the Professor and the Writer; and, finally, the Plague Quarter, a heavily guarded, cordoned-off, former industrial area that marks the beginning/end of the Zone. These settings can be imagined as arranged amphitheatrically around an unnamed port and traversed by bundles of intersecting rail lines, as if in a busy rail hub which is still in use to some extent, as the mesmerizing soundtrack by Russian composer Artemyev (Эдуард Артемьев, 1937) affirms to the viewer. The Zone itself consists of five distinct but interrelated spatial categories: the Battlefield, the Dry Tunnel, the Meatgrinder, the Sand-dunes Shed and, finally, the Room that grants all wishes, which is a tight arrangement of several rooms that include the anteroom, three side chapels and, finally, the Room. Each setting is separated by vague and shifting boundaries from the rest and represents different spatial qualities – that is, different extents of integration and, therefore, different degrees of complicity between human-made and natural elements. Thus, the overall narrative arc of the movie can be reconstructed as a well-planned staging of calculated transitions from the human-made environment represented in the movie's opening sequences, to the natural landscapes of the initial sequences inside the Zone, and back to the human-made spaces of the Room that marks the end of the quest for the three protagonists. This essentially amounts to a process of initiation in a capricious world with fluctuating ambience and physiology, whose intermediate stages arouse the senses by means of subtle spatial contrasts that echo the architectural mise en scène of the baroque.

Beyond the Zone

The Stalker begins his cinematic journey into the magical realm of the Zone in a nameless port; barges and boats inhabit the background of the shot that introduces the Writer. In the previous shot, the Stalker walks across a railyard; his solitary figure is portrayed against the blurred outlines of railway wagons immersed in the morning mist. Finally, the camera cuts to the interior of the port's café-bar, where the Stalker and the Writer meet the Professor, thus concluding the description of the cinematic spaces that exist beyond the Zone. The latter plays a rather significant role, since the journey inside the Zone is bookmarked by two scenes at the café-bar, where the protagonists stand in almost identical postures (Johnson and Petrie 1994: 151), as if they have never left the place. Tarkovsky's laconic cinematography establishes the micro-geography of a fictional terrain: house, railyard, port and café-bar, whose structural components do not occupy the same physical spaces – Mosfilm studio, Tallinn, Moscow (shot depicting the Stalker entering the café-bar) and Mosfilm studio once again. Through the use of shreds of topological evidence, Tarkovsky makes the scene difficult to localize, constructing seemingly seamless spaces by means of continuity of time and action – what Kuleshov outlined in his 1929 essay 'The Art of Cinema' as 'creative geography' (Levaco 1974: 41–124).

The narrative space of the movie describes a formerly active industrial area, populated by abandoned warehouses and factories and crisscrossed by railway lines that stretch out into the emptiness of a highly unwelcoming landscape, opposite to a heavily guarded strip of land that delineates the sealed-off Zone. This spatial arrangement situates the cinematic space that exists beyond the Zone in a privileged realm of spatial ambiguity and mystery that evokes the qualities of a Foucauldian heterotopia, a place that exists outside the routine of daily toil (Alifragkis, 2020; Faubion 1998: 178–9).

The Zone

Once inside the infamous Zone, Tarkovsky constructs a cinematic terrain that defies the laws of physics without resorting to the use of visual effects; traditional storytelling techniques – such as continuity editing, cinematography and sound design – are the only tools utilized for the filmic construction of the oneiric, otherworldly viewing experience of *Stalker* (1979) (Alaniz 2013: 206–7). According to the script, nothing remains dormant once an intruder upsets the equilibrium of the Zone's sensitive ecosystem. When the locomotion dies away, the system settles in a new but equally fragile state of balance, by assimilating the causes of the original disturbance. This is only temporary though, until a new intrusion triggers off bewildering formative processes anew. This makes the Zone a potentially perilous environment for those who are not familiar with the rituals of crossing, such as the Professor and the Writer. The Zone describes a dynamic and adaptive system, whose constantly repositioned structural components, described in more detail in the following text, and their potential for mobility and multiplicity amplifies its mystical vagueness. The ceaselessly escalating entropy of the system results in spontaneous, unpredictable and possibly fatal (according to the Stalker) eruptions of activity. However, the mechanics behind these unnatural activities remain obscure, thus adding to the Zone's significance as a place of myth and ritual. Tarkovsky's *Stalker* (1979) presents us with a temporary crystallization of an extremely fragile and unstable environment, whose erratic behaviour becomes tangible in spatial terms through the singular experience of the Stalker and his two companions, the Professor and the Writer. This research maps one such configuration of the Zone's fluid geography, whose spatial characteristics follow the whims of an inner metabolism that lies beyond human grasp.

The Battlefield

The Stalker warns his companions that any deviation from the prescribed itinerary can become fatal. However, this itinerary is far from fixed; the guide scans the terrain for familiar signs each time he re-enters the Zone. The setting for this, the first spatial category of the Zone, is a former battlefield that still bears the marks of former heavy warfare. This takes place immediately after the memorable sequence with the handcar that marks the ritualistic crossing of the space of the boundary that demarcates the Zone. Once inside the Zone, landmarks, districts, edges, nodes and makeshift pathways, the Lynchian syntax of place imageability (Lynch 1960: 46–90), are in constant movement. What was safe before can become dangerous now. The Stalker trusts nothing but his acute senses, as if crossing an active landmine. Time and again he remains still, sensing the air for potential traps, trying to read his way through the landscape. A light breeze drifting through the dark forest, the lazy flow of the stream, the soft sound of raindrops on thirsty leaves, sunrays making their way through the lush vegetation or the way the grass yields to the weight of his stride become the Stalker's roadmap. A slope points to a possible direction, a clearing in the woods becomes a potential place for rest and a winding riverbank wants to become a route. The Stalker senses the configuration of the landscape and translates the energy that flows underneath the skin of the relief in order to navigate safely towards the Room. He drifts in the currents, the flows of which are as unstable and unpredictable as the powers that generate them are obscure. The parallel between the Stalker's rituals of walking and psychogeography is rather obvious, where data concerning both the physical aspects and the psychology of a place – its special character and nature – are embedded within the place itself and are continuously decoded by the itinerant observer (see Debord 1958a: 15–20). Although the destination of the journey is fixed – the Room – the itinerary changes significantly each time the Stalker enters the Zone, thus making the case for a cinematic, situationist, non-urban *dérive* (Debord 1958b: 11–14). The open-ended playground for this is the natural landscape of the Battlefield, which is nevertheless spotted with rusting pieces of machinery, military equipment and concrete blocks, brought specifically from Moscow (Bessmertny [1977] 2017). Towards the end of the sequence, the dilapidated Jägala-Joa hydropower plant dominates the background, marking one of the many interior pleats of the Zone, where condensed space and time mediate between different spatial categories.

The Dry Tunnel

The narrative space of the Dry Tunnel at the beginning of the second part of the movie – a somewhat ironic reference to a low waterfall depicted in the sequence with the 'looping incident'[2] – constitutes the second spatial category of the Zone. Here, Tarkovsky's elliptical narration functions in a most effective way, with an outstanding economy of expressive means. The sequence of the looping incident roughly comprises four long-take shots, which are typical of Tarkovsky's cinematic style (Martin 2005: 152), interrupted by three extra-diegetic cutaways, with only one of them posing as a possible point of view shot, the wide shot of a rough Yagala River immersed in the mist. The first and last clips of the sequence were shot at the same location, thus completing the 360-degree turn of the protagonists. The deteriorating background belongs presumably to a larger failing structure, whose former use cannot be identified. A minor detail – the check-patterned tiles on the walls and floors – becomes a noticeable feature, since these tiles reappear in several instances. There is great ambiguity about the nature of this space. Is this the interior or the exterior of a formerly functional building?

Tarkovsky's tight framing excludes valuable spatial information from the shot, thus constructing an extremely fragmented narrative space. Gradually the architecture becomes completely baffling; what appears to be an obsolete and out-of-use hydroelectric power station has been decontextualized via abstraction and disorientation, what Shklovsky describes as *остранение* (defamiliarization) (Shklovsky [1917] 1988: 16–30). Yet the camera lingers long enough to suggest that this unintelligible architecture has a unique relationship to the surrounding all-engulfing nature, characterized by a precarious co-habitation rather than a gradual disintegration of the former into the latter. This living ruin becomes much more meaningful in the spatial continuum of the abovementioned Corbusian *promenade architecturale* that sets off from the natural landscape of the Battlefield and culminates in the tightly built, artificial environment of the Room. The following sequence, where the company briefly rests, takes place at the bottom of an artificial canal that scars the face of the earth but also generates precious power by channelling water in the penstock of the nearby plant, thus marking yet another uneasy coexistence between our technological civilization and nature. This echoes, to a certain extent, what Barham describes as an 'antimodernist, antitechnological rhetoric' in Tarkovsky's *Запечатлённое Время* (*Sculpting in Time*, 1986), which also infused his movie *Solaris* (1972), based on Lem's (Stanisław Lem, 1921–2006) same-name novel (1961), where 'a series of structuralist binary oppositions prioritize nature over science, art over technology, irrationality over logic, old over new, spirituality over materialism'. The mystifying, enigmatic, dreamlike atmosphere of the movie – a nostalgic, metaphorical quest for truth and harmony – propels the narration forward and transforms a typical science fiction trope, such as space travel, to a psychological investigation into the labyrinths of memory, loss and nostalgia 'for the earth and for the "ordinariness" of home' (Barham 2008: 265-6).

The Meatgrinder, the Sand-dunes Shed and the Room

Towards the end of their journey, the company reaches the notorious Meatgrinder, the most perilous part of the route and one of the many halls that precede their destination, the Room. This marks the beginning of an architecture of procession: a long, climactic scene that takes place in three distinctive places, a narrow, curbed tube that looks like a sewage pipe and leads to a small water tank, a vast shed whose floor is covered with sand dunes, and the final room where the journey ends.

In the last sequence inside the Zone, Tarkovsky transforms the disjunctive architecture of an industrial carcass into a church (Bird 2008: 68–9). Much of the action is contained in the anteroom and the three adjoining side chapels, a telephone booth, a short flight of stairs that leads to a planked off doorway and, finally, a puzzling crypt, where the remains of a couple rest. At the end of the sequence, where the Professor disarms his bomb, the camera cuts into the interior of the Room and recedes with a slow travelling shot, gradually revealing the familiar check-patterned tiles on the semi-submerged floor and the protagonists, who remain silent on the other side of the *iconostas* – the icon screen that separates the sanctuary from the rest of the church – in the nave, veiled by purifying rainfall. The point of view of the camera becomes a sanctified gaze that, nevertheless, does not reveal the contents of the sacred Room. Thus, the Room, where all wishes are granted, becomes the sanctuary, where the altar, the holy table that in the novel is a golden ball, lies. For Deltcheva and Vlasov the divine is present at the heart of the Zone, inside the Room, which establishes 'a clear-cut borderline between the divine and the earthly world' (Deltcheva and Vlasov 1997: 546). The Room is restricted to the clergy or, as the Stalker informs us, to those who are desperate. The rest, those who are not pure, remain in the anteroom, watching the ceremonial process through the royal doors, the main, axial opening in the *iconostas*. This frame within a frame is the penultimate shot inside the mysterious Zone. Natural elements, such as daylight and rainfall, find a way to perforate the enclosure of this artificial terrain, making it less tight and isolated from the encompassing nature. Efird describes the typically Tarkovskyan architectural setting as 'a dilapidated structure in the process of reconstruction or disintegration, open to the elements and filled with pools of water flashing reflected light on the walls' (Efird 2014: 248). Once again, the outside becomes a structural element of the inside, reminding us the Corbusian maxim 'le dehors est toujours un dedans' (the exterior is always an interior) (Le Corbusier [1923] 1958: 154–60).

In lieu of conclusions: Framing the landscape

The five spatial categories of the Zone described earlier – the Battlefield, the Dry Tunnel, the Meatgrinder, the Sand-dunes Shed and, finally, the Room with its accompanying spaces – can be construed as self-contained and self-sufficient filmic places. They correspond, after all, not only to specific sequences but also to distinct landscapes that exist independently and appear to occupy different physical locations. It never becomes clear how we move from one to another. Even within each sequence, moving across different settings becomes problematic, since there is rarely enough spatial information to facilitate the accurate reconstruction of the set and the camera's itinerary (Johnson and Petrie 1994: 152–3). Tarkovsky resorts to a drastic rearrangement of the physical elements of the landscape, a creative geography consisting of spaces from different locations that are stitched in a loose but nevertheless effective fashion, by virtue of continuity of action. Tarkovsky commented on the Strugatsky brothers' *Roadside Picnic*: 'It seemed to me that this novel could be made into a film with a unity of location, time, and action. This classic unity – Aristotelian in my view – permits us to approach truly authentic filmmaking' (interview with Guerra, in Gianvito 2006: 51).

Deleuze notes, with reference to the construction of cinematic space in Bresson's *Procès de Jeanne d'Arc* (1962), that his interior landscapes are fragmented, tightly framed and without any reference to their spatial coordinates (Deleuze 1997: 108–22). He argues that such spaces do not refer to specific environments; they become 'any-space-whatever'. Deleuze claims that any-space-whatever is not an 'abstract universal' but a 'singular space' that has lost its homogeneity, its qualities as a three-dimensional plane and the relations between its independent particles. As such, its parts can be rearranged and interlinked in numerous ways, without producing incoherent or inconsistent landscapes. Deleuze underlines the predominance of the medium shot in the construction of any-space-whatever and points to its 'spiritual affect'. This is very true about Tarkovsky's camerawork as well. His peripatetic camera follows the protagonists at a distance and usually from behind, revealing little more than fragmented views of the actual spaces they occupy. Even though he often resorts to the use of close-ups, medium shots propel the story forward.

Tarkovsky's cinematic promenades through the fluctuating landscapes of the Zone, which gradually evolve from mainly natural environments to enclosed yet penetrable spaces, are tightly framed. Tarkovsky uses wide shots purposefully. Most of them populate the initial sequences, when the company arrives to the Zone. There, the frame widens to capture the mesmerizing beauty of the graveyard, where rusty tanks and other military vehicles slowly decompose as silent witnesses to humankind's sins. As the story unfolds, wide shots gradually give way to medium shots and expressive close-ups. This coincides with the subtle transition from exterior, to in-between and, finally, interior spaces. Moreover, tighter framing provides greater flexibility over the manipulation of the movie's narrative spaces. The more Tarkovsky zooms-in to his subjects, the more selective his backgrounds grow, and the more elusive and mysterious their corresponding narrative spaces become. When the camera stubbornly refuses to reveal more, the frame becomes tangible in spatial terms. Off-screen space rivals on-screen space in a continuous fight over conceptual predominance. One can sense the tension generated by their friction along the limits of the frame. Tarkovsky's framing technique weaves a condensed landscape that acquires its meaning through the exclusions rather than the disclosures of the camera. Even with close-ups, action is never constrained to on-screen space. Actors often enter and exit the frame in a perpetual renewal of the mise en scène. In some cases, the protagonists exit the frame, only to magically reappear elsewhere in the same travelling shot.

Tarkovsky's settings for *Stalker* (1979) have very little in common, except maybe for being crumpling parts of the same dying structure in the narrative universe of *Stalker* (1979). However, their sublime beauty relies on the power of association triggered by the continuity of action. The calmness of the graveyard that welcomes the protagonists into the Zone, the in-flux geography of the interior/exterior spaces where the looping incident takes place, the ominous dimly lit sewage pipe, the impressive main hall with the sand dunes and the final temple-like arrangement of rooms with the mystical skylight are mere elaborate sets when treated as individual spaces. Only when considered as an orderly succession of locations, as processional architectural events in the sense that architect and theorist Tschumi introduced the term (Tschumi [1981] 1994: xix–xxviii), do they become not only legible as three-dimensional forms but also meaningful in narrative terms. Their subtle transitions become the crucial joints of a premeditated ceremonial succession of spaces, mediated by a series of consecutive thresholds, where the protagonists are persistently put to the test. In this sense, Tarkovsky constructs a monumental architecture that emphasizes the art of walking, not as the leisurely activity of the non-urban *flâneur*, but as an existential experience, that compares to the use of 'architecture as a means of narrative and emotion' in Libeskind's 1999 addition to the Jewish Museum in Berlin (Pavka 2010).

Notes

1. The aesthetics of post-industrial decay, rust and military debris in Stalker is accredited to three production designers: Alexander Boym, Shavkat Abdusalamov (Шавкат Абдусаламов, 1936/9) and, finally, Tarkovsky himself (Martin 2005: 157–8).
2. The Professor complains that he left his knapsack behind, because he was not aware they were moving forward. When the rest realize that the Professor lagged behind in order to fetch it, against the Stalker's warnings, it is too late to do anything, since 'nobody goes back the same way'. They keep on walking, only to find him resting at the same place they split up not so long ago. The Stalker collapses under the realization of their good fortune; obviously, they had fallen into one of the Zone's traps, but they miraculously escaped.

References

Alaniz, J. (2013), '([Post-] Soviet) Zone of Dystopia: Voronovich/Tkalenko's "Sterva"', *The Slavic and East European Journal*, 57 (2): 203–28.

Alifragkis, S. (2017), 'Constructing the Urban Cinematic Landscape: Theo Angelopoulos's Thessaloniki', in T. Kazakopoulou and M. Fotiou (eds), *Contemporary Greek Film Cultures from 1990 to the Present*, 37–69, Bern: Peter Lang.

Alifragkis, S. (2020), 'The Mythical Landscape of Andrei Tarkovsky: Notes on the Interpretation of Cinematic Space in Stalker', in A. Loukaki (ed.), *Urban Art and the City: Creating, Destroying, and Reclaiming the Sublime*, London: Routledge.

Andrei Rublev [Андрей Рублёв] ([1966] 1969), [Film] Dir Andrei Tarkovsky, USSR: Mosfilm.

Bachelard, G. (1994), *The Poetics of Space*, trans. M. Jolas, Boston: Beacon Press.

Bakhtin, M. M. (1981), *The Dialogic Imagination: Four Essays by M. M. Bakhtin*, ed. M. Holquist, trans. C. Emerson and M. Holquist, Austin: University of Texas Press.

Barham, J. (2008), 'Scoring Incredible Futures: Science-Fiction Screen Music, and "Postmodernism" as Romantic Epiphany', *The Musical Quarterly*, 91 (3/4): 240–74.

Bessmertny, S. ([1977] 2017), 'Remembering the Filming of Stalker', *Livejournal*. Available online: https://immos.livejournal.com/80622.html (accessed 19 December 2019).

Bird, R. (2004), 'The Suspended Aesthetic: Slavoj Žižek on Eastern European Film', *Studies in East European Thought*, 56 (4): 357–82.

Bird, R. (2008), *Andrei Tarkovsky: Elements of Cinema*, London: Reaktion Books.

Burns, Chr. L. (2011), 'Tarkovsky's Nostalghia: Refusing Modernity, Re-Envisioning Beauty', *Cinema Journal*, 50 (2): 104–22.

Debord, G.-E., ed. (1958a), 'Formulaire pour un Urbanisme Nouveau', *International Situationniste: Bulletin Central Edite par les Sections de l'International Situationniste*, 1: 15–20.

Debord, G.-E., ed. (1958b), 'Problèmes Préliminaires à la Construction d'une Situation', *International Situationniste: Bulletin Central Edite par les Sections de l'International Situationniste*, 1: 11–14.

Deleuze, G. ([1983] 1997), *Cinema I: The Movement-Image*, trans. H. Tomlinson and B. Habberjam, London: The Athlone Press.

Deleuze, G. (1993), *The Fold: Leibniz and the Baroque*, trans. T. Conley, London: The Athlone Press.

della Dora, V. (2016), *Landscape, Nature, and the Sacred in Byzantium*, Cambridge: Cambridge University Press.

Deltcheva, R. and E. Vlasov (1997), 'Back to the House II: On the Chronotopic and Ideological Reinterpretation of Lem's Solaris in Tarkovsky's Film', *The Russian Review*, 56 (4): 532–49.

Dempsey, M. (1981), 'Lost Harmony: Tarkovsky's "The Mirror" and "The Stalker"', *Film Quarterly*, 35 (1): 12–17.

Durgnat, R. (1990), 'Angelopoulos: The Long Take in "Voyage to Cythera": Brecht and Marx vs. Bazin and God', *Film Comment*, 26 (6): 43–4, 46.

Efird, R. (2014), 'Deleuze on Tarkovsky: The Crystal-Image of Time in "Steamroller and Violin"', *The Slavic and East European Journal*, 58 (2): 237–54.

el-Khoury, R. (1996), 'Introduction', in J.-F. de Bastide (1879), *The Little House: An Architectural Seduction*, trans. and intro. R. el-Khoury, pref. A. Vidler, 19–54, New York: Princeton Architectural Press.

Faubion, J. D., ed. (1998), *Michel Foucault: Aesthetics, Method and Epistemology*, vol. II, trans. R. Hurley and Others, London: Penguin Books.

Gamble, P. (2019), 'Stalker: In Search of Tarkovsky's Soviet Sci-Fi Locations', *BFI*. Available online: https://www.bfi.org.uk/news-opinion/news-bfi/features/andrei-tarkovsky-stalker-locations (accessed 19 December 2019).

Gianvito, J., ed. (2006), *Andrei Tarkovsky: Interviews*, Jackson: University of Mississippi.

Heidegger, M. ([1950] 2002), *Off the Beaten Track*, ed. and trans. J. Young and K. Haynes, Cambridge: Cambridge University Press.

Ivan the Terrible (parts I and II) [Иван Грозный] (1944 and 1958), [Film] Dir Sergei Eisenstein, USSR: Mosfilm.

Johnson, V. T. and G. Petrie (1994), *The Films of Andrei Tarkovsky: A Visual Fugue*, Bloomington and Indianapolis: Indiana University Press.

Le Corbusier ([1923] 1958), *Vers Une Architecture*, Paris: Éditions Vincent Fréal & Cie.

Le Corbusier and P. Jeanneret ([1934] 1995), *Oeuvre Complete de 1929–1934*, vol. II, Zurich: Les Editions d'Architecture.

Lem, S. ([1961] 2003), *Solaris*, trans. J. Kilmartin and St. Cox, San Diego and London: Harcourt.

Levaco, R., ed. (1974), *Kuleshov on Film: The Writings of Lev Kuleshov*, trans. R. Levaco, Berkeley, Los Angeles and London: University of California Press.

Lynch, K. (1960), *The Image of the City*, Cambridge, MA and London: The MIT Press.

Martin, S. (2005), *Andrei Tarkovsky*, Harpenden: Pocket Essentials.

Mumford, L. ([1934] 1955), *Technics and Civilization*, London: Routledge & Kegan Paul PLC.

Nitsche, M. and S. Roudavski with F. Penz and M. Thomas (2002), 'Narrative Expressive Space', *ACM SIGGROUP Bulletin*, 23 (2): 10–3. Available online: https://www.researchgate.net/publication/228958602_Narrative_expressive_space (accessed 19 December 2019).

Norberg-Schulz, C. (1979), *Genius Loci: Towards a Phenomenology of Architecture*, New York: Rizzoli.

Pavka, E. (2010), 'AD Classics: Jewish Museum, Berlin / Studio Libeskind', *ArchDaily*. Available online: https://www.archdaily.com/91273/ad-classics-jewish-museum-berlin-daniel-libeskind (accessed 19 December 2019).

Samuel, F. (2010), *Le Corbusier and the Architectural Promenade*, Basel: Birkhäuser.

Shklovsky, V. ([1917] 1988), 'Art as Technique', in D. Lodge (ed.), *Modern Criticism and Theory: A Reader*, 16–30, London: Longmans.

Solaris [Солярис] (1972), [Film] Dir Andrei Tarkovsky, USSR: Mosfilm.

Stalker [Сталкер] (1979), [Film] Dir Andrei Tarkovsky, USSR: Mosfilm.

Tarkovsky, A. (1986), *Sculpting in Time: Reflections on the Cinema*, trans. K. Hunter-Blair, Austin: Texas University Press.

The Colour of Pomegranates [Цвет Граната] (1969), [Film] Dir Sergei Parajanov, Armenia/USSR: Armenfilm.

The Trial of Joan of Arc [Procès de Jeanne d'Arc] (1962), [Film] Dir. Robert Bresson, France: Agnes Delahaie Productions.

Tschumi, B. ([1981] 1994), *The Manhattan Transcripts*, London: Academy Editions.

11

Architecture Beyond Sight

Filming blindness

Anna Ulrikke Andersen

This chapter consists of a written essay and the film *Architecture Beyond Sight* (2019, 16 mm, Andersen, seventeen minutes seventeen seconds). This film was commissioned by the DisOrdinary Architecture Project on behalf of The Bartlett, University College London (UCL), and is available online at: https://vimeo.com/354967146. An audiovisual transcript by Louise Fryer is available upon request from the DisOrdinary Architecture Project. Written in an essayistic writing style, the following text springs from my presence at the five-day course *Architecture Beyond Sight* held at The Bartlett in July 2019. Here, I reflect upon how my practice as a filmmaker where I use radio microphones and a Bolex H16 film camera opens up a new discussion regarding disability and architecture.

The outline of a hand is drawn with black charcoal on a white surface. Three women are present. Facing the canvas, one of them is drawing the hand of another. Closer to the camera, and out of focus, is the face of a woman talking. It is the partially sighted artist Rachel Gadsden, who in her work tackles the unseen and invisible, and in her mapping workshop, depicted here on film (Figure 11.1), she encourages new methods of mapping by tracing the body in space in ways that do not rely on sight. Doing disability differently, here with charcoal, paper and the presence of bodies, Gadsden is one of the tutors at the five-day study week for blind and partially sighted participants titled *Architecture Beyond Sight*. The course is organized by the DisOrdinary Architecture Project and The Bartlett, UCL.

On day one, I present myself and my equipment to the group of participants. First, I talk about the camera I have chosen to shoot with: a Bolex H16 Reflex. Made in 1959, this Bolex shoots on 16 mm film using a spring-wound clockwork

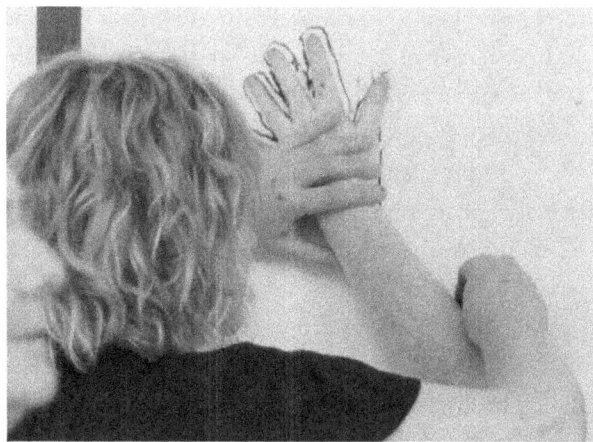

Figure 11.1 Still from *Architecture Beyond Sight* (2019): Two women drawing on a wall [Film], Dir. Anna Ulrikke Andersen, UK.

power system that must be cranked by hand. The clockwork is mechanic and makes a distinct ticking sound. As I demonstrate the cranking and shooting in front of the group, I underscore how the participants would be able to hear me when I prepare the camera and when I shoot. Through sound, the participant could locate me and my camera in space.

I further explain that I will capture sound externally, using two sets of radio microphones, recorded by a Zoom H4n recorder. Each set consists of a small clip-on microphone that is attached to a transmitter by a wire. This is to be worn by the speaking subject, and a separate receiver is connected to the recorder. I ask for volunteers who would consider being recorded as they work on their project throughout the week, and get several positive responses. I later equip two participants with microphones and press record.

I like working with radio microphones. The receiver and recorder can be located away from the transmitter, and I can sit at a distance, in the corner of the room and listen with my headphones. The voices captured appear clear and close, invisible waves sent wirelessly across the room through a domain of chairs, tables, workshop materials, aid equipment and bodies.

'Across the lowly domain of beans and cabbages, the young man was to conduct experiments that were destined to influence the fate of empires' (Archer 1938: 56), Gleason L. Archer writes in his *History of Radio 1926* (1938), discussing the early experiments with long-distance wireless transmission by Guglielmo Marconi. The Italian inventor's early experiments from his father's vegetable garden made long-distance radio transmissions possible from 1895, followed by the first transatlantic transmission in 1901. I read Archer's statement as if change and invention can take place between beans and cabbages, and not necessarily from a place of power, located high above.

I shoot with a 75 mm telephoto lens, the camera located on a tripod, only raised slightly higher than the tables where work takes place. With a shallow depth of field, I capture the hands of the participants working, shuffling through different materials, organizing, cutting, attaching, bending and conjoining. My framing and point of view aim to capture the lowly domain, if not between cabbages and beans, then close by and on the level with the creative process of making and design by disabled bodies, historically marginalized.

Marconi's paternal family was of Italian nobility, and his English-Speaking mother introduced the child to a bilingual and worldly upbringing. Although Archer (1938) describes the nascent stage of wireless technology as rather humble, it would be difficult to argue that Marconi's voice was coming from the marginalized depths of society. In fact, wireless technology around the turn of the century was, in fact, too complicated for most amateurs. In 1918, this was to change, when Elmer E. Bucher at the American Marconi Company published *Practical Wireless Telegraphy: A Complete Text Book for Students of Radio Communication* (1918), making the technology more accessible to the general public. Because even if one of the book's main objectives was to prepare students for examinations to become a licenced wireless operator, the book simultaneously made it easier for amateurs to experiment on their own. This, according to Archer, led to rapid growth in amateur interference in the United States: 'As early as 1906, when President Theodore Roosevelt visited the naval fleet off Cape Cod, the nearby Newport Naval station was unable to communicate messages to him by wireless because of amateur interference' (Archer 1938: 105). As the technology became more accessible, alternative and interfering waves, voices and messages were sent and distributed: powerful enough to silence the president. Radio technology, thus, could be a form of resistance, offering a transmitter of otherwise silenced voices. During the Second World War, the occupying forces of Nazi Germany were aware of – and worried about – the resistance spreading their messages wirelessly and into people's homes. Radios were confiscated at Jersey and Guernsey to avoid the population listening to the BBC, but the German forces' tendency to confiscate radios also led to many of the apparatuses being hidden. Through these illegal radios, voices of resistance could present an alternative to the ruling ideology (Moore 2000: 252).

A radio can challenge our views, as evident in Diana Fuss's work on the deaf and blind activist and author Helen Keller, and the role of radio in her life. Facing illness as a toddler, Keller became blind and deaf. Struggling to communicate with her surroundings, Keller eventually learned the connection between sign and meaning from her teacher Anne Sullivan and was able to communicate. Keller overcame the impossible, or more precisely what her contemporaries considered to be impossible. Photographs of the disabled author often represented the way she navigated a world built for the able, as when a camera captured her window shopping in Paris, as discussed by historian David Serlin (2006), or sitting by her typewriter in front of her radio, as discussed by Fuss (2004).

'To her friends and family, Keller, whose internal vibroscope could pick up even the most distant signals, was a human radio, open like all radio receivers to the danger of telepathic suggestions' (Fuss 2004: 59), Fuss writes. As such, Keller not only enjoyed the radio and the vibrations that came from the apparatus but vibrations at large were important for her to feel a connection to a larger, external world. With her body, she interpreted a set of vibrations and communicative signals, which she transferred into meanings, and her thoughts could be typed out on her typewriter.

Serlin argues that Keller's figure as a *flaneuse* challenges a view of modernity that revolves around 'able-bodied acts such as walking, looking, and hearing' (Serlin 2006: 199). Instead, her interest in fashion with touch, or her mobility in public space, shows a different approach to disability, where Keller enjoys the modern city without being able to see and hear. Serlin suggests that the photographs 'Represent both an epistemological challenge to the vocularcentric contentions of *flânerie* as well as a distinct shift in the generic connections used to depict bodily difference' (Serlin 2006: 2020). As such, Keller's window-shopping challenges how we consider *flânerie*. Showing how Keller's photograph fits into a complex set of representations of disability in modernity, which were to continue to be challenged. Keller's body offers an alternative.

My use of radio microphones builds, draws and gleans upon a long history of various uses and meanings attached. I think of how the disabled body itself has been marginalized historically and how capturing the disabled voice with a radio microphone allows a specific kind of criticality: one that is intimate, mobile and possibly interfering with the establishment.

The disabled body is the point of departure of the DisOrdinary Architecture Project, which was co-founded by Zoe Partington and Jos Boys. The project brings together a range of talented disabled artists and designers around the core idea that disability can be a source of creativity and critique, rather than a problem that must be solved or fitted into a pre-existing system and culture. The way that people who live with disabilities have to navigate and tackle the world and its built environment, the disabled body must often find creative solutions to problems, as discussed by Boys in her book *Doing Disability Differently: An Alternative Handbook on Architecture* (2014). She writes:

> Arguing that starting from disability, does *not* lead to universal or simple design solutions but instead opens up to creative engagement the complex messy and often contradictory intersections of our diverse lives with others, artefacts and material space, and an approach that has ramifications for the very shape of architectural knowledges. (Boys 2014: 4)

Here Boys sees the complexity apparent in the disabled body as offering a shift in architectural knowledge, and challenge the way we design, and speak, think and write about architecture. The DisOrdinary Architecture Project does not seek simple solutions that will make design accessible 'for all', but instead claim that doing disability differently, could bring up alternative views and ideas.

'To have a vision, doesn't require sight,' tutor Mandy Redverse-Rowe claims (Andersen 2019). The notion of 'having a vision', thus, means being creative and aspirational, and this does not necessarily require eyesight. I utilize radio technology to engage with these ideas of vision, creativity, design and the disabled body. Every morning I hand over a fully charged radio microphone and allow the speaking subject to move freely. The speaker does not need to look in my direction to be heard. The microphone captures speech directly from the body of the speaker, a signal that is captured by an external receiver if the transmitter and receiver are kept within reach. They can move around and speak relatively freely and without interruption.

Clarke Reynolds agrees to wear a radio microphone, and I record him speaking eagerly about his design process as he sets out to make a wooden box in the B-Made Workshop in the basement of The Bartlett, 22 Gordon Street, London. The idea is clear: a wooden box with holes, and inside a smaller box containing a series of materials cut into sheets. The materials can be taken out and placed between the inner and the outer layer, and they can be explored through the holes. In this version of a cabinet of curiosity, Reynolds plays with several senses, both offering a cropped visual of the material, and an invitation to reach through the holes and touch. In order to make his box, he must use power tools to saw, sand and drill (Figure 11.2). The recorded conversation

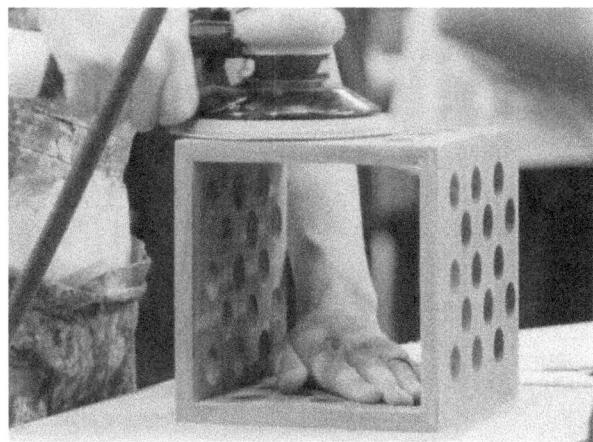

Figure 11.2 Still from *Architecture Beyond Sight* (2019): A man sanding wood using power tools [Film], Dir. Anna Ulrikke Andersen, UK.

captures the safety procedures he must go through to use the tools. He follows these guidelines and cuts the pieces with precision. As Reynolds moves easily around in the workshop, he simultaneously navigates the tools and available aid confidently, evident in the recorded conversation.

'It is as though the practices organizing a bustling city were characterized by their blindness. The networks of these moving, intersecting writings compose a manifold story that has neither author nor spectator, shaped out of fragments of trajectories and alternations of spaces' (de Certeau 1984: 93), critical theorist Michel de Certeau argues. In his book *The Practice of Everyday Life* (1984), he explores a series of practices related to the everyday, including walking in the city and asking how these everyday practices expose power structures; moving around and about, according to de Certeau, relates to power and authorship. Whereas seeing the city from above creates an all-encompassing view, walking in the city is, on the contrary, described as 'resistance, tricky and stubborn'(de Certeau 1984: 93). The embodied and 'blind' knowledge produced through walking and moving about creates new embodied knowledge. This knowledge is linked to space and to looking at how people's movement in space can open up a critical discussion of power structures. He writes:

> First, if it is true that a spatial order organizes an ensemble of possibilities (e.g. by a place in which one can move) and interdictions (e.g. by a walk that prevents one from going further), then the walker actualizes some of these possibilities. In that way, he makes them exist as well as emerge. But he also moves them

about an he invents others, since the crossing, drifting away, or improvisation of walking privilege, transform or abandon spatial elements. (de Certeau 1984: 98)

Here, the walker engages with the spaces already predetermined by the city, and with its structure of knowledge, more importantly, shape something new and rich. The moving subject, thus, can be a form of resistance to predetermined routes. Reynolds moves about and around the workshop, using power tools safely and with precision. Radio technology not only makes a recording of this process possible but also in its very essence makes the movement possible. Here the disabled body moving – and recorded – creates interesting design. His box not only speaks to our visual sense but challenges it – crops it – and invites us to touch.

'I would like to insist on the embodied nature of all vision, and so reclaim the sensory system that has been used to signify a leap out of the marked body and into the conquering gaze from nowhere' (Harraway 1988: 581), Donna Harraway argues in her seminal essay 'Situated Knowledge: The Science Question in Feminism and the Privilege of Partial Perspective' (1988). For her, knowledge is situated and related to power structures, which she aims to challenge. In critiquing the notion of objectivity and the current system of knowledge and ways of seeing, she is critical of how sciences have focused on vision and the eyes as a road to knowledge. Instead, Harraway proposes that a feminist approach to the matter would involve a new sense of vision that is embodied: understanding should come from the body, and not from a conquering gaze.

'Like the radio, the typewriter rendered all its users temporarily blind, immediately equalising Keller's relation to her sighted peers' (Fuss 2004: 61), Fuss writes as she explores the role of architecture in Keller's life and work, in both a literal and a figurative sense. 'Most of the information Keller divined from vibration came from architecture's fundamental design components: walls, windows, doors, stairs, chimneys, and expectably floors' (Fuss 2004: 55). Architecture therefore played a pivotal role in the way Keller experienced and communicated with the world:

> [Doing Disability Differently] proposes that architecture can challenge and shift ideas about, and practices around, disability and ability, that is around diverse occupancies, by designing *from* these complexities and contradictions; by opening up its own internal design discourses to critical investigation; and by creatively exploiting the gaps and openings in architectural theories and practices towards a better understanding of difference. (Boys 2014: 5)

Therefore, the design process itself – including the movement between machines, tools and materials evident in the recorded conversations – reveals certain assumptions of contemporary architectural culture that is ableist, such as the assumption that visual sense is pivotal when using power tools, when simple amendments and a change in culture could make the space accessible to partially sighted or blind designers.

'We are living longer. We are living with more disabilities' (Andersen 2019), tutor Chris Downey states, emphasizing that disability is becoming a more common human experience. As Keller aged, it became much more difficult for her to communicate with the world around her. Fuss describes a series of bronchial colds which affected her olfactory senses, and the amputation of a toe that reduced her ability to sense vibration. 'But the most serious loss of all was the decreased sensitivity of her hands, cropped by arthritis and further disabled by chronic eczema. Like sight and hearing, touch ages. Increasingly infirm, Keller found herself unable to use a typewriter and uncomfortable reading Braille. By the time Keller completed *Teaching* in 1954, she needed to warm her hands continually in order to read a book' (Fuss 2004: 62).

I use my hands, elbows and shoulder to wind my camera: a Bolex H16 from 1959. Each time I wind it up I can shoot for a little less than thirty seconds. As I shoot, it produces a distinct ticking sound: sound reveals where I am, and when I am filming, underscoring that filmmaking takes place and is a spatial practice. For each different shot, I have to move the heavy tripod. After two and a half minutes, I have shot the roll of film, and I must remove the camera from its tripod and load a new film. Each roll is expensive and I must think carefully about my shots, making sure the scene is framed exactly as I want. Filmmaking is a physical practice and the weight of the equipment affects my mobility and determines how long I can shoot before pain and fatigue set in: film roll is limited and so are my energy levels.

On the fourth day of the course, Serlin is invited to give a lecture about Keller and the representations of disability in visual culture. At the outset, he encourages us to get comfortable, move around or lie down, catering to the variety of bodies in his audience. I am initially seated at the very back of the large seminar rooms with my equipment, but I get up from my seat and move down onto the floor, resting my tired body as I listen. The five-day course is almost over, only the final exhibition and feedback session remains. I rest on the floor and let my mind wander. I start thinking about my own position as a filmmaker, and how my film offers a specific form of the cinematic, specifically aimed at tackling architecture and space critically.

Jane Rendell argues that critical spatial practices can be a way to 'challenge criticism as a static point of view, located in the here and now' (Rendell 2010: 18). Building upon de Certeau's attention to the practices of everyday life as having critical potential, Rendell explores critical theory's potential to bring about social and ideological changes; she considers this critical potential in different forms of practices – between art and architecture. She notes how theory tends to involve spatial concepts and she explores how spatial practices negotiate theory in return, delving into the way critical theory offers a way to be self-reflexive and critically expose different forms of power relations. Rendell coins the term 'critical spatial practice' to describe these projects that are both spatial and critical in the way they are made and experienced (Rendell 2006). She considers the critical practices in spatial, temporal and social ways (Rendell 2006: 192). The spaces where encounters with works take place, and the way we talk about them, are of critical potential to Rendell, as she argues how the 'critic encounters the work influences the process of criticism' (Rendell 2010: 12). Critical spatial practices also offer a way to discuss the self and its position in the world and in relation to others. My presence in the room, with or without cameras, microphones or transmitters, matters. Where I am located in relation to others, and how my body is responding to the situation, makes a difference.

As the fourth day comes to an end, I have shot most of my film rolls. What remains is a couple of Kodak 500T film rolls that I will use to shoot interiors on the final day of the course, and two rolls of Kodak 50D which are useful for shooting in daylight. I wake up early the next morning and arrive at The Bartlett before the other participants. I take the lift up to the sixth floor at 22 Gordon Street, and place my camera by a window in one of the corner rooms, overlooking the morning traffic at Euston Road. According to de Certeau, a view from above is linked with power, and 'allows one to read it, to be a solar Eye, looking down like a god' (de Certeau 1984: 92). But de Certeau wishes to challenge the assertion that viewing from above is intricately linked to being all-knowing. He writes: 'The exaltation of a scopic and gnostic drive: the fiction of knowledge is related to this lust to be a viewpoint and nothing more' (De Certeau 1984: 92). This means that knowledge does not necessarily come from above, but instead simply offers one point of view.

The shot from the top floor at 22 Gordon Street is juxtaposed with the voice-over by Downey, who draws attention to how common disability is now, and will be in the future. If we are living longer and with more disabilities, as Downey argues, architectural culture needs to change. The aim is that the five-day study

Figure 11.3 Still from *Architecture Beyond Sight* (2019): A shot of a London street, captured from above [Film], Dir. Anna Ulrikke Andersen, UK.

week will develop into a foundation course in architecture at The Bartlett. Alan Penn, dean at The Bartlett, believes that this could challenge what he experiences as 'a "monoculture" dominated by white architects from mostly affluent backgrounds' (Hall 2019). Involved in decades of architectural education, Penn sees a need to think differently about architectural aesthetics and question the predominant tendency to think about architecture as visual. Through a series of workshops and talks, *Architecture Beyond Sight* aims to rethink architecture removed from visual bias, and to create spaces that speak to all the senses. 'Let's include students with visual impairments and who are blind in architecture and design because it is good for architecture and design' (Andersen 2019), tutor Duncan Meerding's voice states as the visual image shows a seminar room full of empty chairs. Disabled people should not be included in architecture because it is good for the disabled only, but instead, those empty chairs on the top floor at 22 Gordon Street should be filled with a diverse student body because it would benefit an entire culture and profession. In my editing, where I juxtapose the view from above with the voice of a disabled body, I aim to bring together the disabled point of view from below the depths, with the institutional view from above.

The study week *Architecture Beyond Sight* encourages other forms of spatial engagements, and new ways of thinking about the creative, problem-solving or aesthetic processes that are involved in architectural design. Here, doing disability differently invites a new understanding of what it means to have a vision, corresponding to Harraway's embodied and situated attention of knowledge. As a filmmaker, I draw upon Boys's attention to disability and her encouragement to start from the disabled body so as to 'do' disability differently. I also consider Rendell's notion of critical spatial practices as I equip two disabled bodies with radio microphones, and film hands, tools, materials and processes with a 75 mm telephoto lens. Here, a series of critical practices are made and recorded. The film engages with the core thematic of the study week through these practices. I observe how participants move and navigate the spaces, tools, materials, and the advice and encouragement given; I turn to de Certeau to highlight the critical potential of this movement. As I rest my tired body and my worn hands on the corner of the seminar room, I think about how the filming of blindness has, to me, opened up new discussions and ideas about the body in space and the inevitable human experience of chronic or temporary disabilities.

Acknowledgements

The film and essay spring from Architecture Beyond Sight Study Week, which took place at 22 Gordon Street, The Bartlett, UCL, between 22 and 26 July 2019, produced by the DisOrdinary Architecture Project. The project benefited from the support, help and collaboration with the following: students: Vanel Bailey, Terri Balon, Margo Cargill, Daniel Cartin, Gavin Griffiths, Mark Joynson, Fae Kilburn, Zoe Legg, Poppy Levison, Miracle Maduforo, Stephen Portlock, Isabelle Sophie Pua, Clarke Reynolds and Dianne Theakstone; tutors: Duncan Meerding, Chris Downey, Zoe Partington, Mandy Redvers-Rowe and Jos Boys; guest tutors: Rachel Gadsden, Lynn Cox , David Serlin, Shade Abdul, Judit Pusztaszeri and Liz Porter; student assistants: Amy Francis Smith, Alexia Koch, Tahir Mangarah, Hamza Shaikh, Maya Shankla, Rachel Thompson and Emma Yee; project management: Nikki Mangan and Rachel Tyler; and Louise Fryer for transcription. Special thanks to Professor Alan Penn, Professor Barbara Penner, Emily Stone and the B-Made Workshop team, especially James Green from The Bartlett; Zoe Laughlin and Sarah Wilkes from the Institute of Making UCL; and Ria Bartlett and Richard Warren from the British Library.

References

Archer, G. L. (1938), *History of Radio to 1926*, New York: The American Historical Society.

Architecture Beyond Sight (2019), [Film] Dir. Anna Ulrikke Andersen, UK: The DisOrdinary Architecture Project on behalf of The Bartlett, UCL. Available online: https://vimeo.com/354967146 (accessed 20 February 2020).

Boys, J. (2014), *Doing Disability Differently: An Alternative Handbook on Architecture, Dis/ability and Designing for Everyday Life*, Oxon: Routledge.

de Certeau, M. (1984), *The Practice of Everyday Life*, trans. S. Rendall, Berkeley: University of California Press.

Fuss, D. (2004), *The Sense of an Interior: Four Writers and the Rooms that Shaped Them*, New York: Routledge.

Hall, R. (2019), 'Can Blind People Make Great Architects?', *The Guardian*, 2 September 2019. Available online: https://www.theguardian.com/world/2019/sep/02/can-blind-people-make-great-architects (accessed 20 February 2020).

Harraway, D. (1988), 'Situated Knowledge: The Science Question in Feminism and the Privilege of Partial Perspective', *Feminist Studies*, 14 (3): 575–99.

Moore, B., ed. (2000), *Resistance in Western Europe*, Oxford: Berg.

Rendell, J. (2006), *Art and Architecture: A Place Between*, London: I.B. Tauris.

Rendell, J. (2010), *Site-Writing: The Architecture of Art Criticism*, London: I.B.Tauris.

Serlin, D. (2006), 'Disabling the Flâneur', *Journal of Visual Culture*, 5 (2): 193–208.

12

Towards an architecture of the cinematic

Mark E. Breeze

> ... it is architecture that has had the most privileged and difficult relationship to film.
>
> Vidler 1993: 45

Architects, filmmakers and academics have long proclaimed connections between the disciplines and practices of architecture and cinema, as Cairns (2013) and Koeck (2013) have recently elucidated. The academic literature that explicitly focuses on the *architectural* implications of the relationship between architecture and cinema can be broadly categorized in three main areas: broad explorations of notions of place, time, space, narrative and materiality created in *specific films* (e.g. Tawa 2011); broad experiential connections between the disciplines (e.g. Bruno 1997 and 2002; Pallassmaa 2007 and 2012); and how *urban* spaces can not only be understood as exhibiting broad cinematic ideas, but also how such urban spaces are used by *specific filmmakers* (e.g. Alifragkis and Penz 2010, Penz and Lu 2011). However, practising architects who discuss or proclaim cinematic ideas or influences in their built or theoretical work do not tend to name *specific* films, filmmakers or filmmaking approaches as ways of understanding either their *specific* built projects or more general architectural approaches (from Le Corbusier, to Jean Nouvel and Bernard Tschumi, for example). If, as Anthony Vidler succinctly argues, architecture is 'a fundamental site of film practice' (Vidler 1993: 46), what can that mean for how we can understand the practice of architecture differently? Through re-evaluating the early relationship between architecture and cinema, this chapter attempts to offer a different way of understanding both this relationship and its potential implications for the discipline and practice of architecture.

Much of the existing literature implicitly locates a tangible origin of the architecture–cinema relationship in the description of the Acropolis by the trained engineer Auguste Choisy in his 1899 *Histoire de L'Architecture* (see Bruno 1997; Cairns 2013; Koeck 2013; Tawa 2011; Toy 1994; Vidler 1993). Choisy's specific description reveals a nuanced way of understanding ancient Greek architecture by using the cinematic as a tool, technique and way of thinking. It is this reconstruction and revisualization of this ancient architecture that forms the foundation of the architecture–cinema relationship. Choisy's description emphasizes the *experience* at human eye level of approaching and *moving* up and through the *sequence* of buildings:

> Nothing is more apparent than the irregularity of the plan; it makes a balanced ensemble where the symmetry of the masses and the most original variety of details work together. The right wing, with the temple of Victory, form a mass corresponding to that of the left wing: so that for a spectator placed at the foot of the staircase, the two limiting radii . . . reinforce the general axis of the building. . . . This small temple is not orientated parallel to the general composition axis: new irregularity fixes the viewer's gaze, and gives it an importance that its small size would otherwise deny.[1] (Author's translation of Choisy 1899: 414–15)

The architecture is explained through the subjective, three-dimensional, cumulative sequence of visual effects as a human body moves through a particular geography and assemblage of buildings. Significantly, Choisy emphasizes this *performed* experience through his *first* and *only* use of perspective drawings in his whole history of architecture, thereby bringing the reader into the subjective human eye level reality of the experience. He positions the relevant plan directly beneath each perspective to locate and objectify the subjective human experience. These drawings work in tandem with the written description: they are carefully positioned among the text to create a sensation of continuous movement through the Acropolis complex as one moves through the text, with these momentary perspective 'snapshots' highlighting key experiences 'to fix the gaze' at specific points. The effect is a curated performance for the reader to reveal an architecture that is seemingly designed around the human movement through it. The architecture is presented as only having coherence and meaning through its sequenced, shifting imageability.

Choisy does not mention film, cinema or the moving image, but he was writing only four years after the Lumière brothers had screened their first films in Paris, and after both Marey and Muybridge had published several extensive examples of their experiments to capture the motion of animals, humans and objects over time, in static images and short projected sequences. Choisy's argument was in many ways not especially innovative: Viollet-le-Duc had already described Greek architecture as 'mise en scène', a term that cinema later co-opted (Eisenstein, Bois and Glenny 1989: 114). Indeed, Choisy places his understanding of the Acropolis ensemble within what he calls 'the picturesque', a heavily debated term for British architectural thought of the late eighteenth and early nineteenth centuries. Moreover, Ancient Greek and Roman public spaces have long posed an interesting question for architectural theoreticians since the Renaissance, given the predominance of canonical laws of geometry (e.g. symmetry, axiality, repetition and rhythm) in understanding classical architecture and subsequent architectural production. Here, Choisy offers an enticing explanation that normalizes the exception and hybridizes the picturesque by making the irregularity and fluidity of forms seemingly systematic. The innovation of Choisy was how he brought together nascent developments in the moving image with theatrical traditions, to argue architecture as a curated, three-dimensional, active first-person, relational performance.

Choisy presents his argument cinematically in the text: sequenced perspective images among the text mimic nascent cinema's sequenced perspective images between intertitles (first used the year before Choisy's publication). Through this explicit approach, he teases a cinematic reading of the architecture itself, opening up a different way of understanding the architecture. He reconciles forms of the sublime (the towering mass of the Acropolis), and the beautiful (the delicately crafted and proportioned temples), through the irregularity of the picturesque (the layout of the structures in a wild surrounding landscape). But it is much more than this: here the reconciliation and meaning comes from the movement of the *viewer*, curated *by* the forms and placement of the architectures. For this one moment in Choisy's text, architecture is no longer to be understood as a singular, static, passive object or form (which can be conveyed adequately with technical drawings alone), but rather as an active experience through movement. Here the architecture both creates and becomes a constantly shifting, curated individual human *experience* of horizontal and vertical depth; it is revealed through the individual's dynamic movement around and through the interdependent assembled forms, witnessed and performed in the first person. As the placement of *perspective* images of key turning points amongst the descriptive text helps reinforce, there is no static form of meaning, but rather a processional, dynamic, three-dimensional movement that cumulatively creates meaning through its contextual sequencing.² It is a relationally sequenced, experiential, fluid formalism, of shifting imageability.

This is more than just a modified picturesque approach; Choisy argues for architecture as a layered, individual, three-dimensional, moving performance. This cinematic approach operates as a tool and technique to enable a richer way of thinking and conveying the physical experiential qualities and possibilities of architecture; indeed, in choosing one of the most ancient of extant structures as the example, Choisy is showing the universality and foundational nature of this approach.

Sergei Eisenstein's writing on architecture and cinema is indebted to Choisy's work on the Acropolis. Eisenstein, who trained as an architect and engineer before becoming a filmmaker, writes in his posthumously published text 'Montage and Architecture' how 'it is hard to imagine a montage sequence for an architectural ensemble more subtly composed, shot by shot, than the one that our legs create by walking among the buildings of the Acropolis' (Eisenstein, Bois and Glenny 1989: 117). Eisenstein uses this historic example to argue that 'architecture operates as a form of sequential narrative montage', where the 'viewer's engagement with architecture becomes one of glimpses, partial views and momentary glances in sequence . . . a form of "montage computation within an architectural ensemble"' (Eisenstein, Bois and Glenny 1989: 131). It is this experience that Eisenstein – with explicit reference to Choisy's text – describes as 'the most perfect examples of shot design, change of shot, and shot length. . . . The Acropolis of Athens has an equal right to be called the perfect example of one of the most ancient films' (Eisenstein, Bois and Glenny 1989: 117). This is a significant point: architecture as a film – a sequenced, repeatable, visual and emotional, curated experience.

Eisenstein developed a considered theory of montage from early on in his professional life, as his 1923 'Montage of Attractions' work makes clear. 'Montage and Architecture' (written between 1937 and 1940 and published posthumously in 1989) further develops this theory of montage in a more explicitly architectural context.³ Understanding architecture as a system of representation and a site of production of social meaning, Eisenstein was exploring what he called 'cinematographicity' – sequentiality and montage – in architecture, and how the movement of the spectator as a 'material' could bring practical answers for how to understand a building and transform it into a major agent of a cinematic plot (Eisenstein, Bois and Glenny 1989: 113). Importantly, in 'Film Sense' (1942),

Eisenstein explicitly claims architecture as film's predecessor, with its concern for the transition from real to imaginary movement. Bruno (1997 and 2002) elaborates on this theory of mobile embodied spectatorship, highlighting the paradox of the '(im)mobile' cinematic spectator who inherits the camera's point of view, and so moves through an imaginary space: the cinematic spectator is situated in a phenomenological relationship to cinematic space. Eisenstein's broader theory of montage further enriches this understanding, especially given his development of Vertov's insistence on the mobile mechanical eye of the camera lens being free of human immobility. This cinematic approach focuses architects (in designing) and those experiencing the built objects to understand architecture as sequences that shape, frame, orient and move us – both physically *and* emotionally. This is different to the unmediated phenomenological approaches of Norberg-Schulz (1980). Eisenstein's dualistic theory opens us to understanding architecture as a crafted *sequential* phenomenological experience, the basic narrative structure of which is informed by the specific contexts and needs at its moment of inception. However, as soon as it becomes tangible with a physical presence in the world, this architecture is subjectively reconstructed by its users as a montage of real and imaginary sequences, constantly shaping and shaped by its contexts, users and uses, over time. The 'architectural spectator' becomes hyper-mobile, moving freely, looking freely, layering-in and building upon the experiences, emotions and expectations that the architecture constructs. The cinematic constructs sequential affective performances of architectural possibilities, which are subjectively reconstructed and performed through use.

Eisenstein's broader work reveals how his concern with cinema was part of a wider interest in how performative art forms could be made more effective mediums, through a concern with the total effect of a chain of associations, as Taylor (1988) has lucidly shown in his comprehensive collection of Eisenstein's original writings. Indeed, in 'The Montage of Attractions' (1923) he sought to understand how *theatre* could be made more effective, stating that 'the moulding of the audience in a desired direction (or mood) is the task of every utilitarian theatre'; he later used the same arguments for cinema as the 'next dimension of means of expression' (Taylor 1988: 4). It is also in this theatrical work that he developed his key theory of 'attractions', emphasizing the role of the emotional or psychological shocks, which he then applies to cinema.

The key idea of highly curated emotional elements sequenced in a collective chain of associations to create a singular total effect lies at the heart of Eisenstein's approach. Indeed, in 1924 in 'The Problem of the Materialist Approach to Form', he emphasized that the decisive factor 'for art . . . is the maximum intensification of the emotional seizure of the audience' (Taylor 1988: 6), ideas he reaffirmed in both 'The Film Sense' and 'The Psychology of Composition'. Eisenstein constantly searches across these performative arts to describe and formulate his broader performative theory, at one point in 1923 even inventing the non-medium-specific category of 'cinematism' to describe forms of visual articulation (see Eisenstein [1949] 1977).

Sequence and montage lie at the heart of this nascent theory as the means of creating associations, as Eisenstein re-emphasized in 'Beyond the Shot' in 1929.[4] And as he reiterated in 'The Dialectical Approach to Film Form' in 1929, montage is characterized by collisions – be they spatial, graphic, movement, sound or stylistic conflicts – in a cumulative, *superimposed* fashion; each element has a 'dominant' sign, and it is the conflict between those 'dominant' signs that creates the expressive emotive effects (Taylor 1988: 15). Eisenstein further argues in 'The Dialectical Approach to Film Form' that each of these elements is equivalent, becoming what he calls 'common denominators' enabling the 'transference of the basic affective intention from one material to another, from one category of "stimulant" to another'(see Eisenstein [1949] 1977: 45–63). This results in what Eisenstein describes in the 'Fourth Dimension in Cinema' (1929) as 'physiological sensations'. 'I introduce a new uniform formula: "I feel"'. This core concern with the affective closely connects back to Eisenstein's naming of the fundamental shared characteristic of architecture and cinema as the 'ecstatic' (quoted in Vidler 1993: 55): both acts move us mentally.

Eisenstein uses Choisy's text as a starting point to think through the shared characteristics of cinema and architecture as performative arts, and as modes of thinking, tools and techniques in a much broader theory of affective performance. Through his developed theory of montage, Eisenstein argues for architecture as an emotional act that is performed by the mobile eyes and body of the viewer through the cumulative superimposition of a variety of experiential effects of sight, sound, style and movement. This cinematic approach operates as a tool and technique to enable a richer way of thinking and conveying the emotional experiential qualities and possibilities of architecture.

Le Corbusier's built architectural work integrates cinematic techniques, methods and ways of thinking; similarly, his filmic collaborations reveal his constant exploration of the possibilities of the architecture–cinema relationship for both disciplines. He drew heavily on Choisy's work on the Acropolis in his seminal

1924 book *Vers Une Architecture*, in terms of both the ideas and images. The very structure of it is revealing of the transdisciplinary concerns of Le Corbusier: fifteen essays covering a range of disciplines from literature, psychoanalysis and painting to cinematography.[5] Significantly, the structure of the book itself is one of montage – juxtaposed fragments, (often edited) images and a variety of fonts, styles and texts – as he reconstructs architectural meanings in the early twentieth century; allusions to Eisenstein's then developing theories of montage are hard to ignore.

Le Corbusier uses Choisy's work on the Acropolis most explicitly for his third 'reminder to architects', which focuses on the importance of the architectural plan.[6] The chapter begins with Choisy's perspective view on the Acropolis (of the Parthenon, the Erechtheum and the Athena Parthenos from the Propylaea) with the accompanying plan below indicating the position of the viewer. In the Beaux-Arts tradition, Le Corbusier declares the plan as a 'generator'. Mandoul argues that Le Corbusier uses many of the axonometric drawings of Choisy to exemplify this, as the axonometric represents the illustrated building simultaneously in plan, section and elevation, 'thereby making it possible to connect the "generator" with the volumes' (Le Corbusier [1923] 2008: 10). However, this is not strictly the case, and of easily exaggerated relevance to Le Corbusier's text: firstly, only a *sectional* axonometric drawing will show the plan *along with* an elevation *and* a section; and secondly, such sectional axonometric drawings are used only four times Le Corbusier's text – and none of them is from the Acropolis. The more significant element is the use of the annotated locating plan accompanying the subjective viewpoint of the perspective drawing: the emphasis is on the plan as the generator of performed experience through the movement it curates, showing what surrounds the viewer at that point and, in so doing, implying a past (where the viewer has most likely been), a present (where the viewer currently is), and a future (where the viewer can move to). In this sense, the plan provides a spatial and temporal panorama of sorts, acting as a spatial and temporal 'generator', or performance. The plan works as a cinematic tool.

Le Corbusier states directly after the perspective and plan combination (and repeating from the second page of the book) that 'The plan carries within it the essence of the sensation' (Le Corbusier [1923] 2008: 116). Interestingly, it is the Parthenon that Le Corbusier calls 'a machine for stirring emotion', essentially through the composition of forms, and the lack of symbols attached to those forms (Le Corbusier [1923] 2008: 241). Furthermore, Le Corbusier clearly states only several pages before his direct engagement with the Acropolis that 'Architecture: that's for stirring emotion . . . architecture is a matter of "relationships", a "pure creation of the mind"' (Le Corbusier [1923] 2008: 97). Just as with Eisenstein, the core concern for Le Corbusier is with the crafting of sensation and emotion; and for him it is the processional element rooted in Choisy that is the key to creating such a performative architecture.

The processional route that Choisy explicated is synthesized into Le Corbusier's text in two important aspects. His discussion of significant historic examples – such as the Forum of Pompeii for the joy that arises from the act of walking through it – emphasizes both physical movement through a sequence and the movement of the human eye: 'The human eye, in its investigations, is always turning, and man also turns to the right, to the left, clear round. He takes in everything and is drawn toward the center of gravity of the site as a whole' (Le Corbusier [1923] 2008: 224); and 'We must not forget, when laying out a plan, that it is the human eye that observes its effects' (Le Corbusier [1923] 2008: 230). And again, Le Corbusier connects our physical movement through an architecture with being moved affectively: 'Architecture is when there is poetic emotion. Architecture is a plastic thing. Plasticity is what I see and what I measure with our eyes' (Le Corbusier [1923] 2008: 243). As with Choisy, it is a reading of architecture that could be described as using basic conceptual 'cinematic' tools and techniques in its concern with a curated physical movement through a sequence of crafted spaces to create sensations; similarly, he is further developing Eisenstein's discussions of the mobile eye and body.[7] However, as with Choisy, there is never an explicit mention of 'cinema' or 'film' throughout the text; this is a broader conceptual approach, using the cinematic as a mode of thinking the performance of the architecture for human sensation, using its tools and techniques.

The importance of the curated processional route Le Corbusier highlighted so early in his career is evident throughout much of Le Corbusier's later-written and -built work; it is perhaps best exemplified in the Villa Savoye in Poissy, France (1931), which he designed with his cousin Pierre Jeanneret. Benton has shown how the early architectural drawings reveal that in late 1928 Le Corbusier inserted a singular promenade route from the bottom to the top of the villa, replete with ramp access to the roof garden revealing a panorama of the surrounding countryside and the River Seine below (Benton 1987: 198–9). And in his own description of the Villa, Le Corbusier himself guides us through the villa in what he describes as 'la promenade'; it is an architecture whose 'spine' is an ascending walking route from physical arrival at the bottom of the building, weaving up through the building and out on to the roof terrace to the sweeping view at top of the building of the surrounding lands: it is about the experience of gradually ascending through the architecture on a continuous walk to key framed views. It is especially interesting that in this very description Le Corbusier continues:

> Arab architecture gives us a valuable lesson. It is appreciated while walking, on foot; it is while walking, moving from one place to another, that one sees how the arrangements of the architecture develop. This is a contrary to the principle of Baroque architecture that is designed on paper around a fixed theoretical point. I prefer the teaching of Arabic architecture.[8] (Author's translation of original Le Corbusier text in Boesiger 1995: 24)

In explicitly rejecting the approach of 'Baroque architecture' but emphasizing the conceptual similarities of his work with 'Arab architecture', Le Corbusier is positioning his formally unconventional 'new' architecture as part of a long tradition, in effect claiming it to be more historically rooted (and implicitly legitimate) than any baroque architecture.[9] Moreover, in explicitly emphasizing that this is an architecture appreciated on foot, Le Corbusier is implicitly positioning the villa as an architecture of raw experience of the human body, an architecture that is individually performed in person by moving through it. Notably, Gideon describes it as a work 'conceived in motion' (see Cairns 2013: 221). Indeed, immediately after the aforementioned comments on his Villa Savoye, Le Corbusier introduces the now-seminal concept of the 'promenade architecturale':

> In this house, it is about a true architectural promenade, providing aspects constantly diverse, unexpected, sometimes amazing.[10] (Author's translation of Le Corbusier's original text in Boesiger 1995: 24)

The sequence is a continuous one of varying speeds and heights, starting from the arrival in the car from the city, up and under the house to the front door, and then walking through the door and up the looping ramp; the ramp encourages a continuous movement and allows one to look up and around as one moves (as opposed to a stair where one has to watch one's step). The carefully positioned framed views – such as out to the terrace and then to what was originally a clear view to the Seine valley, for example – and the movement up to, around and past them, create this varied and diverse range of aspects. He starts to use cinematic techniques to create key moments in the architecture.

Le Corbusier uses similar descriptions of the journey through many of his other projects, for example his discussion on the Villa Stein de Monzie or the two houses at La Roche. This is architecture as performed movement sequence curated in a certain order by the architect; 'it is a building of ramps, sequences and ceremonial pathways' (Curtis 1987: 18). And in the design of those ramps, sequences and pathways, the architect is implicitly creating a hierarchy of the events. It is an architecture to be experienced as a performance of sorts, as a cinematic experience of sorts: as Colomina states, 'you follow an itinerary and the views develop with great variety' (Colomina 1996: 5).

The notion of the 'promenade architecturale' is clearly related to ideas of the 'path' elaborated by Choisy and Eisenstein, discussed earlier. However, it is much more than just a 'path'. Samuel argues that it can be understood as a formula for creating a circulatory system that shapes narratives of indoor and outdoor space, which Le Corbusier modifies slightly each time in response to site and programme (Samuel 2010). Noting the importance of site in Le Corbusier's work (see Curtis 1987), and how he sought to reconnect and resensitize people with nature (see Samuel 2010), the 'promenade architecturale' can be understood as an experiential strategy to enable the human inhabitant to engage with its ever-changing context. The striking description Le Corbusier gives of the experience of moving through one of his houses at La Roche is revealing in emphasizing the nature of this engagement:

> I enter: the architectural spectacle at once offers itself to the eye. I follow an itinerary and the views develop with great variety; I play with the influx of light illuminating walls or creating shadows[11] (Author's translation of Le Corbusier's original text in Boesiger 1995: 60)

A wide variety of historians have argued this as an essentially passive engagement. For example, Colomina describes the 'architectural promenade' as a construction in 'space and time', designed to 'frame views' (Colomina 1996: 5); similarly, Cairns describes it as a 'linear and dictated route', where 'movement is unchecked and continuous' (Cairns 2013: 230). However, Le Corbusier himself emphasizes that the movement experience itself is more than just a passive engagement – it is also an active engagement on the part of the inhabitant.

Le Corbusier's 'architectural promenade' can be understood as a four-dimensional interactive construction. The architect creates a sequence of movement up, around and through, a particular context, controlling the speed or time of our movement by the choice (and size) of stairs, incline of the ramp and designed moments of pause through the opening up of specific views, and opening out of the ground-plane and ceiling height: it is a curated, sequential, relational, sensory experience that shifts over time, and is dependent on the weather, light and ever-changing physical context. Not only does the body experience these architecturally created effects and affects, but it in turn also creates constantly shifting effects and affects by its own presence, movement and sensory responses. These effects and affects are greatly intensified by the physical centrality of this orienting (and disorienting) spine, given how it intersects with the key spaces across the building and connects the indoors and outdoors both physically and visually.

This is not so much a narrative construction or device as Penz (2004) argues, but rather an interactive, individual performance, which is unique every time. Building on Eisenstein's cinematic approach, the hyper-mobile spectator is an active participant in the inscribed architecture of proliferating possibilities, subjectively engaging and disengaging with the constructed affective sequence, differently each time in the endless varying contexts of light, sound, temperature, touch and smell: not only through the effects and affects on the body through its senses but also through her movement 'on' and 'off' the ramp at varying points, and at different speeds and in different directions, constructing a new sequentiality and montage each time. The architecture becomes an active cinematic form, harnessing cinematic tools and techniques to move beyond a purely cinematic mode of thinking.

The 'architectural promenade' also implicitly opens up a much broader conception of context: it engages us in both the direct architectural context (e.g. the spaces and the materials) and the wider natural context (e.g. the views of the surroundings and the natural environment and the constantly changing light): the natural and architectural context work together to physically move us as bodies and to affectively move us as emotional beings. The 'architectural promenade' brings us into an active and emotional engagement with these contexts. Le Corbusier is explicit in seeking an architecture where 'the emotions aroused by architecture emanate from physical conditions that are ineluctable, irrefutable, forgotten today' (Le Corbusier [1923] 2008: 102). This is not a physical path, but a curated, affective, interactive route which can be freely joined and left at numerous points – shifting our conception of context to something without a physical end. This interactive promenade is without explicit physical or affective end as it engages in the ever-changing natural context above and around us. But this does not mean that the 'architectural promenade' has no purpose beyond this.

In revealing 'diverse, unexpected, sometimes amazing' aspects, this curated movement shows us the physical and conceptual world anew: it crafts understanding and sensation. As Le Corbusier argues, 'the plan carries within it the essence of the sensation.... Architecture is the use of raw materials to establish stirring relationships. Architecture goes beyond utilitarian things' (Le Corbusier [1923] 2008: 86–7). The 'architectural promenade' is central to this, crafting how we move through and experience our surroundings. Through engaging us in an integrated architectural and natural context, Le Corbusier is helping us appreciate the world afresh, as he emphasizes when he asks rhetorically:

> Finally, must one appreciate, when the time comes, what is available and know how to renounce the things that have been learned, to pursue truths that will inevitably develop around new techniques, and at the instigation of a new spirit born of the profound upheaval of the machine age.[12] (Author's translation of Le Corbusier's original text; Boesiger 1995: 60)

Le Corbusier makes no textual reference to Choisy or cinema in the aforementioned work, although clearly there are explicit and experiential connections, as I have discussed earlier. However, there are important personal contextual connections with both Choisy and Eisenstein, which further indicate the strong cinematic undercurrents to his arguments.

Anton Burov – the trained architect who created the intensely modernist sets for *The General Line* (Eisenstein 1929) – introduced Le Corbusier to Eisenstein in late October 1928 in Moscow. Le Corbusier revealingly discussed his time in Moscow in an interview that December:

> Architecture and cinema are the only two arts of our time. In my own work I seem to think as Eisenstein does in his films. I should like to take this opportunity to express all my admiration for Eisenstein's principle of freeing events from all that is uncharacteristic or insignificant. This insistence on essentials not only raises his work beyond mere narrative but also raises everyday events that escape our attention to the level of monumental images, for instance, the procession of *The General Line*, with its 'dynamic porticos' of advancing icons and the sculptural quality of its figures. (Le Corbusier, 'L'Architecture à Moscou', *L'Intransigeant*; Cohen 1992: 49)

Le Corbusier was aligning his architectural work with cinematic concerns and techniques, and he appears keenly engaged with Eisenstein's work and thinking. Moreover, Le Corbusier gave Eisenstein a copy of his book *L'Art Décoratif d'Aujourd'hui* at this meeting, inscribing it explicitly with the same statement that 'I seem to think as M. Eisenstein does when he makes films' (Cohen 1992: 49). Also, as I noted earlier, it was around this time at the end of 1928 that Le Corbusier added the 'architectural promenade' to the drawings for Villa Savoye (Benton 1988: 198–9). Certainly Le Corbusier is vague on specifics of the architecture–cinema relationship, elusively stating that he '*seems* to think' as Eisenstein does (author's italics), and failing to elaborate what that thinking is beyond 'freeing events from all that is uncharacteristic or insignificant', and an 'insistence on essentials' – comments which are remarkably open to interpretation. This is not about a direct translatability between disciplines, but rather a fluid discussion and shared development of conceptual tools and techniques around new overlapping thematic directions in their disciplines, focused around the performance of sequenced movement.

Eisenstein similarly emphasizes these broader overlapping disciplinary and thematic concerns, highlighting the shared role of composed movement:

> At the basis of the composition of the architectural ensemble . . . lies that same unique 'dance' which is the basis of the creation of works of music, painting and film montage. (Eisenstein [1949] 1977: 98)

A decade after meeting Le Corbusier, Eisenstein reiterates the heritage of cinema in his discussion about the problem of representing the full multidimensionality of a phenomenon:

> Only the film camera has solved the problem of [fixing the total representation of a phenomenon in its full visual multidimensionality] on a flat surface, but its undoubted ancestor is architecture. (Eisenstein, Bois and Glenny 1989: 117)

Both Le Corbusier and Eisenstein emphasized that their disciplines were closely related conceptually. Both built from Choisy's description of the ascending path through the Acropolis to create different but related arguments about affective performance. Neither Eisenstein nor Le Corbusier sought to directly literalize elements of the other discipline, or co-opt one into the other. Indeed, in 1933 Le Corbusier explicitly noted the distinctness of cinema as 'positioning itself on its own terrain . . . becoming a form of art in and of itself, a kind of genre' (Vidler 1993: 112). Le Corbusier and Eisenstein recognized the broad, shared conceptual concerns of architecture and cinema, and so explored how they could push new directions in their respective disciplines by harnessing the techniques, tools and thinking of the other. Further understanding Le Corbusier's subsequent direct engagement with the cinematic medium is therefore especially revealing.

In 1930 Le Corbusier began collaborating on a series of documentary films on his own recent work and that of Auguste Perret and Robert Mallet-Stevens: *Bâtir*; *Trois Chantiers*; and *Architecture d'Aujourd'hui*. Le Corbusier worked closely on the films with the then relatively unknown 26-year-old film director Pierre Chenal to promote a new architectural agenda and to convey the physical experience of that; indeed, the titles of the films explicitly emphasized the importance of building (rather than just theorizing), while the films themselves emphasized the experience of moving around the buildings. Significantly, Le Corbusier himself stated 'everything is Architecture' in film's architectonic dimensions of proportion and order (see Abel 1988: 112–13): this was about seeing, understanding and beginning to experience new architectural possibilities across media and across scales, using all tools and techniques available. It was about performing new realized and realizable architectural possibilities for a wider audience.

The documentaries not only performed the architecture but also used cinematic techniques to perform the theories that underlay the architecture. For example, Penz elucidates how the final film in the trilogy – *Architecture d'Aujourd'hui* – performs Le Corbusier's Villa Savoye as 'a non-literal explication of Le Corbusier's Five Points (1927) through camera movement' (Penz 2013: 408). Cinematic techniques from both Hollywood and Eisenstein were used (and misused) as Chenal and Le Corbusier (who co-scripted the film) sought to simultaneously express both the human experience of a specific architecture and the theoretical underpinnings to that architecture, all within a broader narrative of the potentials and nature of new directions in architecture at a variety of scales. Penz shows how the stylistic shift from the non-sensory, purely visual Eisensteinian montage logic of the first part of the film switches in the scene where the figure walks up the ramp on the roof of Villa Savoye: here the film cuts to a form of Hollywood logic, where the time is determined and measured by movement. This crafted shift in styles enables us to experience both the sensation of the 'architectural promenade', as well as the rational key elements of Le Corbusier's Five Points – the use of pilotis, horizontal picture windows, a free plan, a free façade and a roof garden (Penz 2013: 409). Le Corbusier and Pierre Chenal are using cinematic tools and techniques to perform the sensations and the logic of this performative architecture – as an individual and a communal experience. It is not so much that the 'building is a cinematic framing device for the modern eye', as Colomina argues (1996: 5), but rather that the cinematic medium enables the affective, sensorial, theoretical and practical experiences of the building to be simultaneously performed, a-temporally and a-geographically. Emphasizing the symbiotic nature of the architecture–cinema relationship, Le Corbusier is using an idea of the cinematic to interweave the practical, affective and theoretical experiences and intentions of his built architecture, thereby enabling it to be performed forever more, anywhere and anytime.

The core origins of the nuanced architecture–cinema relationship open up a different way of thinking architecture's past, present and future. Both disciplines are explorative, explanatory and performative acts of the imagination, with their own techniques, histories and theories. Both dynamically challenge, create and reflect our experiences of – and engagement with – the world. Through their intersections, they reconstruct each other's possibilities. As the work of Choisy, Eisenstein and Le Corbusier shows, cinematic tools, techniques and modes of thinking help us to understand and create a different conception of architectural possibility, both theoretically and in practice. These cinematic approaches re-centre the subjective human experience and emphasize architecture as a performative act that constantly shapes, frames, orients and moves us – both physically and emotionally – just as we shape it through our bodily presence, experiences and use of it. The cinematic opens us to architecture as a subjective performance of spatial, social, theoretical and experiential possibilities curated by the design and its fluid contexts. The cinematic in this sense can become an enabling condition for a different mode of architectural understanding and practice – architecture as a form of the cinematic.

Notes

1 Author's translation of the original text: '*Rien n'est en apparence plus irrégulier que ce plan: en fait c'est un ensemble équilibré, où la symétrie des masses s'associe à la plus originale variété de détails. L'aile de droite, avec le temple de la Victoire, forme une masse qui répond a celle de l'aile de gauche: si bien que, pour un spectateur placé au pied de l'escalier, les deux rayons limites . . . s'inclinent également sur l'axe général de l'édifice. Si l'architecte a tronqué l'aile droite, ce fut pour respecter l'enceinte de la Victoire aptère et permettre au temple V de se dessiner tout entier sur le ciel. Ce petit temple n'est point orienté parallelement a l'axe général de la composition: irrégularité nouvelle qui fixe sur lui le regard, et lui rend une importance que l'exiguité de ses dimensions semblait lui refuse.*'

2   If there is a narrative, it is only in the most basic sense of an ordered sequence. It is important to note that cinema has not yet developed its formal narratological tools at this point in the late nineteenth century.

3   Although it is beyond the limits of this chapter to discuss in detail the arguments around the origins and context of 'Montage and Architecture', it is worth noting that Bois convincingly positions it as part of Eisenstein's long-standing interest in painting and the articulation of images, and his search for a non-medium-specific new category between painting and cinema – 'cinematism' (Eisenstein, Bois and Glenny 1989).

4   Eisenstein was working within a context of experimental Russian filmmakers (re) forming and assimilating Constructivist and Futurist ideas. For example, Pudovkin explored fracturing traditional constructions of space and time to dramatize events in his experimental narrative films (Pudovkin 1970): Pudovkin's 'architectonic model' of using montage to link film strips as building blocks in a series is not too dissimilar to Eisenstein's own approach. Similarly, Kuleshov manipulated traditional conceptions of space and time using 'relational editing' to craft a different visual language (see Kuleshov and Levaco 1974: 51–2). And finally, Vertov, who understood film as a documentary medium (as part of the Kinoks movement), similarly explored the fragmentation and reconstruction of space and time to alter 'perception of the world' and manipulate 'the mechanics of the eye' (Cairns 2013). Eisenstein's nascent affective theory of performance was implicitly informed by and reacting to this context.

5   Cohen has elucidated in the introduction to Goodman's recent translation that the book was in fact originally a collaborative creation in 1920 of Le Corbusier (Charles-Édouard Jeanneret), the painter Amédée Ozenfant and the publicist and poet Paul Dermée in their journal *L'Esprit Nouveau*. Le Corbusier took it over and it became a promotional tool for his work and ideas, to win recognition as an intellectual and architectural reformer (Le Corbusier [1923] 2008: 1–5).

6   Given Corbusier's commitment to standardization, it is not surprising that he co-opts Choisy to emphasize that even an irregular layout can be normalized and standardized.

7   Of course, the *physical* 'cinematic' tools and techniques available when Le Corbusier, Eisenstein and Choisy were each writing was different, but the argument here is rooted in the underlying core conceptual tools and techniques.

8   Author's translation of the original text: '*L'architecture arabe nous donne un enseignement précieux. Elle s'apprécie à la marche, avec le pied; c'est en marchant, en se déplaçant que l'on voit se développer les ordonnances de l'architecture. C'est un principe contraire à l'architecture baroque qui est conçue sur le papier, autour d'un point fixe théorique. Je préfère l'enseignement de l'architecture arabe.*'

9 Le Corbusier's dismissive and simplistic use of the term 'baroque' is deliberately facile for dramatic effect. The baroque took many forms across a wide expanse of time, and as Vidler (2001) argues, baroque space already held qualities of modern space.
10 Author's translation of the original text: *'Dans cette maison-ci, il s'agit d'une véritable promenade architecturale, offrant des aspects constamment variés, inattendus, parfois étonnant.'*
11 Author's translation of the original text: *'On entre: le spectacle architectural s'offre de suite au regard: on suit un itinéraire et les perspectives se développent avec une grande variété; on joue avec l'afflux de la lumière éclairant les murs ou créant des pénombres.'*
12 Author's translation of the original text: *'Encore, faut-il savoir apprécier, quand l'heure sonne, ce qui est à disposition et il faut savoir renoncer aux choses que l'on a apprises, pour poursuivre des vérités qui se développent fatalement autour des techniques nouvelles et à l'instigation d'un esprit neuf né du profond bouleversement de l'époque machiniste.'*

References

Abel, R. (1988), *French Film Theory and Criticism: A History/Anthology, 1907–1939*, Princeton: Princeton University Press.
Alifragkis, S. and F. Penz (2010), 'Fragmented Utopias – Architecture, Literature and the Cinematic Image of the Ideal Socialist City of the Future: Dziga Vertov's *Man with a Movie Camera*', in J. Harris and R. Williams (eds), *Regenerating Culture and Society: Architecture, Art and the Urban Style within the Global Politics of City Branding*, 117–41, Liverpool: Liverpool University Press & Tate Liverpool.
Benton, T. (1987), *The Villas of Le Corbusier*, New Haven: Yale University Press.
Boesiger, W. (1995), *The Complete Architectural Works in 8 Volumes: Le Corbusier and Pierre Jeanneret*, 11th edn, Basel: Birkhäuser.
Bruno, G. (1997), 'Site-Seeing: Architecture and the Moving-Image', *Wide Angle*, 4 (19): 8–24.
Bruno, G. (2002), *Atlas of Emotion: Journeys in Art, Architecture, and Film*, New York: Verso.
Cairns, G. (2013), *The Architecture Of The Screen: Essays In Cinematographic Space*, Bristol: Intellect.
Choisy, A. (1899), *Histoire de L'Architecture*, Paris: Gauthier-Villars.
Cohen, J.-L. (1992), *Le Corbusier and the Mystique of the USSR: Theories and Projects for Moscow, 1928–1936*, trans. K. Hylton, Princeton: Princeton University Press.
Colomina, B. (1996), *Privacy and Publicity; Modern Architecture as Mass Media*, Cambridge, MA: MIT Press.

Curtis, W. J. R. (1987), *Le Corbusier: Ideas and Forms*, 2nd edn, London: Phaidon Press.
Eisenstein, S. ([1943] 1975), *The Film Sense*, ed. and trans. J. Leyda, Orlando: Harcourt Brace & Company.
Eisenstein, S. ([1949] 1977), *Film Form: Essays in Film Theory*, trans. J. Leyda, Orlando: Harcourt.
Eisenstein, S. (1977), 'Piranesi, or The Fluidity of Forms', trans. R. Reader, *Oppositions*, Winter (11): 84–110.
Eisenstein, S., Y.-A. Bois and M. Glenny (1989), 'Montage and Architecture', *Assemblage*, 10: 111–31.
Koeck, R. (2013), *Cine-Scapes*, London: Routledge.
Kuleshov, L. V. and R. Levaco (1974), *Kuleshov on Film*, Berkeley: University of California Press.
L'Architecture D'Aujourd'hui (1931), [Film] Dir. Pierre Chenal. Paris.
Le Corbusier ([1923] 2008), *Toward an Architecture*, 2nd edn, ed. J.-L. Cohen, trans. J. Goodman, London: Frances Lincoln.
Norberg-Schulz, C. (1980), *Genius Loci: Towards a Phenomenology of Architecture*, New York: Rizzoli.
Pallasmaa, J. (2007), *The Architecture of Image: Existential Space in Cinema*, 2nd edn, Helsinki: Rakennustieto.
Pallasmaa, J. (2012), *The Eyes of the Skin: Architecture and the Senses*, 3rd edn, Chichester: Wiley.
Penz, F. (2004), 'The Architectural Promenade as Narrative Device: Practice Based Research in Architecture and the Moving Image', *Digital Creativity*, 15 (1): 39–51.
Penz, F. (2013), 'L'Ombre de L'Acropole: La Ville Savoye Construite Par Le Cinema', in R. Amirante, P. Tournikiotis and Y. Tsiomis (eds), *L'Invention d'un Architecte: Le Voyage en Orient de Le Corbusier*, 407–13, Paris: Éditions de la Villette.
Penz, F. and A. Lu, eds (2011), *Urban Cinematics: Understanding Urban Phenomena Through The Moving Image*, Bristol: Intellect.
Pudovkin, V. (1970), *Film Technique and Film Acting*, trans. I. Montague, New York: Evergreen Press.
Samuel, F. (2010), *Le Corbusier and the Architectural Promenade*, Basel: Birkhäuser.
Tawa, M. (2011), *Agencies Of The Frame: Tectonic Strategies in Cinema and Architecture*, Newcastle: Cambridge Scholars Publishing.
Taylor, R., ed. (1988), *Eisenstein Selected Works, Volume 1: Writings 1922-34*, London: British Film Institute.
Toy, M., ed. (1994), *Architecture + Film*, London: Wiley Academy.
Vidler, A. (1993), 'The Explosion of Space: Architecture and The Filmic Imaginary', *Assemblage*, 21: 44–59.
Vidler, A. (2001), *Warped Space: Art, Architecture, and Anxiety in Modern Culture*, Cambridge, MA: MIT Press.

Index

Note: Page numbers followed by "n" refer to notes.

1963 (film, 1983)   26–8
Abdusalamov, S.   175 n.1
Abercrombie, M.   2, 115
absolutism   42
actualities   80
Adventures of Ideas (Whitehead)   70 n.3
aesthetic geology   58
aesthetics   57, 80, 85
   architectural   187
   authentic   133
   non-standard   46
   of post-industrial decay   175 n.1
Agora, or things indifferent (video, 2015–16)   26
algorithmic social control   158
Alice in Wonderland (Carroll)   57
Alifragkis, S.   10
All Thoughts Are Equal (Ó Maoilearca)   43, 46, 47
American Marconi Company   180
American Society of Cell Biology (ASCB)   117
analogism   9, 98, 102
Andersen, A.   11
Anderson, H. C.   57
Andrew, D.   75
Andrei Rublev (Андрей Рублёв) (film, 1969)   161
Angelopoulos, T.   164
Anti-Badiou (Laruelle)   52
anti-philosophy   45
Antonioni, M.   94
Archer, G. L.   179–80
architectonics of cinema   95–7, 103
Architects' Data (Neufert)   95
Architecture Beyond Sight (film, 2019)   178–88
architecture–cinema relationship   11, 190–206

Architecture d'Aujourd'hui (film, 1930)   2, 203
area studies   86–7
Arnheim, R.   4
Artemyev, E.   167
art-house cinema   49
'Art of Cinema, The' (Kuleshov)   168
ASCB, *see* American Society of Cell Biology (ASCB)
aspect perception   26
audiovisual media   128–33
augmented reality   7, 132
Augustine   25
authorship   87, 157, 186

Badiou, A.   2, 52
Baier, A.   53 n.2
Balázs, B.   4
Barham, J.   171
Baroque architecture   198
Barthes, R.   5, 6
Bartlett, The   187
Bâtir (film, 1930)   203
Bauchau, P.   50–1
Baudrillard, J.   5, 7
Bazin, A.   3, 4, 8, 9, 55–9
Beaufoy, S.   147
behavioural tangent   48–52
Benjamin, W.   3, 5
Benning, J.   60
Berger, R.   158
Bergin, J.   126
Bergson, H.   2, 18
beur cinema   78
Big Data   116
biomedical science   107–18
Bird, B.   8
Birdsong (Faulks)   151
Black Death, The (film, 2016)   134

Black Lives Matter   88
Blanchot, M.   59
Block, B.   100
B-Made Workshop   182
Boetticher, B.   55–6
Bois, Y.-A.   192, 193, 202, 205 n.3
Bolex H16 camera   11, 178, 185
Boulez, P.   69
Boyhood (film, 2014)   101
Boyle, D.   148
Boym, A.   175 n.1
Boys, J.   181, 188
Bresson, R.   173
British Academy   89
British Empire Cancer Campaign   114
Bruno, G.   194
Bucher, E. E.   180
Burch, N.   2, 4
Burov, A.   201

CAD software   102
Cahiers du cinema (magazine)   55, 57
Cairns, G.   190, 199
Camera Recording its Own Condition (7 Apertures, 10 Speeds, 2 Mirrors) (photographs, 1971)   24
Campbell, J.   135
canonical laws of geometry   192
Canti, R.   2, 113–14, 116
Canudo, R.   2
Carpenter Center for the Visual Arts, Harvard University   23
Carrel, A.   112–13
Caston, E.   157
Catalogue Raisonné of Everyday Life Activities (Penz and Schupp)   102
Cavell, S.   5, 6, 8, 32–5, 84
Celldance   117
Center (Inside Out) (video, 2013–14)   22–4
chambre obscure (or *camera obscura*)   58
chaosmosis   62, 70
Chase, The (film, 1950)   108–9
Cheese Mites (film, 1903)   112
Chenal, P.   203
Choisy, A.   11, 191–3, 195–6, 201, 202

cinema, *see also* film; *individual entries*
   architectonics of   95–7, 103
   of attractions   80
   beur   78
   cultural differences in   97–8
   early   80
   everyday life through cinema, understanding   93–4
   national   78, 88
   as philosophy   44
   world   87
Cinéma 2: L'image-temps (Deleuze)   59
Cinema du Look   50
Cinémathèque Française   78
cinematic aided design approach   92–105
cinematic forms   42–3
'Cinematic Interpretation of Spatiality: A Workshop and Seminar on Cinematic Architecture'   103
cinematic thinking   31, 86, 122–36
cinematism   195, 205 n.3
cinematographicity   193
Cinemetrics   99
cinemicroscopy, *see* microcinematography
Citizen Kane (film, 1941)   55
Clément, R.   55
Cocteau, J.   2
Code, B.   134
cognate disciplines   75, 82, 83–4
cognitive polyphony   64
Cohen, J.-L.   201, 202, 205 n.5
Collins, F.   117
Colomina, B.   199, 203–4
Colour of Pomegranates, The (Цвет граната) (film, 1969)   162
Comandon, J.   112, 118
common denominators   195
Concept of Nature, The (Whitehead)   70 n.3
Conceptual Art in Britain 1964–1979 (exhibition, 2016)   24
Confessions (Augustine)   25
Conley, T.   8
Cooper, I.   93
Corpus Christi Mystery Plays   133
costume   79, 125, 129, 134
'Could You Love a Chemical Baby?' (Burke)   114

Crin blanc (Bazin)   56
critical spatial practices   11, 186, 188
cross-referencing   77–9, 85, 86
Cultivation of Living Tissue, The (film, 1932)   113–14
cultural differences, in cinema   97–8
cultural heritage   122–36

Dasein   59
data mining of filmic archive   94–5
Davis, G.   146
Dear, N.   149
de Certeau, M.   183–4, 186, 188
Deleuze, G.   2, 4, 5, 8, 9, 17–18, 57–63, 70 nn.2, 3, 83, 173
De l'exercitation (Montaigne)   60
Deltcheva, R.   166, 172
Deng, W.   104
Department of Architecture, University of Cambridge   92
Dermée, P.   205 n.5
Derrida, J.   70 n.6
Descola, P.   97–9
Det Perfekte Menneske (The Perfect Human) (film, 1968)   47–52
'Dialectical Approach to Film Form, The' (Eisenstein)   195
Die Nibelungen (film, 1924)   123
Die Stadt von Morgen (film, 1930)   2
digital image   22–4
digital methodology, for filmic data analysis   98–100
disability in architectural design   11
discipline
    mapping   75–90
    surveying   76–80
DisOrdinary Architecture Project   178, 181–2
Doing Disability Differently: An Alternative Handbook on Architecture (Boys)   182
Douglas, K.   123
Downey, C.   185–7
Dulac, G.   2
Dumoncel, J.-C.   63
Duncan, M.   112

early cinema   80
Ebert, R.   154
écriture feminine   130
Edda   124
    Völuspá (The Seeress's Prophecy)   129, 130
Egan, J.   157
Eisenstein, S.   5, 11, 23, 53, 162, 193–5, 197, 199–202, 205 nn.3, 4
Elements of Architecture (Koolhaas)   96
Emerson   35, 39
Emersonian perfectionism   35
Epstein, J.   2
ethics   85
European languages, film studies in   86–7
event, definition of   59–60
everyday life through cinema, understanding   93–4
externalism   51

Faulk, S.   151
feminist film theory   79, 88
Film Form, The (Eisenstein)   55
filmic archive, data mining of   94–5
filmic data analysis, digital methodology for   98–100
filming blindness   178–88
filmology   78
film(s), *see also* cinema; *individual entries*
    criticism   80–3, 89
    event   55–71
    form   80
    heritage   79
    history   80
    and modern languages   86–7
    movements   80
    non-philosophy   43–4
    philosopher   52–3
    of philosophy   46–8
    and philosophy/film-philosophy   83–6, 89
    ride   80
    as a site of post-occupancy studies   92–3
    studies   75–90
    theory   75
    trick   80

'Film Sense, The' (Eisenstein)   193–4, 195
Final Cut Pro   24
Finehair, K. H.   128
Five Obstructions, The (film, 2003)   8, 46–9, 51
    creative constraints   47
Five Points, The (Le Corbusier)   203
Flaherty, R.   57
flâneur   135, 174, 181
Fleischer, R.   123, 130, 135
Ford, J.   55
Foster, C.   10
Foucault (Deleuze)   59
Fox Searchlight   147
framing   1, 3, 5, 6, 20, 99, 100, 101, 165, 171
franchising   157, 158
Friday Evening Discourse, The Royal Institution   114
Full Monty, The (film, 1997)   147
Fury (film, 1936)   9, 65–8
Fuss D.   181, 185

Game of Thrones (TV series, 2013–19)   126, 129, 135
Garden Stroll: Illusive Realm (film, 2018)   103–4
Gelassenheit   161
General Line, The (film, 1929)   201
Gerber, J.   99
Gerwig, G.   149
Gesta Danorum (Grammaticus)   126
GFP, *see* green fluorescent protein (GFP)
Gideon, S.   198
Godard, J.-L.   94
Good Morning (film, 1959)   101
Gotland Law   127
Grammaticus, S.   126–9
Greenaway, P.   6
green fluorescent protein (GFP)   109–10
Gunning, T.   3

Halle, A. de la   133
haptic visuality   82
Harraway, D.   184
Harrison, R.   112
headword tracker   78

Heath, S.   5–6
Heimskringla (Sturluson)   123
heritage film   79
heterotopia   168
Hislop, I.   123
Histoire de L'Architecture (Choisy)   191
Historien om Danmark (History of Denmark) (TV miniseries, 2017)   130
    Sen midelalder (TV episode, 2017)   131
History of Radio 1926 (Archer)   179–80
History of the Kings of Britain (Monmouth)   127
Hjort, M.   49

idea   17–29, 48–52
identity   76, 88–90
If Buildings Could Talk (film, 2010)   93
image   17–29
immersion   124–6
Impression, soleil levant (artwork, Monet, 1872)   26
interpretation   126–8
intersectionality   88
Interval (moving-image installation, 2019)   26–8
intervalometer   19, 20
intuition   8, 18, 24, 27
Ivan the Terrible I (Иван Грозный I) (film, 1944)   162
Ivan the Terrible II (Иван Грозный II) (film, 1958)   162

Jackson, P.   129
Jarmusch, J.   94
Jeanne Dielman, 23, quai du commerce, 1080 Bruxelles (film, 1975)   94
Jeanneret, P.   197
Jenkins, H.   157
Jewish Museum, Berlin   174
Journal of Visualized Experiments (Jove), The   117

Keller, H.   181, 184, 185
Kiarostami, A.   56
Killing Cancer – Cytotoxic T-Cells On Patrol (film, 2014)   117

Kingdom Come, Deliverance (video game, 2018)   134
Kitchen Stories (film, 2003)   95
Kjellström, A.   129
Kodak 50D film roll   186
Kodak 500T film roll   186
Koeck, R.   190
Koolhaas, R   95–6
Kracauer, S.   3, 4
Kren, K.   22
Kriemhild's Rache (*Kreimhild's Revenge*) (film, 1924)   123
Kuhn, A.   9
Kuleshov, L.   5, 168, 205 n.4

La Fabrique des Images (exhibition, 2010)   98
La Fille de l'eau (*The Whirlpool of Fate*) (film, 1925)   55
Lang, F.   9, 65–9, 123, 124
Langer, S.   3
La Règle du jeu (*The Rules of the Game*) (film, 1939)   55
L'Art Décoratif d'Aujourd'hui (Le Corbusier)   201
Laruelle, F.   8, 42–7, 52–3
L'Eclisse (*The Eclipse*) (film, 1962)   96–7
Le Corbusier   11, 23, 165, 166, 171, 172, 190, 195–204, 205 nn.5, 6, 206 n.9
Leech-Wilkinson, D.   153
Lefebvre, H.   99, 104
Leibniz, G.   64, 69, 70 n.4
Leigh, M.   94
Le Pli: Leibniz et le baroque (Deleuze)   8, 58, 59, 70, 70 nn.2, 3
Les jeux interdits (*Forbidden Games*) (Clément)   55, 57
L'Espace littéraire (*The Space of Literature*) (Blanchot)   59
Lessig, L.   157
Leth, J.   8, 46–51
Libeskind   174
Lichtung Test No. 1 (video, 2017)   26
Little Women (film, 2020)   149
Livingston, P.   49
Loach, K.   94
Lodbrok, R.   123, 126
Logan, J.   151–2

Lord of the Rings (Tolkien)   129
Louisiana Story, The (film, 1948)   57
Louw, R.   24, 25
Lowder, R.   22
Lu, A.   92, 103
Lucas, G.   135
Lumière   55, 63, 64, 69, 70 n.1, 191
Lütgert, S.   99
Lynes, K. G.   48

McCarthy, T.   152–3
MacDonald, J. R.   114
Magnificent Ambersons, The   55
Malkovich, J.   84
Mallet-Stevens, R.   203
Malory, T.   133
Marconi, G.   179
Marey, É.-J.   1, 2, 5, 111, 118, 191
Margrete – Queen of the North (film, 2020)   131
Martin, R. R.   126
Masur, T.   117
materialism   42, 45, 171
'materiality of theory' approach   42
Medawar, P.   114–16, 118
Medieval Defenders (video game, 2016)   134
mental experience   18
Metamorphosis (Ovid)   61
metaphor   4, 92, 104
Metchnikoff, I.   111
#MeToo movement   89
Metz, C.   3, 4
microcinematography   9, 107–18
mise-en-scene   79
modern languages studies, film and   86–7, 89
'Montage of Attractions, The' (Eisenstein)   193, 194
Montaigne, M.   60
moral perfectionism   32–4
moving image   1, 2, 5, 7–9, 11, 12, 18–19, 21, 26, 62, 64, 80, 94, 98, 103, 111, 112, 162, 191, 192
Mulhall, S.   4, 8
multimedia   117, 146, 157
multiplicity   45, 60, 169
Münsterberg, H.   2, 4–6

Muybridge, E.   1–3, 5, 6, 111, 118, 191
mythopoeia   10, 129, 135

narrative study   88
national cinema   78, 88
naturalism   9, 94, 98, 102
Nature (journal)   114
neo-realism   58
Newell, M.   146
Nibelungenlied (film, 1924)   123, 126, 128
Nietzsche, F.   35, 36
non-philosophy   42–7, 52
non-standard philosophy   8, 43, 46, 47
Norberg-Schulz, C.   165, 194
Norwegian Film Institute, Script Fund   131
Norwegian National Film School   132
Nouveaux Essais (Deleuze)   58
Nouvel, J.   190
Nouvelle Vague   78

Ó Maoilearca, J.   8, 53 n.3
on-demand consumption   157
ontology   8, 9, 22–4, 31, 36, 40–2, 82, 97–100, 166
Ott, J.   112, 118
Oxford Dictionary of Film Studies (Kuhn and Westwell)   9, 75
Ozenfant, A.   205 n.5
Ozu, Y.   94, 101

Painlevé, J.   1
Paisan (film, 1947)   58–9
Pan.do/ra database technology   99
Partington, Z.   181
Pascal, B.   60
Penn, A.   187
Penz, F.   9, 92, 200
perceptual experience   18
Perec, G.   94, 102
perfectionism   32–41
   American   40
   Emersonian   35
   moral   32–4
Perret, A.   203
Persuasion (film, 1995)   149–50
Petric, V.   99
phenomenology   20–2, 82, 85, 194

Philosophical Investigations (Wittgenstein)   26
physicalism   45
Pierce, L.   29 n.3
Plague, The (video game, 2015)   134
Plague Tale: Innocence, A (video game, 2019)   134
plasticity   197
Plato   34, 39
Plato's Phaedrus (video, 2016)   26
Plus Ultra   35
polyphony   69
Post-Occupancy Evaluation - Where Are You? (Cooper)   93
post-occupancy studies, film as a site of   92–3
post-structuralism   88
Practical Wireless Telegraphy: A Complete Text Book for Students of Radio Communication (Bucher)   180
practice-based approaches to spatial cultural differences   103–4
Practice of Everyday Life, The (de Certeau)   183
Princess Tale, A (2016)   134
'Problem of the Materialist Approach to Form' (Eisenstein)   194–5
Procès de Jeanne d'Arc (film, 1962)   173
Process and Reality (Deleuze)   70 n.3
production design   79
pro-filmic space, locating   163–5
promenade architecturale   165, 171, 198–202
Proust, M.   9, 62–3
psychoanalysis   32, 82, 196
   Lacanian   42
psychoanalytic film theory   78, 81, 84, 85
'Psychology of Composition, The' (Eisenstein)   195
Pudovkin, V.   205 n.4
Pyramid (video, 2016)   24–5

Quantitative Cell Biology   116
Queens Game (2000)   132–5
Queens of the North (interactive drama, 2011)   131
queer theory   88
Qu'est-ce que la philosophie? (Deleuze)   59, 70 n.2

Qu'est-ce que le cinéma? (What Is Cinema?)
(Bazin) 55, 59
Quo Vadis? (film, 2013) 123

radio technology 180
Ragnarsson, E. 125
'read-only' culture 157
'read-write' culture 157
realism 85, 161, 162
Rear Window (film, 1953) 97, 98
Redverse-Rowe, M. 182
Refractions of Reality: Philosophy and the Moving Image (Ó Maoilearca) 42
relativism 42
Rendell, J. 186, 188
Renoir, J. 48
repérage 164
Republic (Plato) 34
Reynolds, C. 184
Richter, H. 2
ride films 80
Ride Lonesome (film, 1959) 56
Roadside Picnic (*Пикник на Обочине*) (Arkady and Boris Strugatsky) 163, 173
Rodowick, D. N. 5, 8
Rogers, D. 108
Rohmer, E. 93–4
Romeo and Juliet (film, 1968) 155
Roosevelt, T. 180
Rose, F. 157
Rosenberger, H. 113
Rublev, A. 161–2
RuneCast (2007) 130
Ruttmann, W. 2

Saga of the Völsungs (Crawford) 128
Salmer fra kjøkkenet (Kitchen Stories) (film, 2003) 94–5
Salomon, B. 61
Salt, B. 99
Samuel, F. 199
Schindler's List (film, 1993) 155
Schupp, J. 9
Science (journal) 113
Scientific American (journal) 111
scientism 45
screen, as barrier and support 31–41

screenplay
 as empirical experience 153–4
 as sequence of prompts of varying emphasis 154–6
 as time-specific address 148–53
screenwriting
 as literary art 145–59
 as model for performativity of all writing 156–9
Sculpting in Time (*Запечатлённое Время*) (film, 1986) 171
self-coincidence 34
self-overcoming 34, 35, 37, 39
self-perfecting 34
Selsjord, M. 130
Sen midelalder (TV episode, 2017) 131
Sense and Sensibility (film, 1995) 149
Serlin, D. 181, 185
Shklovsky, V. 171
Siegfrieds Tod (film, 1924) 123
Sieling, C. 131
simulation 124–6
'Situated Knowledge: The Science Question in Feminism and the Privilege of Partial Perspective' (Harraway) 184
Skyfall (film, 2012) 151–2
Slumdog Millionaire (film, 2008) 148
Smith, M. 49
Sobchack, V. 6
Solaris (film, 1972) 165
Song of Ice and Fire (Martin) 126
Soul City (Pyramid of Oranges) (sculpture, 1967) 24
Southcote Road: Frame Displacement (film, 1982) 19–23
spatial cultural differences
 practice-based approaches to 103–4
 systematic analysis of 100–3
Spielberg, S. 135, 155
Stagecoach (film, 1939) 56
Stalker (film, 1979) 10
 Battlefield, the 169–70
 Dry Tunnel, the 170–1
 landscape, framing 172–4
 Meatgrinder, the 171–2
 pro-filmic space, locating 163–5
 Room, the 171–2
 Sand-dunes Shed, the 171–2

three-dimensional plateau, choreography of 165–7
Zone in 161–75
Stewart, J. 97, 98
stillness 20, 23
Stramer, B. 9
Strangeways Research Laboratory 113–15
stratigraphy 58, 59
structuralist approach to image analysis 99
Sturluson, S. 123–4
Svendsen, Z. 155
symbolism 3, 4, 162
systematic analysis of spatial cultural differences 100–3

Taichung (film, 2012) 21–3
Tarkovsky, A. 10, 56, 161–75
Tarr, B. 23, 56
Tavernier, B. 63–4
Teaching (Keller) 185
technicity 18
theory 18, 45
thinking democracy 44–6
'Third Meaning, The' (Barthes) 6
Thomas, K. S. 146
Thomas, M. 9–10
Thor (film series, 2011–19) 124
three-dimensional plateau, choreography of 165–7
Thunberg, G. 135
Timaeus (Deleuze) 62
time 133–6
time image 83
Tokyo Twilight (film, 1957) 97, 98
Tolkien, J. R. R. 129
Tomorrowland: A World Beyond (film, 2015) 8, 32, 34–41
T-pins 36, 40, 41
transcendence 42, 48
transmedia 157
trick films 80
Trois Chantiers (film, 1930) 203
Tschumi, B. 190
Turin Horse, The (Bazin) 56

Ufa-Pavillon 122, 123, 125, 135

UK Equality Act 2010 88
Ultramicroscope Time-Lapse of Syphilis Parasite (film, 2010) 112
Unseen World, The (film series, 1903) 112

Vala (2001–3) 129, 130
Vers Une Architecture (Le Corbusier) 196
Vertov, D. 2, 4, 5, 23, 194
Vidler, A. 190, 206 n.9
Viking Life (multi-screen installation) 125
Viking Planet, Oslo 122, 124–6, 131, 135
Vikings, The (TV series, 1958) 123, 126, 128, 130, 135
Villa Savoye, Poissy 197
Villa Stein de Monzie, La Roche 199
Viollet-le-Duc 192
Virilio, P. 3
virtual reality (VR) 124
Visual Story, The (Block) 100
Vlasov, E. 166, 172
Völuspá (*The Seeress's Prophecy*), see Edda
von Harbou, T. 123
von Trier, L. 8, 46, 48–9, 53 n.1
VR, *see* virtual reality (VR)
Vuillermoz, E. 2

Walt Disney Corporation 112
Waterloo (film, 2012) 19–23
Welles, O. 23
West, K. 148
Westwell, G. 9
What Cinema Is! (Andrew) 75
'What is the Creative Act?' (Deleuze) 17
Whitehead, A. N. 59, 64, 70 n.4
Win Win (McCarthy) 152–3
Wittgenstein, L. 26
Wollen, P. 3
Woman's Lot, A (video game, 2019) 134
world cinema 87
Writers Guild of America 147
writing 147–8

Yousafzai, M. 135

Zeffirelli, F. 155